JAPAN'S DEPENDENCE

ON THE WORLD ECONOMY

JAPAN'S DEPENDENCE ON THE WORLD ECONOMY

THE APPROACH TOWARD ECONOMIC LIBERALIZATION

BY LEON HOLLERMAN

PRINCETON, NEW JERSEY
PRINCETON UNIVERSITY PRESS
1967

TO JEREMY

PREFACE

Of central concern in the modern world is the conflict between the interests of the individual and the interests of the state. A specific form of this conflict occurs in the encounter between the activities of government in the process of economic planning and the prerogatives of the individual according to the rules of an enterprise system. Japan's experience since World War II affords an interesting example of such an encounter. Its sharp edges have been concealed by the fact that until recently Japan has enjoyed an unusually high rate of growth, in which the objectives of government and business could both be accommodated. Moreover, in the case of Japan, there has been a substantial degree of identity rather than conflict of interests between government and business—especially big business—in the planning process.

The accord of interests in planning, however, was disturbed by economic constraints of a structural kind which, having long been latent, became critical in 1965. The embarrassment of these internal constraints was heightened by the fact that in that year Japan was more vulnerable than ever before on the international plane, where liberalization (*jiyūka*) had been brought formally to an advanced stage. The purpose of this book is to identify the structural difficulties of Japan's economy during the process of liberalization and to evaluate the policies with which liberalization has been associated. Some light may thereby be cast on the meaning of "planning" in relation to "free enterprise" within the Japanese milieu.

My procedure begins with an analysis of changes in the structure of Japan's foreign trade in relation to changes in the structure of its industrial production during the postwar period. Next, in terms of performance, special attention is given to sources of stability and instability in the Japanese economy. Finally, at the policy level, a history of the approach toward liberalization is presented and a review of institutional arrangements and the outlook within government and business is compiled on the basis of extensive personal interviews with Japanese ministry officials and business leaders.

As a "middle-advanced country" (*chūshin koku*) Japan's experience is of considerable interest to other lands now in the early stages of economic development. In addition to the lessons usually cited, however, my analysis suggests that as liberalization proceeds in the international sector, Japan's domestic economy is becoming steadily more centralized and subject to more, rather than less, official control. In other words, "liberalization" does not necessarily imply a liberal economy in Japan. Partly, this reflects the effort to find defenses for the domestic economy against growing pressures from abroad. Partly, it arises from the natural instinct of bureaucrats to establish new prerogatives in lieu of those which liberalization has dismantled. Partly, it results from the reassertion of traditional paternalist impulses on the part of a government which sees economic difficulties unfolding.

After World War II the question was asked, "Does Japan have a viable economy?" At the current stage of Japan's transition, the query becomes, "Can Japan achieve stable growth?" The present study finds ingredients of the answer within the context of Japan's dependence on the world economy. In the approach toward liberalization on the international plane, the ambivalence of some of Japan's policies reflect the uncertainties of this dependence.

I am deeply grateful for the Fulbright Fellowship and for the grant from the Social Science Research Council through the American Council of Learned Societies which made it possible for me to spend two years—August 1963 to August 1965—in Japan. The present study was substantially completed during that period, in which I enjoyed one of the most happy and meaningful experiences of my life. Chapter 1 of the study is a revised version of my paper, "Japan's Place in the Scale of Economic Development," published in *Economic Development and Cultural Change*,

January 1964. Chapter 2 is a revised version of my paper, "What Does 'Dependence' Mean in International Trade?" published in *Kyklos*, Vol. XIII, 1960, Fasc. 1. Permission to use the material incorporated here has kindly been given by the editors of those journals.

I also greatly appreciate the facilities and hospitality extended by Hitotsubashi University to which I was attached by the Fulbright Commission as a research scholar. Professors Iochi Ryotaro, Shinohara Miyohei, and Tsuru Shigeto[1] of the University's Economic Research Institute took particular pains to make me feel welcome.

Officials of the Keidanren (Federation of Economic Organizations), Keizai Doyukai (Japan Committee for Economic Development), The Bank of Japan, the Ministry of International Trade and Industry, the Ministry of Finance, the Ministry of Foreign Affairs, the Bank of Tokyo, the Export–Import Bank of Japan, the Japan Development Bank, the Economic Planning Agency, the National Diet Library, and other official agencies, as well as innumerable executives of business firms, were cordial and generous beyond any reasonable expectation. In particular, I must mention the names of Harada Akira, Hayashi Yujiro, Hiyama Hiroshi, Horie Shigeo, Horikoshi Teizo, Ihara Takashi, Inaba Hidezo, Iwasa Yoshizane, Mizukami Tatsuzo, Ōkita Saburo, Segawa Masahisa, Shimomura Osamu, Watanabe Takeshi, Yamashita Seiichi, and Yoshino Toshihiko.

I am especially grateful to my friends Professors Hemmi Kenzo, Kimura Motokazu, Kojima Kiyoshi, and Ohkawa Kazushi for including me in their circle and for encouragement and guidance which only another foreigner who has attempted to immerse himself in Japanese affairs could sufficiently appreciate.

For instruction and advice, as well as for warm friendship and hospitality during the period of my stay in Tokyo, I am deeply indebted to Theodore and Mitsuko Cohen.

[1] In the preface only, Japanese names are written in the Japanese manner, with surname first.

PREFACE

I would also like to express my thanks to Kobayashi Kinichi, who has been my friend and research assistant for many years. Needless to say, none of the above is to be necessarily associated with any of the opinions or conclusions presented here. Finally, I greatly appreciate the patient help of Frances Reed, who did an impeccable job of typing the manuscript.

Leon Hollerman

Hitotsubashi University, Tokyo
August 1965

CONTENTS

xi

CONTESTS

TABLES

xiv

JAPAN'S DEPENDENCE

ON THE WORLD ECONOMY

PART I : STRUCTURE

The structure of an economic organism—whether of a country or a firm—tends to condition its behavior and response to events within its environment. In order to place the details of the Japanese economy in perspective, I begin this section with an attempt to systematically compare Japan with other countries in terms of various structural characteristics or indicators of the degree of development. Chapter 1 concludes that the chief distinction between Japan and other countries whose per capita income is greater than its own, is that they also have a higher per capita level of foreign trade than does Japan. This leads, in Chapter 2, to a discussion of various concepts of foreign-trade dependence. Here it is shown that within a particular situation alternative methods of evaluating dependence may yield conflicting or even opposite results. Also, in the case of Japan, some of the usual methods of evaluation have a downward bias. The discussion of foreign-trade dependence is followed in Chapter 3 by an analysis of the interdependence among output, exports, and productivity in the Japanese economy. Evidence is adduced to reject, for the case of Japan, E.A.G. Robinson's thesis that a nation's exports are concentrated within the channels of its technical advance. Since exports pay for imports, Japan's deviant structure of exports in relation to the Robinson hypothesis presents a handicap to the process of import liberalization. As an alternative explanation of the mechanism of Japan's export expansion, the hypothesis of supply-oriented exports is presented.

Chapter 4 identifies the industries in which growth has occurred as expressed in terms of the ratio of value added to the total value of manufacturers' shipments of various commodities. Here we find that in all manufacturing, the trend value of the ratio has not noticeably increased over time. Also, as compared with other industries, the value added ratio in the heavy and chemical industries, in which investment has been concentrated during recent

3

years, is no higher than in industry at large. Moreover, this ratio in exported goods has been no greater than that within total manufactures. In view of Japan's deficient home supply of industrial raw materials, the failure of the value added ratio to rise means that the brunt of import liberalization must be borne by increases in the sheer volume of exports without substantial help from increases in earnings per unit of exports. This at once constitutes an obstacle to import liberalization and provides a congenial environment for the mechanism of supply-oriented exports.

Part I concludes with the finding that the imbalance in Japan's resource structure is reinforced by various types of imbalance in its commodity trade. In the first place, despite the remarkable growth in Japan's exports, its imports have increased at an even greater rate. Thus its total commodity trade has been persistently unbalanced during the postwar period. Second, geographically, the imbalance has been concentrated in trade with the United States. Third, in trade with the United States, as in Japan's total trade, there is no confirmation of the hypothesis that increases in exports correspond with increases in productivity in particular industries.

---

1 · JAPAN'S PLACE IN THE SCALE OF ECONOMIC DEVELOPMENT

The attempt to evaluate Japan's place in the scale of economic development reveals a paradox. In terms of a set of variables for which data have been presented by Norton Ginsburg, Japan is in many respects among the most developed countries in the world.[1] On the other hand, in terms of half of the criteria of backwardness described by

[1] Ginsburg, *Atlas of Economic Development* (Chicago, 1961).

4

H. Leibenstein, Japan may be classified as a backward country.[2] Especially, Japan is backward as measured by the key criterion of per capita national income. In analyzing this situation, I will first compare Japan's economic dimensions with those of all other countries, using Ginsburg's data for 47 variables in my calculations. Second, in terms of the same variables, Japan will be compared with only those countries whose per capita GNP exceeds its own. The similarities and differences between comparisons based on all countries, as contrasted with those based on higher-income countries, yield a structural explanation of Japan's backward characteristics. In particular, the comparison reveals the role of foreign trade as a key determinant of Japan's place in the scale of economic development.

TABLE 1

Japan's Percentile Rank Among All Countries in Terms
of Specified Indicators of Economic Development

Class of indicator	Description of indicator	Japan's percentile rank[a]
VII	Export dependency on raw materials (raw materials as percent of exports)	97.6
VI	Waterpower development (proportion of potentials developed)	97.6
III	Post-primary school enrollment (percentage of total population in secondary and higher education)	96.6
VI	Commercial fertilizer consumption (kilograms per hectare of cultivated land)	96.5
II	Density of population (persons per square kilometer)	96.0
III	Daily newspaper circulation (per 1,000 population)	96.0

[2] Leibenstein, *Economic Backwardness and Economic Growth* (New York, 1957). I am indebted to the Planning Bureau (then directed by Saburo Ōkita) of the Economic Planning Agency for its help in classifying these characteristics for the case of Japan as of the year 1961.

[a] A high percentile rank means a relatively high degree of advancement.

5

TABLE 1 (*cont.*)

Japan's Percentile Rank Among All Countries in Terms
of Specified Indicators of Economic Development

Class of indicator	Description of indicator	Japan's percentile rank[a]
IV	Rice yields (100 kilograms per hectare)	94.9
VI	Gross energy consumption (I) (millions of megawatt-hours)	93.1
V	Intensity of railway use (I) (million freight ton-kilometers per railway kilometer)	91.9
VII	International trade turnover (I) (imports and exports in millions of U.S. dollars)	91.4
IV	Energy potentials (I) (trillions of kilowatt-hours)	90.9
I	Gross national product (I) (billions of U.S. dollars)	90.9
III	Urban population (I) (percent of population in cities of 20,000 or more)	90.2
VI	Hydroelectric generation (kilowatt-hours per capita)	89.3
V	Railway density (I) (kilometers per 100 square kilometers)	89.2
II	Physicians and dentists (per 100,000 population)	88.1
III	Literacy (percentage of adults literate)	87.9
V	Road density (I) (kilometers per 100 square kilometers)	83.7
VII	Trade with the North Atlantic Region (percent of total exports)	82.3
IV	Wheat yields (100 kilograms per hectare)	81.6
VI	Electricity generation (kilowatt-hours per capita)	80.6
V	Intensity of railway use (II) (million freight ton-kilometers per 100,000 population)	79.2
V	Railway density (III) (kilometers per person to population distance)	78.9
VI	Commercial energy consumption (II) (as percent of gross consumption)	78.7
II	Infant mortality (infant deaths per 1,000 live births)	77.6

6

TABLE 1 (cont.)

Japan's Percentile Rank Among All Countries in Terms
of Specified Indicators of Economic Development

Class of indicator	Description of indicator	Japan's percentile rank[a]
VI	Petroleum refining capacity (barrels per day per 1,000 population)	75.0
III	Agricultural population (percent of active population in agricultural occupations)	74.7
VI	Consumption of steel (metric tons per 1,000 population)	74.5
VI	Commercial energy consumption (I) (megawatt-hours per capita)	73.9
III	Primary school enrollment (proportion of children 5-14 in primary school)	70.4
II	Population growth (annual rate, 1953-57)	70.4
VI	Gross energy consumption (II) (megawatt-hours per capita)	68.1
III	Urban population (II) (population of largest city as a percentage of the total population of the four largest)	60.1
II	Youthfulness of population (proportion in age group 5-14)	58.7
IV	Energy potentials (II) (millions of kilowatt-hours per capita)	55.2
IV	Cultivated land (III) (percent of land cultivated)	54.2
V	Motor vehicles density (II) (vehicles per 100 kilometers of roads)	52.2
V	Railway density (II) (kilometers per 100,000 population)	50.7
I	Gross national product (II) (U.S. dollars per capita)	48.4
VII	International trade turnover (II) (imports and exports in U.S. dollars per capita)	39.4
V	Motor vehicles density (I) (motor vehicles per 1,000 population)	38.9
V	Road density (II) (kilometers per 100,000 population)	27.8
II	Food supply (calories per capita per day)	26.3
VII	International mail flow (pieces dispatched per 1,000 population)	11.3
VI	Commercial energy consumption (III) (annual rate of change per capita, 1937-54)	10.8

7

TABLE 1 (*cont.*)

Japan's Percentile Rank Among All Countries in Terms
of Specified Indicators of Economic Development

Class of indicator	Description of indicator	Japan's percentile rank[a]
IV	Cultivated land (I) (hectares per capita)	5.0
IV	Cultivated land (II) (hectares per capita agricultural population)	2.8

SOURCE: Calculated from data presented by N. Ginsburg. Most of the data are for the years 1955 and 1956. The number of countries ranked in terms of the various indicators varies from a minimum of 79 to a maximum of 136. Ginsburg's classification of the variables is as follows:

I   Gross national product
II Population
III The organization of population
IV The resource endowment
V   Accessibility
VI Technology and industrialization
VII External relations

JAPAN COMPARED WITH ALL OTHER COUNTRIES

For each of a set of 47 variables, Ginsburg[3] ranked all of the countries for which data were available. Data for each variable were ranked either in ascending or descending order of magnitude, according to which more appropriately reflected a descending order of development. Using the ordered data, the first step is to compute Japan's percentile rank among the countries specified for each variable. The percentile rank formula is:

$$PR = 100 \left\{ 1 - \frac{R - 0.5}{N} \right\}$$

where R = country rank, and N = number of countries ranked. After obtaining Japan's percentile rank for each

[3] Ginsburg, *Atlas.*

8

variable, these results have been ranked in turn, forming Table 1.

The components of Table 1 describe the factors of Japan's development; therefore it is interesting to find which of the original items have become the leading and which the lagging indicators of that table. An outstanding fact is that 98 percent of the countries of the world rely more heavily than Japan on raw material exports in relation to total exports. In this sense, Japan is almost the most "developed" country in the world; but of course this indicator also reflects Japan's poverty in natural resources. Imbalance in the resource structure has in turn led to exploitation of those means which are available, and this is expressed in the second indicator: in terms of domestic potential, Japan's development of water power also exceeds that of 98 percent of the countries of the world. The dimensions of development in which Japan's leading accomplishments are found lie precisely along an intensive rather than an extensive scale. The eighth indicator on the list—gross energy consumption—is the first on the extensive plane, but at the same time, it reflects the intensity-bias of Japan's processing activities.

At the other end of the list are found the complementary indicators of the deficits of this poorly endowed, intensively developed economy. Only 26 percent of the countries of the world have a smaller food supply in calories per capita per day, and in terms of cultivated land per capita Japan is almost the most poorly endowed country in the world.[4] Also at the lower end of the list is an indicator which deserves special mention, that of per capita international trade turnover, which reflects the influence not only of the capacities of Japan but also of the policies of other countries. Both of these factors are necessary to explain why, on a per capita basis, Japan's trade is so low.

Finally, encompassing and summarizing the other meas-

[4] Altogether, no clear pattern emerges in terms of Ginsburg's categories I through VII, each category being represented at least once in the extremities of the list.

9

ures of development is the measure of per capita income. Japan's per capita GNP lies only in the 48th percentile (although its aggregate GNP falls in the 91st percentile). Here we return to the anomaly noted above: relatively high development in terms of various indicators other than the critical one, combined with mediocre performance in terms of the key indicator. The anomaly is enhanced by the fact that Japan also scores fairly high in those indicators other than per capita GNP which most consistently discriminate between high and low income countries.[5]

Japan's economy thus yields a mixed result in terms of performance. For in 38 cases out of the total of 47 indicators Japan's performance outranks that of more than half the countries in the world; indeed, for 13 indicators, its development exceeds the level of more than 90 percent of the countries in the world. Nevertheless, Japan's percentile rank in per capita GNP is mediocre. We have here a clear numerical expression of the paradox with which we started. In Japan a unit of advance in terms of the usual dimensions of economic development yields a disproportionately small increment in per capita GNP.

Saying that there is a deficiency in income, of course, is merely another way of saying that there is a deficiency in output. The indicators which express qualitative refinement and intensive exploitation of human and natural resources describe the overall level of output. But they say nothing about output per capita. In terms of individual workers, given its methods and the man-resource ratio,

---

[5] Indicators with the greatest power of discriminating between high and low income countries are the following (each is on a per capita basis): GNP, daily newspaper circulation, physicians and dentists, electricity generation, and consumption of steel. They were selected in terms of the degree to which the group of upper income countries remains intact when ranked respectively by indicators other than income. I have devised the discrimination ratio concept as follows: (1) Countries are ranked according to their degree of development in terms of the given indicator, the most developed being listed first; (2) The number of countries among the first 50 listed which also appear in the list of those 50 countries with the highest per capita GNP is taken as the numerator; the denominator is 50.

Japanese intensive exploitation is accompanied by various forms of disguised unemployment. Since Japan is obliged to exploit marginal and submarginal resources, there develop situations in which intensive exploitation reinforces disguised unemployment in reducing per capita output: these are technological consequences of Japan's unbalanced resource structure.

JAPAN COMPARED WITH MORE DEVELOPED COUNTRIES

Taking then per capita GNP as the key indicator of the level of development, let us extend our analysis by comparing Japan with only those countries which surpass Japan in terms of this criterion.

On this basis of comparison, in which Japan's per capita GNP has been reduced to the bottom percentile rank, a striking result emerges. Once again there is the same paradox. It would be reasonable to expect a very low standing for Japan's other percentile rankings. But the situation in most cases is in fact comparatively favorable (see Table 2). Indeed, as before, for more than half of the indicators (27 out of 47), Japan's development exceeds that of half of the countries whose per capita GNP exceeds its own. This is an even more dramatic expression than before of the disparity between Japan's percentile rank in per capita income and its percentile ranks in most other indicators.

Having been calculated in terms of different sets of countries, the rank order percentile of a given indicator

TABLE 2

Japan's Percentile Rank in Terms of Specified Indicators Among Those Countries Whose Per Capita GNP Exceeds That of Japan

Class of Indicator	Description of indicator	Japan's percentile rank
VII	Export dependency on raw materials (raw materials as percent of exports)	94.3
VI	Waterpower development (proportion of potentials developed)	94.3

11

TABLE 2 *(cont.)*

Japan's Percentile Rank in Terms of Specified Indicators Among Those
Countries Whose Per Capita GNP Exceeds That of Japan

Class of indicator	Description of indicator	Japan's percentile rank
VI	Commercial fertilizer consumption (kilograms per hectare of cultivated land)	92.7
III	Post-primary school enrollment (percentage of total population in secondary and higher education)	90.8
III	Daily newspaper circulation (per 1,000 population)	90.6
II	Density of population (persons per square kilometer)	90.6
VII	Trade with the North Atlantic Region (percent of total exports)	88.3
V	Intensity of railway use (I) (million freight ton-kilometers per railway kilometer)	87.5
IV	Rice yields (100 kilograms per hectare)	87.5
I	Gross national product (I) (billions of U.S. dollars)	86.7
VI	Gross energy consumption (I) (millions of megawatt-hours)	86.7
IV	Energy potentials (I) (trillions of kilowatt-hours)	81.5
VII	International trade turnover (I) (imports and exports in millions of U.S. dollars)	79.8
III	Urban population (I) (percent of population in cities of 20,000 or more)	77.7
V	Railway density (I) (kilometers per 100 square kilometers)	74.0
VI	Hydroelectric generation (kilowatt-hours per capita)	74.0
II	Physicians and dentists (per 100,000 population)	71.3
IV	Wheat yields (100 kilograms per hectare)	68.9
III	Literacy (percentage of adults literate)	68.4
V	Road density (I) (kilometers per 100 square kilometers)	63.5
III	Urban population (II) (population of largest city as a percentage of the total population of the four largest)	60.2

TABLE 2 (cont.)

Japan's Percentile Rank in Terms of Specified Indicators Among Those
Countries Whose Per Capita GNP Exceeds That of Japan

Class of Indicator	Description of indicator	Japan's percentile rank
II	Population growth (annual rate, 1953-57)	60.2
II	Infant mortality (infant deaths per 1,000 live births)	56.7
VI	Electricity generation (kilowatt-hours per capita)	56.1
VI	Commercial energy consumption (II) (as percent of gross consumption)	53.6
III	Agricultural population (percent of active population in agricultural occupations)	52.1
V	Intensity of railway use (II) (million freight ton-kilometers per 100,000 population)	51.1
V	Railway density (III) (kilometers per person to population distance)	49.0
III	Primary school enrollment (proportion of children 5-14 in primary school)	44.8
VI	Consumption of steel (metric tons per 1,000 population)	43.6
IV	Cultivated land (III) (percent of land cultivated)	42.7
VI	Commercial energy consumption (I) (megawatt-hours per capita)	41.5
VI	Gross energy consumption (II) (megawatt-hours per capita)	37.8
IV	Energy potentials (II) (millions of kilowatt-hours per capita)	37.5
VI	Petroleum refining capacity (barrels per day, per 1,000 population)	35.7
II	Youthfulness of population (proportion in age group 5-14)	33.0
V	Motor vehicles density (II) (vehicles per 100 kilometers of roads)	28.1
V	Railway density (II) (kilometers per 100,000 population)	17.7
V	Road density (II) (kilometers per 100,000 population)	15.3
VII	International trade turnover (II) (imports and exports in U.S. dollars per capita)	13.8

13

TABLE 2 (*cont.*)

Japan's Percentile Rank in Terms of Specified Indicators Among Those
Countries Whose Per Capita GNP Exceeds That of Japan

Class of Indicator	Description of indicator	Japan's percentile rank
v	Motor vehicles density (I) (motor vehicles per 1,000 population)	13.5
vi	Commercial energy consumption (III) (annual rate of change per capita, 1937-54)	7.4
iv	Cultivated land (I) (hectares per capita)	5.2
vii	International mail flow (pieces dispatched per 1,000 population)	5.2
ii	Food supply (calories per capita per day)	1.2
iv	Cultivated land (II) (hectares per capita agricultural population)	1.1
i	Gross national product (II) (U.S. dollars per capita)	1.0

SOURCE: Same as Table 1.

differed in Table 1 as compared with its value in Table 2.
As an alternative to comparing the rank order percentiles
of given indicators, let us now compare the sequence of
given indicators in the two tables respectively. If the
sequences are not the same in the two lists, the differences
should be systematically related to the sources of backwardness. At first glance, the sequences are notably similar.
However, there are exceptions, which are shown in Table 3.

The differences in percentile rank order sequence of the
indicators in Table 2 as compared with Table 1 show that
in contrast to the higher income countries, Japan "overtrades" with the rich countries of the North Atlantic
Region (Western Europe and Anglo-America), has a higher
primacy rate in its principal city (Tokyo) than they, and
has a higher rate of population growth.[6] On the other

---

[6] However, this is accounted for by the high concentration of the
Japanese population in the reproductive age groups. "On a basis
standardized for differences in age structure, fertility in Japan is at

TABLE 3

Comparison of Tables 1 and 2

Indicator	Position in percentile rank order sequence		
	Table 1	Table 2	Difference
Table 2 compared with Table 1:			
RISE IN RANK ORDER SEQUENCE			
Trade with North Atlantic Region (percent of total exports)	19	7	+12
Urban population (II) (population of the largest city as a percentage of the total population of the four largest)	33	21	+12
Population growth (annual rate, 1953-57)	31	22	+ 9
FALL IN RANK ORDER SEQUENCE			
Petroleum refining capacity (barrels per day, per 1,000 population)	26	35	— 9
GNP (per capita)	39	47	— 8

hand, its per capita petroleum refining capacity is lower in relation to the high income countries than it is in relation to all other countries; and finally, of course, its per capita GNP status in Table 2 is at the bottom of the list.

Here we see new light on our paradox. Japan's trade partners among rich countries take a relatively higher proportion of its exports than they take from each other. Yet notwithstanding that Japan already "overtrades" with the North Atlantic countries, its trade with them is at the same time *insufficient* to enable foreign trade to play the role it must play in Japan's economy if it is to compensate for the unbalanced resource structure and thus raise per

present below that of most other industrialized countries, and a continuation of present trends in mortality and fertility would result in the cessation of further growth of the population within the foreseeable future." United Nations Secretariat of ECAFE, *Economic Bulletin for Asia and the Far East*, XII (Sept. 1961), 13.

capita national income above a backward level. Why is any potential increase in Japanese foreign trade largely restricted to the North Atlantic Region? It is because the poor countries elsewhere have insufficient purchasing power to substantially expand their trade with Japan. Rich countries can expand trade with the poor countries because they can provide the necessary finance, while Japanese trade is restricted primarily to those countries that can supply their own finance.

The relative preponderance of Tokyo in relation to the population size of other Japanese cities is another illustration of Japan's economic imbalance. It reveals the reinforcing effect of an absolute surplus of population in the country at large (associated with the high rate of population growth), combined with a relative excess of population in Tokyo.

Japan's low level of petroleum refining capacity implies a low level of mechanization—another mark of a labor-intensive economy.[7] For example, Japan's per capita use of automobiles is low, as would be expected in a poor country with poor roads, and thus the demand for motor fuel is low.

For a complete picture, we must take account not only of the differences in rank order sequence of indicators in Table 1 as compared with Table 2, but also of similarities at the bottom of both lists. That is, in which economic respects is Japan consistently disadvantaged? First, in terms of cultivated land per capita, Japan is practically the poorest of all countries. Second, in terms of international trade turnover per capita, whereas Japan ranks in the 39th percentile among all countries, it ranks only in the 14th percentile among those countries whose per capita income exceeds its own.

[7] As an average, however, the calculation takes no account of Japan's dual economy, in which some activities are highly modern and mechanized, whereas others are backward and unmechanized. Petroleum refining capacity, moreover, is increasing steadily at the present time in accordance with the advance of heavy and chemical industry as emphasized in the current long-range economic plan.

16

In summary, there is a population which is already too large and yet at the same time is still increasing. The counterpart of excessive population is found in an extreme scarcity of arable land. We find a relative imbalance of foreign trade combined with an inadequate level of foreign trade. Finally, there is a relatively low level of petroleum refining capacity.

Putting aside the agricultural and demographic variables for the moment, it may be argued that Japan's relatively low petroleum refining capacity is primarily an expression of its poverty, whereas the low per capita level of foreign trade helps explain why that poverty persists. For restricted access to the world economy reinforces the domestic limitations from which poverty arises.

CONCLUSION

Our point of departure was a paradox: Japan is a country at the head of the list according to some criteria of the degree of economic development, and at the bottom of the list according to others. In terms of half the absolute criteria of backwardness, as compiled by Leibenstein, Japan was still backward as of 1961. I then attempted to examine in relative terms the structure of distinctions between Japan and all other countries, on the one hand, as contrasted with distinctions between Japan and high income countries on the other.

As shown by the data, the consequence of the relation between Japan's natural poverty and its highly dynamic social institutions has been that the indicators which reveal a high degree of Japanese development are primarily those that reflect the degree of intensive exploitation of resources. Intensive exploitation has in fact been carried to marginal or submarginal levels, for as was seen, in Japan a unit of advance in terms of technological and demographic indicators is associated with a smaller increment of national income than is observed in most other countries. Thus economic efficiency is not necessarily found in "develop-

17

ment" which takes place by the exploitation of inadequate and unbalanced resources.

Therefore, in order to transcend backwardness and achieve sustained growth, more is required of Japan than the "critical minimum effort" specified in Leibenstein's thesis. Even when the proportional increase in income is fairly large (as has been the case following the period to which my data refer), the absolute increase is small, for Japan remains limited by the domestic resource structure. The classical prescription for a country with an abundance of labor, both unskilled and skilled, is to project its competitive power upon the international plane. Surprisingly, however, the level of Japanese foreign trade on a per capita basis is among the lowest in the world. Moreover, the ratio of total Japanese foreign trade to national income is also peculiarly low.[8] There are two things to be said about this.

First, it would be naïve, given Japan's recent percentage increases in national income, to infer from the low ratio of foreign trade to national income that Japan's dependence on foreign trade is low. This inference has sometimes actually been drawn, with consequent policy recommendations that future Japanese development should be staked primarily on expansion of the home market as opposed to the foreign market. But this inference is entirely misconceived. As analyzed above, foreign trade stands out as one of the principal bottlenecks which inhibit attainment by Japan of consistent levels of development in its various dimensions. For a poor and overpopulated country such as Japan, foreign trade is a basic and independent income determining factor.

Second, and this follows directly from my preceding remark, not only Japan's decisions, nor even Japan's decisions primarily, but rather the decisions of other countries will

[8] During 1956-58, the ratio of imports to national income was 14.1 percent. By 1970, the projection is that it will rise only to 16.7 percent, according to the Japanese Government, Economic Planning Agency, *New Long-Range Economic Plan of Japan, 1961-70* (Tokyo, 1961), p. 75.

determine the level of Japanese per capita foreign trade and thus the level of Japanese income.

For various reasons, as described below, the ratio of foreign trade to national income may underestimate Japan's dependence on foreign trade. In particular, as emphasized in this chapter, if per capita foreign trade were higher, per capita national income and total national income would be higher, but the ratio of foreign trade to national income would not necessarily rise.

---

2 · CONCEPTS OF FOREIGN TRADE DEPENDENCE

Concepts of foreign trade dependence might be classified as either quantitative or qualitative. In the preceding chapter I referred to an example of the former type, namely a relation between the per capita level of income and the per capita level of foreign trade. Qualitatively, dependence might be expressed, for example, in terms of the degree of stability or instability to which an economy is subject, due to influences arising from abroad. Also, the degree of complementarity between the domestic and the international sectors of an economy may express a qualitative aspect of its dependence. For example, *particular forms* of foreign commodities (or capital or technology) may be essential to the very existence of an economy—just as vitamins, oxygen or hormones are essential to a healthy human organism—regardless of the quantitative dimensions it has attained.

When we distinguish imports from exports, various dimensions of dependence emerge. Thus "dependence" on imports may be *low* because the average propensity to import is low; but "dependence" on imports may be *high* because a high volume of basic foreign commodities is consumed for which no import substitutes are available. On the other hand, "dependence" on exports may be *low* be-

19

cause the average propensity to export is low; but "dependence" on exports may be *high* because the ratio of value added in domestic production to the total value of exports is high. Thus a recent conflict of opinion appeared in the almost simultaneous statements of two authorities. Professor G. C. Allen observed, "It may surprise those who have accepted uncritically the proposition that Japan is exceptionally dependent upon international trade to learn that the relation between her trade and national income is now one of the lowest in the world."[1] According to Professor Jerome B. Cohen, however, "Some observers, noting the lower percentage of exports to national income erroneously conclude that Japan is less dependent on foreign trade than it was in the thirties. Nothing could be further from the fact."[2] Although both writers were expressing a "quantitative" point of view, the conflict arose from an emphasis in one case on the role of foreign trade in its pecuniary aspect as distinguished from its logistic aspect in the other. For Cohen's position was based on the fact that during a specified six-year interval, industrial production increased 100 percent while the consumption of imported raw materials increased by 134 percent.

Another example of conflicting interpretations with regard to pecuniary as contrasted with the logistic view of dependence concerns a pair of ratios constructed for the purposes of a study prepared under the direction of Arthur B. Hersey in the U.S. Department of State. They are:[3]

$$1 \qquad \frac{\text{originated exports}}{\text{national income}}$$

[1] G. C. Allen, *Japan's Economic Recovery* (London, 1958), p. 175.
[2] Jerome B. Cohen, *Japan's Postwar Recovery* (Bloomington, Ind., 1958), p. 111.
[3] U.S. Department of State, *The Place of Foreign Trade in the Japanese Economy*, Intelligence Research Report OCL-2815 (Washington, D.C., 1946), hereafter referred to as the Hersey Study. "Retained imports," used for final consumption in Japan, are the difference between total imports and imports required for exports. The excess of exports over imported materials used for exports—that is, the component of exports added by domestic production—is "originated exports."

20

$$2 \quad \frac{\text{retained imports}}{\text{national income}}$$

Referring to Ratio 1, which was about 15 percent in Japan during the 1930s, Professor W. W. Lockwood writes, "Retained imports furnished about 15 percent of the national income."[4] Thus he implies that the ratio is not only an indicator of Japan's dependence but a measure of the gains from trade as well. However, this raises a methodological difficulty.

In deriving both originated exports and retained imports, Hersey excludes what he refers to as "offsets." As applied to imports not treated as materials for exports, offsets are defined as "estimated quantities against which there were equal quantities of the same or similar exports."[5] For the logistic purposes of the Hersey Study it was entirely appropriate to exclude offsets from the estimate of imports necessary to achieve minimum per capita rations for a population of given size. In estimating the contribution of foreign trade to national income, however, we must take account of them. That offsets do make such a contribution can be appreciated merely from the fact that an apple in April does not have the same value as an apple in September. Offset shipments give rise to money incomes received by the traders who ship them and thus they reflect increments to national income. Throughout the economy, offset shipments contribute to national income by means of the additional infra-marginal transactions which they make possible.[6]

4 W. W. Lockwood, *The Economic Development of Japan* (Princeton, 1954), p. 385.

5 Hersey Study, Vol. I, Part 1, xiv. Depending on the point of view, an exchange of "similar" commodities may be regarded as either offsetting imports or offsetting exports.

6 An interesting example of the role of offsets was illustrated in the design of Japan's postwar bilateral trade agreements. When both Japan and its would-be trade arrangement partner were short of some particular commodity, Japan would sometimes contract to export it in order to receive back some other commodity which was also in short supply. The former deficit commodity would then be restocked by Japan through trade with some third country.

21

Quantitatively, offset transactions are an important component of Japanese trade because of both their size and their volatility. According to Hersey, they amounted to nine percent of total exports in 1930 and seven percent in 1936. By my estimate, they amounted to two percent of total exports in 1950 and 11 percent in 1954.[7]

In general terms, quite apart from the case of Japan, Ratios 1 and 2 above have an additional idiosyncrasy as measures of dependence; namely, they do not yield a consistent interpretation of the balance of payments. Before illustrating this, it should be noted that a rise in either 1 or 2 would be interpreted as an increase in the degree of dependence. That is, in 1 the rise is understood to mean an increase in relative dependence on export markets; in 2 a rise is understood as a relative increase in dependence on imports of commodities from abroad.

As a particular instance, suppose that while "dependence" in both 1 and 2 have risen, real net product and real net income remain constant. There is no consistent interpretation of this event in terms of the balance of payments, for whereas increased "dependence" in 1 is accompanied by an *increase* in foreign exchange receipts, increased "dependence" in 2 is accompanied by a *loss* of foreign exchange. In practice, moreover, if we are told that originated exports have risen, we may have no basis for knowing in which direction the accompanying change in retained imports will go. Neither, incidentally, is there any relation between the degree of dependence and the achievement of equilibrium in the balance of payments.

Suppose we allow income to vary. Now if we are told that the value of either Ratio 1 or Ratio 2 has changed, we need to know whether change has taken place in the numerator, the denominator, or both. Conceivably, the ratios may even remain constant and yet their component values may have changed. Given the summary value of a particu-

[7] Leon Hollerman, "Japanese National Income and International Trade: A Structural Analysis," (unpub. diss., University of California, Berkeley, 1957).

lar ratio, therefore, it may be difficult to estimate the direction of combined net change in foreign exchange receipts from one point of time to another, and at least as difficult to ascertain whether a specified change in the "dependence" level of one is accompanied by either a rise or a fall in the "dependence" level of the other. In short, there is no necessary consistency in either the direction of change in foreign-exchange receipts or in the direction of change in the summary "dependency" description of either ratio as compared with the other through time.

The ratios are nevertheless often used to expound the objectives of Japan's economic plan. An example of the contradictions which arise in this context may be worth mentioning. Suppose, for example, that in accordance with the objectives of the plan, the structure of Japan's industry is changed so that with a given total of textile goods output, artificial fiber textiles partly displace cotton fiber textiles. In this case, the real volume of imports will decline; assume that real net income remains constant. In this case, Ratio 2 declines. Therefore "dependence" *declines*. On the other hand, in terms of Ratio 1, after displacement of cotton fiber textiles by artificial fiber textiles, the originated value component of a given volume of textile exports will rise. Again assume that real net product remains constant. In this case, "dependence" has *increased*. Progress toward the accomplishment of the plan is thus susceptible of contrary evaluations so far as "dependence" is concerned. The moral is that Ratios 1 and 2 are not consistent aggregate measures of change in the degree of international trade dependence.

As a further complication, sometimes both quantitative and qualitative aspects of dependence are included in a single evaluation. An example again occurs in the Hersey Study in the context of its "dependent industry" formula, which takes account of the qualitative degree of international complementarity as well as the quantitative dimensions of Japanese industries. The distinction between "dependent" and "domestic" industries arises from the cutting of a continuum. Where the principal raw material used in the exports of a particular industry is imported in a volume equal to or greater than the volume embodied in exports, the industry is classified as "dependent." Where the principal raw material used in an export product is produced domestically in sufficient volume for exports as well as for domestic utilization, the industry is classified as "domestic." For 1930 Hersey found that less than half of Japanese exports were included in the category of dependent industries. In 1950, on the other hand, according to my estimate in which Hersey's criteria were used, 75 percent of total Japanese exports were produced by dependent industry.[8] This result contrasts strikingly with the inference which might be drawn from the fact that total Japanese exports in 1950 were only one-third their real volume of 1936. The latter inference would disregard the degree of dependence in terms of complementarity between the domestic and international sectors of the economy.

Below, I will distinguish import dependence from export dependence and analyze dependence in terms of individual industries. By means of this disaggregative approach we may hope to achieve greater coherence among the various indicators of dependence.[9]

3 · OUTPUT, EXPORTS, AND PRODUCTIVITY IN JAPANESE ECONOMIC DEVELOPMENT

As already anticipated, two alternative views may be distinguished in analyses of the role of foreign trade in Japan's economic development. One, referring to the fact that by far the greater part of Japan's total output has al-

[8] Hollerman, op.cit., p. 162.
[9] For further details, see my article, "The Logistic View Versus the National Income View, of Foreign Trade Dependence," *Hitotsubashi Journal of Economics*, Vol. I, No. 1 (Oct. 1960).

ways been absorbed by the home market, affirms that "the idea that the drive for foreign markets was the motor force of Japanese industrialization is nothing but a literary invention."[1] On the other hand, a recent study of the rate of growth of industry in Japan as compared with the rate of growth of exports concludes that "the latter seems to have a leading, causative role in industrial development."[2] In a sense, intermediate between the two is the position of Professor E.A.G. Robinson who has sought to explain *how* exports increase and suggested some "causal connections" between the growth of exports and the growth of national income.

Robinson observes that regardless of the size of the ratio of foreign trade to national income, exports make imports possible and that growth in turn is either fed or choked off by particular bottleneck imports which are available only to the extent that they can be paid for by exports. Most importantly, however,

> through the expansion of foreign trade, further scope may be given . . . for the process of increasing productivity per man-year by transfer of part of the working population into those activities where productivity is higher. At any time productivity tends to increase for two separate reasons: first, because in all industries technical progress is leading to a more efficient use of resources; second, because resources are increasingly concentrated in those industries where it is higher. My point is that increasing foreign exports are likely to be concentrated in those industries where relative productivity is highest and thus to raise the rate of growth of the national income and the power to accumulate.[3]

[1] W. W. Lockwood, *Economic Development of Japan*, p. 309.
[2] Miyohei Shinohara, *Growth and Cycles in the Japanese Economy* (Kinokuniya, Tokyo, 1962), p. 46.
[3] E.A.G. Robinson, "Foreign Trade in a Developing Economy," in *Economic Development with Special Reference to East Asia*, proceedings of a conference held by the International Economic Association, edited by Kenneth Berrill (Macmillan and Co., Ltd., New York, 1964).

In testing the links of his causal chain with regard to Japan, Robinson contents himself with observing that during the phase of its modern development between 1868 and 1900, "Japan enjoyed a rising export ratio," namely from three percent in 1868-72 to 13 percent in 1908-12.[4] However, according to our calculations as shown below, there is some doubt that this thesis holds true for the case of Japan.

In accordance with the implications of the preceding chapters I propose to proceed by an analysis of the inter-relations among exports, output, and productivity on a disaggregated basis. I am especially interested in Robinson's thesis because it states the case for the classical theory of international trade.

PRODUCTIVITY IN RELATION TO OUTPUT

Is it true that historically Japanese output expanded by a transfer of resources from less efficient to more efficient industries? First I prepared a rank order arrangement of ten major manufacturing industries in terms of the in-crease in their respective indexes of deflated gross output during the interval 1909-36.[5] Then I prepared a rank order list of the same industries in terms of the increase in their respective indexes of productivity per person engaged during the same interval.[6] Comparison of the two lists yields a coefficient of rank correlation of only .45. Beginning with 1929, value added in manufacturing was reported for the first time by the Census of Manufactures. Using data for value added instead of gross output, and performing the same calculations for the year 1961 in relation to 1936,

4 Robinson, op.cit., p. 5.

5 1909 is the first year for which Census of Manufactures data are available. 1936 is a typical prewar year commonly used for "standard" comparisons. In an attempt to assure the stability of our results, the analysis which follows includes a series of alternative representative periods.

6 The productivity index per person engaged was computed by dividing the deflated value of gross output or the deflated amount of value added (depending on which was available) by the number of persons engaged in each industry respectively and expressing the result as an index.

we obtain a rank order correlation coefficient of only .25. Again, performing the same calculations for the year 1961 in relation to 1948, we obtain a rank order correlation coefficient of only .30. In each case, therefore, the proportion of variation in output statistically explained by corresponding changes in gross output or value added per person engaged is very low, not significantly different from zero. In view of the low degree of correlation between relative increases in productivity and relative increases in output in given industries, it is of interest to identify those industries in which growth in output was greatest, as contrasted with those in which increases in productivity were greatest.

1936 compared with 1909

In 1909 textile products were far and away the most important industry, contributing 51 percent of total gross output in manufacturing. In terms of gross output per person engaged, however, chemical and allied products was the leading industry. At that time, per-person-engaged gross output in textiles was only 28 percent of the output in chemicals.

By 1936, textiles remained the leading industry in terms of gross output, but its share of total output had declined to 29 percent. Machinery was second, having increased its share from 5 percent in 1909 to 20 percent in 1936. In terms of gross output per person engaged, however, the metal industries were the leader in 1936. As shown in Table 4, moreover, the industries that made the greatest relative advance in total gross output between 1909 and 1936 were not highly correlated with those which made the greatest relative advance in output per person engaged.

There is a further point to be noted, however, in the comparison of results for 1936 with those of 1909. The two industries—machinery and metals—which led the list in terms of proportional output increases likewise led the list in terms of increased output per person engaged. They were second and third, respectively, in their contribution to total output at the later date. The chemical in-

27

TABLE 4

Rank Order Performance of Japanese Manufacturing Industries During Specified Periods in Terms of (A) Relative Increase in Value Added in Manufacturing,[a] (B) Relative Increase in Value Added Per Person Engaged[a]

Industry	Rank order of industry					
	1936 compared with 1909		1961 compared with 1936		1961 compared with 1948	
	A[b]	B[b]	A	B	A	B
Food and kindred products	9	7	8	9	6	9
Textiles	7	4	9	2	9	8
Lumber and wood	6	8	1	1	8	7
Printing and bookbinding	4	3	2	5	2	5
Chemical and allied products	3	9	7	4	7	1
Ceramics, stone and clay	5	6	5	6	5	4
Metals	1	2	6	8	4	3
Machinery	2	1	3	7	3	2
Miscellaneous manufactures	8	5	4	3	1	6
Coefficient of rank correlation:	.45		.25		.30	

[a] Deflated by Wholesale Price Index (1934-36 = 1).
[b] Rank order is in terms of relative increase in deflated value of gross output.

NOTE: The rank order designations in this table differ from those in corresponding columns of Tables 5 and 6 because of differences in the number of items ranked.

SOURCE: Calculated from *Kogyo Tōkei Gojyu Nen Shi* [History of the Census of Manufactures], Ministry of International Trade and Industry, 1961 and *Kogyo Tōkei Chosa Kekka* [Preliminary Results of Tabulation, Census of Manufactures, 1961], Ministry of International Trade and Industry, 1963.

All Census of Manufactures data in these tables were deflated by the Bank of Japan Wholesale Price Index (1934-36 = 1). The sectoral breakdown of the index is not available prior to 1931. However, for binary comparisons following 1931, supplementary calculations were performed using the sectoral breakdown of the index. A discussion of these calculations, which conform with the results of Tables 4-6, appears at the end of this chapter.

dustry, which was third in terms of increased proportional total output was lowest in terms of proportionate increased output per person engaged.

1961 Compared with 1936

Between 1936 and 1961 there is a bit of encouraging news for the Robinson thesis, concerning highly correlated increases in both output and productivity within individual

28

TABLE 5

Rank Order Performance of Japanese Manufacturing Industries During Specified Periods in Terms of (A) Relative Increase in Value Added Per Person Engaged, (B) Relative Increase in Domestic Exports from Japan

Industry	Rank order of industry					
	1936 compared with 1909		1961 compared with 1936		1961 compared with 1948	
	Aa	B	A	B	A	B
Foodstuffs	5.5	5	8	7	18	14
Textiles:	2	2	2	8		
textile mill products					15	18
apparel					17	8
Lumber and wood:	7	1	1	2		
lumber and wooden products					16	16
furniture and fixtures					10	1
pulp, paper and paper products					14	7
Publishing, printing and allied products	b		b		9	5
Chemicals and allied products:	8	7	4	5		
chemicals					1	13
petroleum and coal					b	
rubber products					6	2
leather					19	15
Ceramic, stone and clay products	4	8	5	4	7	19
Metals:	1	3	7	3		
iron and steel					3	6
nonferrous metals					8	11
fabricated metal products					12	12
Machinery:	5.5	4	6	1	5c	17c
electrical machinery and supplies					4	3
transportation equipment					2	4
meters and measuring instruments, etc.					13	9
ordnance and accessories						b
Other manufactures	3	6	3	6	11	10
Coefficient of rank correlation:	.18		—.07		.34	

a Value added statistics being unavailable prior to 1929, the comparison between 1936 and 1909 is made in terms of the value of gross output.
b No exports during one or both of the years being compared.
c For machinery other than those types listed below.
SOURCE: Same as Table 4.

industries. The lumber and wood industry, which leads the list in terms of its relative increase in value added since 1936 also leads the list in terms of the relative increase in value added per person engaged. In absolute terms, however, this industry contributed only 8 percent of the value added of total manufacturing output. By 1961, machinery was the leading industry in terms of total output, but whereas it was third in terms of the size of relative increase in total value added since 1936, it was only seventh in terms of the rela-

29

TABLE 6

Rank Order Performance of Japanese Manufacturing Industries During Specified Periods in Terms of (A) Relative Increase in Value Added in Manufacturing, (B) Relative Increase in Domestic Exports from Japan

Industry	1936 compared with 1909		1961 compared with 1936		1961 compared with 1948	
	Aa	B	A	B	A	B
Foodstuffs	8	6	7	7	12	14
Textiles:	6	4	8	8		
textile mill products					16	18
apparel					15	8
Lumber and wood:	5	3	1	2		
lumber and wooden products					18	16
furniture and fixtures					9	1
pulp, paper and paper products					10	7
Publishing, printing and allied products	b		b		3	5
Chemicals and allied products:	3	8	6	5		
chemicals					13	13
petroleum and coal						b
rubber products					7	2
leather					17	15
Ceramic, stone and clay	4	2	4	4	8	19
Metals:	1	5	5	3		
iron and steel					4	6
nonferrous metals					14	11
fabricated metal products					2	12
Machinery:	2	1	2	1	6c	17c
electrical machinery and supplies					19	3
transportation equipment					11	4
meters and measuring instruments, etc.					5	9
ordnance and accessories						b
Other manufactures	7	7	3	6	1	10
Coefficient of rank correlation:	.31		.81		.19	

a Value added statistics being unavailable prior to 1929, the comparison between 1936 and 1909 is made in terms of the value of gross output.

b No exports during one or both of the years being compared.

c For machinery other than the types listed below.

SOURCE: Same as Table 4.

tive increase in value added per person engaged. The textile industry was at the bottom of the list in terms of relative increase in total value added between the two dates, but due to the transformation of the industry away from its historically based emphasis on natural fibers towards chemical fiber output, its relative increase in value added per person engaged was second greatest among all industries.[7]

[7] If within a particular industry labor shifts from small, inefficient units of production to large, modern units, the efficiency of the in-

1961 Compared with 1948

1948 was the first year in which the Census of Manufactures data were compiled according to the commodity classification system now in effect. It also was a year in which rehabilitation had superseded relief as a principal objective of the Occupation authorities. However, during the postwar period following 1948, there is no clearer evidence than during longer periods or earlier periods of the kind of correspondence between growth in output and growth in productivity described by Robinson. Miscellaneous manufactures was the industry which made the greatest advance in the relative increase of value added to total output, but it was only sixth in terms of the degree of its relative expansion of value added per person engaged.

PRODUCTIVITY IN RELATION TO EXPORTS

If international trade is governed by the rule of comparative advantage, and if other countries are not improving their competitive position at a faster rate than the country being studied, Robinson's account of the "causal connections" between increased productivity and increased exports in particular sectors would seem to be convincing. In the case of Japan, however, for the fairly lengthy periods under review, these connections are as weak or weaker than they were in the relation between productivity and total output observed above.

In order to compare relative changes in manufacturing productivity with relative changes in exports within each industry, it was necessary to first recompile the record of Japan's export statistics at the most refined available level of detail into the industrial categories of the Census of Manufactures.[8] The reclassification presented several diffi-

---

dustry may apparently increase without any technological advance at all. In steel production, there is no possibility of such a shift because only large plants exist in the industry. This is one conceivable reason why the textile industry may show up well in productivity comparisons with the heavy and chemical industries.

8 The code for exports is found in *Yushutsu Nū Tōkei Hinmoku*

culties. In the first place, the descriptions in the foreign trade commodity classification are not always strictly comparable with those in the classification of the Census of Manufactures. Second, each of these codes has been changed several times during the interval of time under review.[9] Regarding coverage of the data, several distinctions were observed. In recompiling the export commodities, re-exports were excluded and only domestic exports were tabulated. Also, exports of unmanufactured primary goods were excluded inasmuch as only manufacturing industries are included in this analysis.[10] Finally, prewar exports to former colonial areas (Korea and Formosa) were excluded in order to maintain consistency with the analysis of Chapter 7 below.

As mentioned above, the correlation of relative increases in productivity with relative increases in exports for major manufacturing industries yields very poor results. Intuitively—as well as from the claims of various writers— I would have expected the opposite. In the case of the relation between increased productivity and increased total output of individual industrial sectors, the low correlation might be attributed to special needs of the economy for expansion in bottleneck sectors regardless of productivity inducements. With regard to exports, however, it is sur-

Hyō (Fu Tōkei Fugō Hyō) [Statistical Classification of Commodities for Japanese Foreign Trade, 1964], published by *Nihon Kanzai Kyokai Hakko* [Japan Tariff Association]. It is organized chiefly in terms of the nature of materials rather than the structure of industries. The Census of Manufactures code is published as the *Standard Industrial Classification for Japan, 4th Revision, May 1957*, Statistical Standards Bureau, Administrative Management Agency, December 1958.

[9] One instance of the vagaries of classification might usefully be cited. Chemical fibers (rayon, acetate, and synthetic) are included in the chemical industry. However, yarn, thread, and fabric made from chemical fibers are included in "Textile Mill Products, Except Apparel and Other Finished Products Made from Fabrics and Similar Material," and apparel made from chemical fibers is included in "Apparel and Other Finished Products Made from Fabrics and Similar Materials."

[10] Exports of wholly unprocessed primary goods amounted to less than 2 percent of total domestic exports during each of the years studied.

prising that the largest relative advances did not occur in those industries in which relative improvements in productivity were greatest. For the period 1909-36, the coefficient of rank correlation was only .18; for the period 1936-61, it was —.07, for the period 1948-61, .34.

Of course it can be argued that if important industries show parallel increases in productivity and output or in productivity and exports, this is more important for the well-being of the economy at large than merely a high rate of correlation between these types of increase among all industries. In the short run this may well be true, but it is not the point being pursued here. Instead, we are attempting to find out whether among the industries of the economy at large there occurs the kind of reallocation of resources that theory predicts. It should be emphasized that there is no reason why the theory should be confirmed in the case of important industries any more than in the case of lesser ones. Therefore it is appropriate that our correlation analysis take account of all industries rather than merely those that are principal revenue earners.

1936 Compared with 1909

During this period the relative productivity advance of the leading industries is not badly correlated with their corresponding advance in exports. For example, in terms of relative advance in productivity the leading industries were metals and textiles; these were third and second, respectively, in relative expansion in exports. However, the leading industry in terms of relative export expansion was lumber and wood, which ranked only seventh in relative productivity increase.

1961 Compared with 1936

The greatest relative productivity advance during this period was accomplished in lumber and wood products; in terms of relative export expansion, however, this industry ranked second. Textiles, the second ranking industry in productivity increase ranked eighth in export expansion.

33

The leading industry in relative export expansion was machinery; its rank was sixth in relative productivity increase.

1961 Compared with 1948

For this comparison, because of the more detailed categories presented by the Census of Manufactures, the industry breakdown is more refined than for the two periods previously reviewed. The degree of correlation, however, is consistently poor. It is interesting that the chemical industry was the leader in terms of relative productivity advance, while it was thirteenth in relative export expansion. The leader in relative export expansion was furniture and fixtures, which ranked tenth in improvement in relative productivity.

OUTPUT IN RELATION TO EXPORTS

Thus far, for the periods and industries specified, the analysis here does not reveal any special relation between relative increases in productivity and relative increases in either output or exports. On the evidence thus far, it would be difficult to ascribe, as Robinson does, a leading role to exports in the process of improving productivity.

In the relation between exports and output, however, we find somewhat clearer evidence for appraising the relative importance of the foreign market in contrast with the home market as factors in Japanese economic development. For the period 1909 to 1936, the coefficient of rank correlation is low, namely .31. For the period 1948 to 1961, it is .19. But for the period 1936 to 1961, which is probably the most meaningful period for the purpose at hand, the coefficient is .81. This means that 66 percent of the variation in the dependent variable may be statistically attributed to fluctuation in the other variable. In connection with further evidence to be shown, this result is consistent with my hypothesis, discussed below, concerning the role of supply-oriented exports in Japanese economic development. It is also consistent with the fact, for

34

which evidence will be shown in the following chapter, that growth and innovation in Japan during the postwar period have occurred primarily in response to the home market—with particular emphasis on import substitution—rather than to the incentives of producing for the foreign market.

SUPPLEMENTARY CALCULATIONS

As a check on the results of this chapter for periods in which a sectoral breakdown of the WPI is available, the results for 1961 as compared with 1936 and for 1961 as compared with 1948 were recomputed, using the sectoral breakdown. The results, which conform with those already discussed, are as follows.

In Table 4, the coefficient of rank correlation for 1936-61 was increased from .25 to .33; for 1948-61, it was increased from .30 to .67. Neither of these higher results is statistically significant at the five percent level.

In Table 5, the coefficient of —.07 for 1936-61 was raised to +.05; the coefficient of .34 for 1948-61 was reduced to .26.

In Table 6, the coefficient of .81 for 1936-61 was reduced to .57; the coefficient of .19 for 1948-61 was raised to .41.

---

4 · ECONOMIC PLANNING AND ECONOMIC STRUCTURE

Three statistical results were especially noted in the preceding chapter. First, it was shown that the path of Japan's growth has not necessarily been in accord with the pattern of increases in economic productivity. Second, we found that Japan's export expansion has not necessarily been in accord with the pattern of increases in productivity and conceivably not in accord with changes in comparative advantage. Third, instead, we found that exports had a tendency to expand simply in accordance with output. Since these results are rather challenging, it would seem desirable to support them with further evidence. In seeking this evidence, we obtain at the same time a cross-section view of the structure of economic growth in Japan following World War II.

THE KINDS OF INDUSTRIES WHICH HAVE GROWN

The Economic Planning Agency and its predecessors have described one of their basic objectives as that of "boosting the industrial structure to a higher level."[1] The "higher level" industries are those marked by a high degree of processing or value added per unit of raw material input as well as per person engaged—in other words, the industries of higher productivity. They include the metal, machinery, and chemical industries, which are largely based on imported raw materials. Enormous investments in these industries have been sponsored both directly and indirectly by the government, and it is planned that traditional products such as natural fiber textiles and sundry goods will be substantially displaced by them, especially in export trade.

Japan's progress towards the goal of increasing output per unit of input may be measured in terms of the relation between value added in manufacturing[2] and the total value of manufacturers' shipments. According to this measure, the performance of the economy at large should improve steadily over time, and the industries whose expansion has been assisted through "administrative guidance" should perform particularly well.[3]

With regard to both of these expectations, however, the record is disappointing. According to figures of the

[1] Japanese Government, Economic Planning Agency, *New Long-Range Economic Plan of Japan, 1958-62* (Tokyo, 1957), p. 15.

[2] Value added = Value of production—Cost of materials—Value of excise taxes included in Value of shipments—Value of depreciation. *Supplement to the Monthly Statistics of Japan: Explanatory Notes*, Statistical Standards Bureau, Administrative Management Agency, January 1963, p. 46.

[3] We assume that regardless of the restrictions (indicated in note 6) under which the value added ratio has been calculated, the figures in Table 8 correctly approximate both the time trend of the ratio and the comparative degree of value added by various industries.

Ministry of International Trade and Industry,[4] in the economy as an aggregate, the ratio of value added to total value of manufacturers' shipments was lower in 1961 than during the prewar "normal" year of 1936. In 1961, the ratio was 33.1 percent, as compared with 35.0 percent during 1936. (See Table 7.)[5] Immediately after World War II, curiously enough, the ratio temporarily soared to an all-time high of over 50 percent. Probably this reflected the fact that the customary network of subcontracting relationships had not yet been revived. When subcontracting was re-established, subassemblies were counted as raw materials by the prime contractor. In this connection, it should be noted that planning policy is also designed so that "the 'limping' development of major and small enterprises may be terminated and the dual structure of the nation's economic structure liquidated."[6] Inasmuch as the subcontracting system would likewise be largely liquidated along with the dual structure, it is clear that the objectives of the plan create a built-in bias in favor of a higher rather than a low ratio of value added to the total value of manufacturers' shipments. Taking account of this bias, the level of accomplishment by 1961 is doubly disappointing.

In the record of individual industries (Table 8) we are able to see the sources of the disappointing result at the aggregate level. Among officially encouraged industries, chemicals delivered the best performance in terms of the ratio of value added to value of manufacturers' shipments. However, the ratio of 41.2 percent for 1961 was still not very impressive as compared with the figure of 38.8 percent for the larger, more miscellaneous, and therefore "lower" category of "Chemicals and Allied Products" during 1936.

4 Released in preliminary form in May 1963.

5 It is usually claimed that the standards of the prewar "normal" economy were reattained by Japan in 1953. The above is only one of various dimensions in which this is not true. Another example is the case of deflated value added per person engaged in manufacturing. By this critical measure, the level of 1936 was not reattained until 1960.

6 New Long-Range Economic Plan, 1958-62, p. 77.

37

TABLE 7

Total Value of Shipments[a] and Value Added in Japanese Manufacturing, by Year, 1929 to 1961
(millions of current yen and percent)

Year	A Total Value of shipments	B Value added	C B/A	Year	A Total Value of shipments	B Value added	C B/A
1929	7,739	2,896	37.4	1950	2,294,109	730,455	31.8
1930	5,987	2,223	37.4	51	4,027,969	1,178,853	29.3
31	5,160	2,025	39.2	52	4,616,107	1,299,850	28.2
32	5,069	2,468	41.3	53	5,708,235	1,686,205	29.5
33	7,857	3,029	38.6	54	6,053,989	1,895,682	31.3
34	9,371	3,461	36.9				
1935	10,816	3,893	36.0	1955	6,561,887	2,098,597	32.0
36	12,236	4,288	35.0	56	8,473,910	2,543,668	30.0
37	16,328	5,334	32.7	57	10,226,879	3,016,819	29.5
38	19,620	7,065	36.0	58	9,880,929	2,865,353	29.0
39	24,793	9,398	37.9	59	11,888,785	3,645,482	30.7
1940	27,093	10,456	38.6	1960	15,293,704	4,887,125	31.6
41	30,458	11,968	39.3	61	18,732,911	6,194,787	33.1
42	32,039	13,690	42.7				
1946	84,266	46,238	54.9				
47	288,108	147,892	51.3				
48	825,072	353,054	42.8				
49	1,442,329	510,779	35.4				

[a] Shipment data for 1929 through 1947 are reported as "value of gross output." For this period also, statistics refer to establishments engaging five or more persons; thereafter, establishments engaging four or more persons are included.

SOURCE: *Kogyo Tōkei Gojyu Nen Shi* [History of the Census of Manufactures], Ministry of International Trade and Industry, 1961, and *Kogyo Tōkei Chosa Kekka* [Preliminary Results of Tabulation, Census of Manufactures, 1961], Ministry of International Trade and Industry, 1963.

TABLE 8

Ratio of Value Added in Manufacturing to Total Value of Manufacturers' Shipments[a] in Japan
During Selected Years 1929 to 1961
(percent)

Industry	1929	1936	1948	1949	1953	1958	1961
Total manufactures	37.4	35.0	42.8	35.4	29.5	29.0	33.1
Foodstuffs	43.7	36.5	30.2	23.6	18.8	20.9	23.7
Textiles	27.1	22.4					
textile mill products			48.1	33.4	22.9	21.7	28.4
apparel and other textile products			37.4	31.8	25.4	29.5	29.3
Lumber and wood	28.2	25.4					
lumber and wooden products			42.9	35.4	26.6	28.0	28.1
furniture and fixtures			47.7	46.0	38.5	38.3	38.2
pulp, paper and paper products			37.7	28.3	32.6	26.8	33.2
Publishing, printing and allied products	47.7	49.4	58.9	48.9	48.1	52.8	52.6
Chemicals and allied products	41.7	38.8					
chemicals			39.6	36.7	37.2	31.8	41.2
petroleum and coal products			42.0	30.5	25.4	11.9	20.1
rubber products			48.3	41.1	35.4	36.2	40.9
leather and leather products			53.1	31.0	20.9	26.7	27.4
Ceramic, stone and clay products	50.9	54.9	46.2	42.6	47.2	42.0	46.5
Metals	35.5	32.7					
iron and steel			41.5	32.6	24.1	20.8	28.0
nonferrous metals			32.3	25.8	24.6	22.6	23.4
fabricated metal products			47.6	42.1	31.8	36.6	37.3
Machinery	67.5	58.3	50.3b	48.0b	38.9b	40.3b	38.9b
electrical machinery and supplies			45.7	44.3	42.9	40.3	39.5
transportation equipment			48.9	42.3	35.4	29.7	30.8
meters and measuring instruments, etc.			53.1	45.0	40.1	42.1	41.3
ordnance and accessories			—	—	42.2	26.6	46.5
Other manufactures	37.0	30.6	42.6	35.3	33.4	34.4	34.4

a Shipment data for 1929 through 1947 are reported as "value of gross output." For this period
also, the statistics include establishments engaging five or more persons; thereafter, they include
establishments engaging four or more persons.
b Includes only nonelectrical machinery not elsewhere specified.

SOURCE: Calculated from sources given in Table 7.

On the basis of the "norm" for 1936, the subcategories of
the machinery industry were distinctly disappointing. In
the prewar year, the ratio of value added to the value of
manufacturers' shipments of all machinery had been
58.3 percent, but in 1961 the highest figure among the
components (excluding ordnance) was 41.3 percent for
meters and measuring instruments. Such as it is, the latter

figure owes much to the success of photographic and optical goods, which are included in meters and measuring instruments. Transportation equipment has a ratio of only 30.8 percent.

The worst performance was delivered by iron and steel and nonferrous metals—industries which are highly dependent upon imported raw materials. As compared with the 1936 ratio of 32.7 percent for Metals as a whole, the ratio of 28.0 percent for iron and steel and 23.4 percent for nonferrous metals places these commodities well below the average for manufacturing in general; indeed, they rank among the lowest five industries on the list. Since the ratio of value added in manufacturing to the total value of manufacturers' shipments reflects the degree of an industry's power to produce national income (though not necessarily the level of reward to its entrepreneurs), it is evident that some industries which have been leaders in the race for output expansion have been far from best in terms of maximizing the use of Japan's economic resources. In analyzing this ingredient of Japan's remarkable rate of aggregate growth, therefore, we come to the same conclusion as in the preceding chapter.[7]

Another pertinent measure of the success of the programs for rationalization and technical innovation of recent years is the percentage of raw materials cost in manufacturing shipment value. In contrast to what we would expect, by 1962 the ratio had declined less than six percent from its peak level (68.6 percent) of a decade earlier.[8]

[7] The conclusion assumed, however, that various factors excluded from this analysis either remained constant or were mutually self-cancelling in their effect on the value added ratio. These include industrial organization and institutional arrangements, relative prices among industries and the relation between prices of inputs and prices of outputs in particular industries, industrial technique and the degree of integration of the productive process at the level of the firm.

[8] Calculated from sources given in Table 7 and from Census of Manufactures, *Report by Industries*, Ministry of International Trade and Industry, December 1964, p. 10. The latter is in Japanese, the title only being given in English.

THE EFFECT ON EXPORTS

As mentioned above, it is an objective of government planning to encourage those exports which have a high degree of value added per unit of raw material (especially imported raw material) input. Commodities of this type would be those in which there is a high ratio of value added in manufacturing to the total value of manufacturers' shipments. However, we have seen that on the average this ratio was lower in 1961 than it was in 1936. Is it possible nevertheless that it has risen in the export sector taken separately?

The answer requires that the export statistics be recompiled in terms of the categories of the MITI[9] Census of Manufactures. For it may be assumed for each commodity group taken separately that the relation of value added to value of total shipments in Japanese manufactured goods exports will be the same as the relation between value added and value of shipments in Japanese manufacturing in general. However, the ratio (A) of total value added to total value of shipments in all Japanese manufacturing will not be the same as the ratio (B) of total value added to total f.o.b. value of Japanese manufactured goods exports shipments because of differences in the relative importance of the component groups comprising each total respectively. From the point of view of the income-earning power of Japan's exports in relation to the income-earning power of Japanese output in general, our question may be rephrased simply as follows: to what extent do these two ratios differ?

The recompilation of exports in terms of the Census of Manufactures categories has already been done as described in the preceding chapter. Next, the ratio of value added to value of shipments as calculated above for each major commodity category in the Census of Manufactures was applied to the corresponding categories as compiled from the export statistics. The sum of the amounts of value

[9] Ministry of International Trade and Industry.

added in each export category estimated in this manner enables us to calculate a weighted average ratio of value added to the total value of export shipments from Japan.

TABLE 9

Ratio of Value Added to Total Value of Shipments During Selected Years, 1929 to 1961 (A) in Total Japanese Manufacturing, (B) in Japanese Exports

Year	A In total manufacturing	B In exports
1929	37.4	30.9
1936	35.0	29.4
1948	42.8	45.6
1949	35.4	35.0
1953	29.5	28.5
1958	29.0	28.2
1961	33.1	32.6

SOURCE: Calculated as explained in text.

These figures also are consistent with the results found in the previous chapter. For it might have been hoped that although Column A has not risen appreciably in recent years Column B would nevertheless reveal an increase in Japan's international competitive power resulting from the tremendous expansion of its "modern" industries—those whose products have a high degree of value added by manufacturing. If anything, we find instead that Japan's exports have a slightly lower degree of value added than obtains within Japanese manufactured products as a whole.

The discrepancy is in the same direction, although not as wide, as during the prewar period. It is clear that by 1961 highly processed goods, which per unit sold are rich earners of foreign currency, did not yet predominate in Japan's export pattern. The figures show, moreover, that Japan earned only very slightly more national income per unit of exports sold in 1961 than it did in 1936. The present analysis thus reveals a fact which, due to Japan's favorable terms of trade, has tended to be masked in recent years. These findings also conform with the results of the preceding chapter. Given a low correlation between relative increases in productivity and relative increases in exports, it seems consistent to find that the average level of value added in exports has been lifted rather little by the modern industries in which rationalization and technological change have been concentrated.

SUPPLY-ORIENTED EXPORTS:[10] A HYPOTHESIS

Although Japan's export expansion has been poorly correlated with the pattern of increases in productivity, as the final chief result of the preceding chapter we found a moderately high correlation between relative increases in output and relative increases in exports. Before investigating the way in which this relationship might have come about, it is of interest to calculate the change through time in the proportion of the total output of various industries accounted for in each case by exports.

In order to express the basic substance of this change, I have estimated the ratio of value added in domestic exports to the total value added in manufacturers' shipments for each industry respectively.[11] (See Table 10.) In 1929 22 percent of the value added in Japanese manufacturing was embodied in exports; by 1961 the ratio had declined to 8 percent. The trend in aggregate, however, according to the selected years covered by my data, seems somewhat ambiguous, for the figures alternately rise and fall.

Nevertheless, there are some clear trends at the individual industry level.[12] Within the textile category, textile

[10] This descriptive term for my hypothesis was suggested by Professor Kazushi Ohkawa. Needless to say, his suggestion in no way commits him to the hypothesis itself.

[11] It should be noted that the results are considerably different from the simple ratio of the value of exports to the value of production.

[12] Before tracing these trends it should be noted again that I refer only to the relative importance of exports within each industry at a specified moment of time. Whether the absolute size of the industry has increased or diminished is not my concern at this point.

TABLE 10

Ratio of Estimated Value Added[a] in Domestic Exports of Manufactured Goods from Japan to Value Added in Total Manufacturers' Shipments[b] During Selected Years 1929 to 1961
(percent)

Industry	1929	1936	1948	1949	1953	1958	1961
Total manufactures	22.1	17.9	6.7	11.6	7.7	10.1	8.0
Foodstuffs	11.6	15.4	2.8	3.9	5.6	6.4	4.4
Textiles	47.6	41.8					
textile mill products			26.9	32.1	13.2	19.0	18.1
apparel and other textile products			9.1	30.2	36.1	80.9	51.1
Lumber and wood	14.8	15.3					
lumber and wooden products			2.7	5.1	4.4	10.1	5.7
furniture and fixtures			*	0.1	0.8	6.4	0.8
pulp, paper and paper products			7.4	1.3	1.0	2.9	3.3
Publishing, printing and allied products	—	—	*	0.1	0.7	0.7	0.8
Chemicals and allied products	9.4	8.0					
chemicals			1.9	1.6	4.6	4.8	4.7
petroleum and coal products			—	24.1	3.1	1.8	1.8
rubber products			0.3	9.2	2.5	6.1	6.3
leather and leather products			0.6	7.9	3.6	0.7	0.9
Ceramic, stone and clay products	25.6	26.5	20.1	20.5	13.7	12.8	10.8
Metals	6.5	7.7					
iron and steel			2.2	8.9	8.1	10.0	6.7
nonferrous metals			1.3	13.4	3.5	4.7	2.5
fabricated metal products			5.3	14.3	6.4	9.2	6.7
Machinery	5.4	10.9	1.4[c]	8.2[c]	6.1[c]	7.3[c]	1.7[c]
electrical machinery and supplies			2.6	4.0	2.5	5.8	10.9
transportation equipment			2.3	8.3	12.1	16.4	10.1
meters and measuring instruments, etc.			7.7	18.7	16.4	19.7	20.2
ordnance and accessories	—	—	—	—	3.0	21.6	31.7
Other manufactures	70.4	69.4	14.5	39.5	24.0	23.9	19.1

* Less than one-half the unit.

a See text for explanation of the method of estimation. The purpose of this table is to measure the importance to various individual industries of exports in terms of value added as distinguished from the total value of production exported.

b Manufacturers' shipment data for 1929 through 1947 are reported as "value of gross output." For this period also, the statistics include establishments engaging five or more persons; thereafter, they include establishments engaging four or more persons.

c Includes only nonelectrical machinery not elsewhere specified.

SOURCE: Estimates of value added in domestic exports calculated from *Nippon Gaigoku Bōeki Nenhyo* [Annual Return of the Foreign Trade of Japan], Ministry of Finance. Manufacturers' shipment statistics from *Kogyo Tōkei Gojyu Nen Shi* [History of the Census of Manufactures], Ministry of International Trade and Industry, 1961; and *Kogyo Tōkei Chosa Kekka* [Preliminary Results of Tabulation, Census of Manufactures, 1961], Ministry of International Trade and Industry, 1963.

mill output is steadily becoming less dependent on exports, while apparel and other textile products are becoming more dependent. Cheap labor in Hong Kong, India, and elsewhere have progressively displaced Japan in basic textiles, but Japan remains competitive in garments and more highly finished textiles. Indeed, with 51 percent of its value added being exported in 1961, the latter is more highly export-dependent than any other major Japanese industry.

Within the heavy and chemical goods industries, the degree of dependence on exports seems to have been fluctuating uncertainly or rising slowly during recent years, but the actual degree of dependence is very slight, sometimes even being well below the prewar degree of dependence. For example, in 1961 less than 5 percent of the value added in chemical production was exported, as compared with 8 percent for "Chemical and Allied Products" during 1936. In iron and steel and in fabricated metal products, the degree of dependence in 1961, about 7 percent, was approximately the same as for Metals during 1936. In electrical machinery and supplies and in transportation equipment, the degree of dependence in 1961 was about 11 percent, approximately the same as in the more inclusive Machinery category during 1936. Meters and measuring instruments, however, exported 20 percent of their value added. In the case of Other Manufactures, which include a high proportion of sundry goods, the decline from 1936 when 69 percent of value added was exported, to 1961 when only 19 percent was exported, is in accord with the plan to reduce the role of these goods in the export pattern.

On the whole, despite the fact that the quantity of exports practically quadrupled during the decade prior to 1961, these figures show that Japanese industry in the postwar period has become less, rather than more, export-oriented. The domestic boom was the principal ingredient of the growth rate; although exports increased in size they decreased in proportion to the national income.[13]

[13] In 1960, exports were 12.8 percent of the national income, as compared with 23.1 percent during 1936. (The Bank of Japan, Sta-

45

As the next step in the analysis, therefore, we must examine the way exports have grown in relation to the way national income has grown. There is a distinct difference, moreover, in the way in which national income itself has grown during the postwar, as compared with the prewar, period. As measured by the deflated value of gross industrial output, Japan weathered a depression following World War I in 1920-22 and again in 1930-32. In the important individual case of the textile industry, beginning with 1937 there was an additional prolonged episode of low-level production. In contrast, following World War II, with the exception of a decline in 1949 that was turned into a boom by the Korean conflict, Japan's aggregate industrial activity maintained a persistent and spectacular rise into the 1960s.

Despite the differences between the interwar and postwar periods, however, it will be recalled that our analysis shows a very low correlation between exports and productivity in *both* periods. This is consistent with the assumption that, in general, innovations are developed—or imported—primarily in response to opportunities in the home market rather than in the export market.[14] Furthermore, my correlations suggested that there may be some association between expansion in output and expansion in exports. Remaining, then, is the question: Does expansion in exports lead or lag expansion in output? If we assumed correctly that innovations are developed primarily for the home market, it is reasonable to assume further that expansion in exports lags expansion in output.

In order to take account of the differences between the interwar and postwar periods respectively, we return to the data with the above question expressed in the following

tistics Department, *Historical Statistics of the Japanese Economy* [Tokyo, 1962], p. 90.) A key point is the fact that in terms of value added, the ratio of manufactured exports to total manufacturing output was even less during both years.

[14] Indeed, both before and after World War II, the introduction of new technology has often been based on the administrative policy of "catching up" rather than upon the economic forces of comparative advantage.

form: During a period marked by depressions, such as that following World War I, do increases in exports occur primarily when pressure to export becomes more intense through the increasing availability of excess capacity, or do they occur primarily at other times? On the other hand, during a period of more or less sustained growth in output, such as that following World War II, does the rate of increase in exports rise when the rate of increase in total output slackens?

First, then, for the prewar period, I identified periods during which excess capacity existed in each of the principal categories[15] of output specified by the Census of Manufactures. My method was to find newly attained peaks in the deflated value of gross output which were followed by periods of decline. Until output was restored to the former peak, I inferred the existence of a period of excess capacity. The amount of excess capacity at any given time may be said to equal the difference between actual output at that time and the amount of output at the former peak.[16] Next we referred to our compilation of the corresponding export series for each of the output categories. The interrelation between changes in exports and the onset of excess capacity was then observed.

Between 1919 and 1942, within the eight categories of the breakdown, 60 percent of the occasions in which exports increased were also occasions in which excess capacity existed. Moreover, 82 percent of the occasions in which new export peaks were attained were found to occur during periods of excess capacity.

In contrast with the interwar period, during a period of general buoyancy marked by occasional "saucering out" of booms, such as that following World War II, the problem

15 Eight categories—food, textiles, lumber, chemicals, ceramics, metals, machinery, and miscellaneous goods—are included in this analysis. Printing and publishing are omitted as being essentially a domestic rather than an export industry.

16 This method has been suggested by Lawrence R. Klein in his Osaka lectures for periods in which excess capacity statistics are not available.

is to find whether export increases are or are not synchronized with declines in the rate of increase of industrial activity. Let us take account of several important examples.

In the case of textile mill products, export increases occurred during six of the eleven years 1950-61. In every instance except one, these coincided with declines in the rate of increase of deflated value added in the output of textile mill products.

The iron and steel industry is another important example, in several respects. First, the industry itself accounts for a large proportion of total output and occupies a highly important place in Japan's program for economic development. Second, iron and steel were characterized by greater fluctuations in output following World War II than any other industry of comparable importance. During 1950-61, there were six years in which iron and steel experienced a decline in the rate of increase of deflated value added. In each of these cases, exports of iron and steel increased during the same year, in the following year, or both. In no case did exports increase during any other year.

Conclusions based on these results are necessarily tentative and require further study and testing. As a working hypothesis, however, it may be suggested at this stage that exports seem to be impelled by increases in output capacity. In the effort to hold their relative share of sales amid implementation of the income-doubling plan, many producers in recent years have expanded their productive capacity ahead of the realized growth of the domestic market. In these cases especially, extra efforts to export became imperative. However, because of the greater profits available in the protected domestic market prior to liberalization, these efforts would be made only after initial efforts had been made to expand sales at home. Another factor in the situation is the life-contract system which forces manufacturers with permanent employees to continue working even when prices are lower than average total cost, so long as they are higher than average variable cost. Thus for various institutional as well as statistical reasons, the hypothesis of output-oriented exports has an air of plausibility.

---

5 · THE STATUS OF LABOR–INTENSIVE INDUSTRY[1]

Historically, the labor-intensive sector has played a key role in Japan's economic development. But it constitutes an anachronism in Japan's present stage of transition. Although some modern industries are labor-intensive, in general this quality often serves to distinguish progressive from backward industries. The distinction is summarized in the phrase "dual economy." In both a technological and a welfare sense, it has long been an objective of the planning authorities that "the dual character of the nation's economic structure [be] liquidated."[2]

The advanced, capital-intensive sector of the economy is identified with the heavy and chemical industries. Consistently, since even before the end of the Occupation, Japan's government and business leaders have cooperated in a massive program to expand the role of these industries, in which, for technological reasons, the possibilities of substituting labor are slight. Consequently, their rate of advance in productivity and their contribution to national income in terms of value added have been enhanced.

Besides the direct action of authorities, several additional factors have tended to accelerate the relative displacement of the labor-intensive sector. A structural factor has been the shortage of skilled labor.[3] At the policy level

---

[1] The term "labor-intensive" in this chapter refers simply to the degree of value added by labor rather than to the capital/labor ratio.

[2] Japanese Government, Economic Planning Agency, *New Long-Range Economic Plan of Japan, 1958-62*, p. 77.

[3] Because of the presence of a large number of workers in activities of relatively low productivity, it may be argued that in general Japan still has a relatively abundant labor supply.

on the international plane, the twin programs of import liberalization and exchange liberalization have exposed Japan to new competition, especially among the modern industries. Accordingly, they have been impelled to innovate and rationalize at a faster pace than they otherwise might.[4]

Indeed, during the period of liberalization, Japan's growth rate has been among the highest in the world. Partly, the reason seems to be that increases in competitive power were taking place prior to, rather than after, implementation of the various categories of liberalization. At any rate, the disturbances and distress which had been feared as a result of liberalization largely failed to materialize. Since the so-called degree of liberalization reached 92 percent by August 1963, it may be assumed that by that date the industrial adjustments attributable to it had already been mostly completed. This fact—in view of the lag in publication by the MITI of comprehensive statistics concerning Japanese industry—is a convenience for the present analysis. Complete figures are available only through the calendar year 1961, by which date adjustments due to liberalization may be considered to have reached an advanced stage.

Using the most recent figures available, then, I would like to evaluate the character of Japan's recent growth in terms of the status of labor-intensive industry. The question may be asked in two parts: (1) What changes have occurred in the degree of labor-intensiveness in Japanese industries; and (2) What changes have occurred in the relative importance of the various labor-intensive industries as such?

There are two aspects to the measurement of (1). First, we may compare the change over time in the relation of the most labor-intensive industries, as compared with the

[4] Concerning the "conflict between planning and liberalization," it is interesting that in the present instance their objectives have been mutually reinforced. Moreover, in fulfilling the obligations of Japan's membership in IMF, GATT, and OECD, liberalization appears to be a method of making a virtue out of a necessity.

relation of the most capital-intensive industries to the average degree of labor-intensiveness in the economy at large (Table 11). The most labor-intensive industries in Japan are:[5] apparel (42.4), lumber and wooden products (55.5), furniture and fixtures (56.8), textile mill products (61.1), and miscellaneous manufactures (62.8). In each of these cases, the proportion of deflated value added per person engaged in the respective industry to the average value added per person engaged in Japanese industry at large *declined* or remained almost stationary between 1953 and 1961. The same is true of almost every other industry whose value added per person engaged was less than the average for all industry in 1953. The transportation equipment industry (which includes shipbuilding, in which recent technological advance has been outstanding) was a notable exception: its proportion rose from 91.5 percent in 1948 to 124.0 percent in 1961. Machinery, particularly electrical, also showed an improvement.

At the other end of the scale, the most capital-intensive industries in 1961 were[6] petroleum and coal products (316.6), chemicals (202.1), iron and steel (163.7), nonferrous metals (140.3), and transportation (124.0). In each of these cases, with the exception of nonferrous metals (a depleted industry), the proportion of value added in relation to that for industry at large *increased* substantially between 1953 and 1961. In other words, the amount of value added per person engaged was being increased so rapidly by the capital-intensive industries that though every industry without exception registered some increase in value added per person engaged between 1953 and 1961, the labor-intensive industries were being left further and further behind in terms of the rising average.

[5] In parentheses is shown deflated value added per person engaged in the specified industry as a percentage of deflated average value added per person engaged in total Japanese manufacturing during the calendar year 1961.

[6] For figures in parentheses, see note 5 above. This classification of capital-intensive industries is consistent with one given by the Ministry of International Trade and Industry, *Analysis of Current Japanese Industry*, 1959, p. 167.

TABLE 11

Comparative Degree of Labor-Intensiveness Among Japanese Industries During Specified Years 1948 to 1961

Industry	1948			1953		
	A	B	C	A	B	C
Total Manufacturing	750		100.0	1,030		100.0
Foodstuffs	911	14	121.5	992	11	96.3
Textiles						
textile mill products	595	5·	79.3	723	5	70.2
apparel and other textile products	451	1	60.1	511	1	49.6
Lumber and wood						
lumber and wooden products	556	4	74.1	564	3	54.8
furniture and fixtures	482	2	64.3	520	2	50.5
pulp, paper and paper products	1,081	19	144.1	1,511	18	146.7
Publishing, printing and allied products	912	15	121.6	1,238	15	120.2
Chemicals and allied products						
chemicals	1,063	18	141.7	1,832	20	177.9
petroleum and coal products	908	13	121.1	2,818	21	273.6
rubber products	796	12	106.1	1,141	13	110.8
leather and leather products	948	17	126.4	739	6	71.7
Ceramic, stone and clay products	744	10	99.2	1,099	12	106.7
Metals						
iron and steel	935	16	124.7	1,411	17	137.0
nonferrous metals	1,127	20	150.3	1,806	19	175.3
fabricated metal products	704	9	93.9	817	9	79.3
Machinery[a]	689	8	91.9	872	10	84.7
electrical machinery and supplies	747	11	99.6	1,268	16	123.1
transportation equipment	686	7	91.5	1,163	14	112.9
meters and measuring instruments, etc.	641	6	85.5	763	8	74.1
ordnance and accessories	—	—	—	749	7	72.7
Other manufactures	536	3	71.5	568	4	55.1

Column headings:

A: Value added per person engaged, in deflated yen (1934-36 = 1).

B: Rank order of labor-intensiveness.

C: Value added per person engaged in specified industry as a percentage of average value added per person engaged in total Japanese manufacturing.

Against this background, the answer to part (2) of my question above is very surprising. For in assessing changes in the relative importance of Japanese industries, we find that between 1953 and 1961 the aggregate value added in those industries which were most labor-intensive—and most laggard in reducing labor-intensiveness—increased proportionately about as much as the value added by their opposite numbers in the advancing "modern" sector.

To illustrate this point, I have arbitrarily split the continuum between labor-intensive and capital-intensive in the middle of the list of industries (Table 12). The ten

TABLE 11 (Continued)

Comparative Degree of Labor-Intensiveness Among Japanese Industries During Specified Years 1948 to 1961

Industry	1959			1961		
	A	B	C	A	B	C
Total Manufacturing	1,435		100.0	2,052		100.0
Foodstuffs	1,153	7	80.3	1,741	9	84.8
Textiles						
textile mill products	884	4	61.6	1,253	4	61.1
apparel and other textile products	620	1	43.2	870	1	42.4
Lumber and wood.						
lumber and wooden products	761	3	53.0	1,139	2	55.5
furniture and fixtures	633	2	44.1	1,166	3	56.8
pulp, paper and paper products	1,703	14	118.7	2,375	16	115.7
Publishing, printing and allied products	1,632	13	113.7	2,219	14	108.1
Chemicals and allied products						
chemicals	2,926	20	203.9	4,148	20	202.1
petroleum and coal products	5,066	21	353.0	6,497	21	316.6
rubber products	1,349	11	94.6	2,134	18	104.0
leather and leather products	1,004	5	70.0	1,491	6	69.4
Ceramic, stone and clay products	1,266	9	88.2	1,985	11	96.7
Metals						
iron and steel	2,485	19	173.2	3,359	19	163.7
nonferrous metals	2,300	18	160.3	2,879	18	140.3
fabricated metal products	1,148	6	80.0	1,683	8	82.0
Machinery[a]	1,536	12	107.0	2,069	12	100.8
electrical machinery and supplies	1,889	15	131.6	2,323	15	113.2
transportation equipment	1,998	16	139.2	2,545	17	124.0
meters and measuring instruments, etc.	1,247	8	86.9	1,507	7	73.4
ordnance and accessories	2,146	17	149.5	1,936	10	94.3
Other manufactures	1,289	10	89.8	1,289	5	62.8

a Includes only nonelectrical machinery not specified elsewhere.

SOURCE: Calculated from *Kogyo Tōkei Gojyu Nen Shi* [History of the Census of Manufactures], Ministry of International Trade and Industry, 1961, and *Kogyo Tōkei Chosa Kekka* [Preliminary Results of Tabulation, Census of Manufactures, 1961], Ministry of International Trade and Industry, 1963. Includes enterprises engaging four or more persons only. Deflation was done by Wholesale Price Index (1934-36 = 1) from The Bank of Japan.

most labor-intensive industries contributed 35.8 percent of the total deflated value added in Japanese manufacturing in 1953; in 1961 they contributed slightly less, 31.3 percent. The same calculations for the ten most capital-intensive industries show that in 1953 they contributed 58.3 percent of total deflated value added; in 1961 they contributed slightly more, 63.9 percent.[7] In view of the extraordinary priorities in terms of allocations, subsidies,

7 From Table 12 it may also be seen that the 1961 relatives in the labor-intensive category exceed their partner relatives in the capital-intensive category in exactly half the cases listed.

TABLE 12

Value Added in Japanese Manufacturing Industries During 1961: Relatives Based on Deflated Magnitudes, 1953 = 100

Rank order of intensiveness in 1961a	Labor-intensive industries		Capital-intensive industries	
	Industry	1961 relative	Industry	1961 relative
1	Apparel	292	Petroleum and coal	290
2	Lumber and wood	294	Chemicals	309
3	Furniture and fixtures	433	Iron and steel	371
4	Textile mill products	217	Nonferrous metals	291
5	Miscellaneous manufactures	495	Transportation equipment	403
6	Leather and its products	337	Pulp, paper	275
7	Meters, measuring instruments	454	Electrical machinery	626
8	Fabricated metal products	511	Publishing, printing	284
9	Foodstuffs	307	Rubber products	378
10	Ordnance	17	Nonelectrical machinery	534

a The continuum between labor-intensive and capital-intensive industries was arbitrarily split in the middle of the list of industries. Ceramic, stone, and clay products were omitted in order to balance the number of items in the lists. The 1961 relative for this industry is 181. (The value of the relative is the index level based on 1953 = 100.)

SOURCE: Calculated from the sources given in Table 11.

and finance bestowed on the capital-intensive industries in recent years, this performance seems less impressive than figures for the size of investment would lead us to expect.

This reveals that the drive to promote capital-intensive industries and to liquidate labor-intensive ones has been only partly successful. It suggests that the progress of the economy in generating reserve power for the output of capital-intensive exports leaves something to be desired. At the same time, Japan is losing its comparative advantage in labor-intensive industry to the less-developed countries. Their competition will increasingly be felt by Japan both at home and in third markets, for, as will be seen below, small industry, which is essentially labor-intensive, plays a substantial role in Japanese exports. This combination of circumstances presents a possible source of difficulty in Japan's balance of trade and accordingly is a threat to its import liberalization program.

---

6 · ECONOMIC STRUCTURE AND UNBALANCED TRADE

Our inquiry leads next to a question concerning the distribution of Japan's foreign trade in relation to the results already observed.

As mentioned above, Japan's leading trade partners are among the rich countries of the North Atlantic region. Even during 1934-36, Japan sold 23 percent of its exports to North America. During the five-year period centered on 1961, the proportion was 33 percent. But during both periods the merchandise trade between Japan and North America was highly unbalanced, primarily in favor of the United States. Imports from North America during the five years centered on 1961 were 42 percent of total imports.

It is a commonplace that Japan's natural resource position is heavily in deficit. However, is it desirable that the resource deficit should enter the accounts principally as a deficit in Japan's merchandise trade with the United States? In a world of truly multilateral relations, of course there would be no need for trade between any two regional areas to be bilaterally balanced. In fact, however, total trade has been unbalanced and Japan has been obliged to pay its debts by capital loans. A preponderant proportion of these happens to be short-term loans, which places Japan in a vulnerable position.[1]

Aside from the financial burden of the deficit, the nature of its structural repercussions on Japanese industry is of equal or even greater importance. These repercussions take effect through institutional action by which Japan's national need to export is transformed into actual exports by private firms. One of the principal ingredients of Japan's high growth rate in recent years is the relatively unnoticed and little known nature of this institutional action. Hitherto, the exchange control system has been one of its chief instruments. During brief periods, in order to obtain desirable import licenses, firms have been impelled to export almost without regard to profit or loss on exports. The credit control system works in a similar manner. Because of the way in which domestic credit is restricted and channeled, firms are forced to obtain export contracts— accompanied by letters of credit—which they use either to finance production or to finance short-term loans to others at high rates of interest. These are institutional aspects of what has been described above as "supply-oriented exports."

Given Japan's deficit position in the world economy, the

[1] The imbalance of trade as financed by capital inflow has been a net benefit to growth and not intrinsically bad. However, the extent of short-term usance credit provided by foreign (mostly United States) banks for the financing of Japanese imports amounted at the end of 1965 to approximately the total amount of Japan's foreign exchange reserves. The increase in the United States discount rate at that time made it possible—subject to the availability of funds—for Japanese importers to borrow more cheaply at Japanese banks than in the United States. Theoretically, this jeopardized Japan's entire supply of foreign exchange. Other aspects of Japan's vulnerability on this score are discussed below.

56

responsibility for the way in which it responds to the situation is, of course, primarily Japan's. At the same time, its choice of means depends on the way in which established international institutions either work or fail to work in helping it find a state of equilibrium.

At the moment, however, I would like to assess the nature of the accommodation already reached. Specifically, I would like to know whether exports induced in the manner described above do or do not result in distortions in the structure of Japanese production. As a small beginning in the attempt to answer this question, I will repeat in the case of Japan's exports to the United States some of the analysis which has been performed above with regard to Japan's total exports.

My first set of calculations is an attempt to test the theory that "increasing foreign exports are likely to be concentrated in those industries where relative productivity is highest. . . ."[2] By means of rank correlation analysis, I have compared the relative increase in productivity per person engaged in Japanese manufacturing industries with the relative increase in the value of exports of each of these industries to the United States. In order to perform the analysis it was necessary first to recompile at the most refined available level of commodity detail the statistics of the *Nippon Gaigoku Bōeki Nenhyo* [Annual Return of the Foreign Trade of Japan] into the categories of the *Kogyo Tōkei Hyō Sangyo Hen* [Census of Manufactures, Report by Industries].[3] Categories for each of the major industries specified by the Census of Manufactures were utilized and all data were deflated by the Bank of Japan Wholesale Price Index (1934-36 = 1).

For various representative intervals I obtained a set of uniformly negative results, and for several postwar periods taken separately I obtained positive but uniformly poor

---

2 E.A.G. Robinson, "Foreign Trade in a Developing Economy."
3 See *Yushutsu Nū Tōkei Hinmoku Hyō* [Statistical Classification of Commodities for Japanese Foreign Trade], published by Nihon Kanzei Kyōkai [Japan Tariff Association] (Tokyo, 1964.)

results, as shown in Table 13. As in the analysis of Japan's total exports, in the case of Japan's exports to the United States I have found no confirmation of the hypothesis that increases in exports correspond with increases in productivity in particular industries. Since Japan's trade with the United States is such an important part of its total trade, it may be presumed moreover that the characteristics of Japan's trade with the United States largely determine the total result.

TABLE 13

Relative Increase in Productivity in Relation to Relative Increase in Exports to the United States During Specified Periods

Period	Coefficient of rank correlation
1936-1949	—0.53
1936-1953	—0.60
1936-1958	—0.02
1936-1961	—0.35
1949-1961	0.31
1953-1961	0.33

Evidence at this point in favor of the alternative hypothesis of supply-oriented exports is also not good, but it is better than the evidence just presented for the classical hypothesis. Rank correlation coefficients were calculated for the relative increase in value added by each major Japanese manufacturing industry in relation to the relative increase in the value of exports by the same industries to the United States. All data were deflated by the Wholesale Price Index and the relation was calculated for two strategic intervals of time, 1936-61 and 1953-61. The results are shown in Table 14.

TABLE 14

Relative Increase in Output in Relation to Relative Increase in Exports to the United States During Specified Periods

Period	Coefficient of rank correlation
1936-1961	0.50
1953-1961	0.52

In the preceding chapters I have attempted to analyze the structure of Japan's foreign trade in relation to the structure of Japanese industry. Next I will consider economic performance in the foreign trade sector as such.

PART II: PERFORMANCE

In Part II I examine the details of Japan's actual foreign trade performance during the period in which liberalization was introduced.

Consistent with the implications of Part I, in which various structural anomalies were found in the relation of trade to production, and despite the fact that as shown there the degree of Japan's foreign trade dependence is often underestimated, I find that the chief source of growth during the postwar period was in the domestic market rather than abroad. Prior to liberalization, Japan's new industries found many opportunities for import substitution without being deterred by the necessity for attaining world competitive standards in the protected home market. Import liberalization, however, implies this very necessity, not only for the defense of the home market but also so that exports may be expanded sufficiently to pay for the increased imports which liberalization entails, most of which are industrial raw materials for which no import substitution is possible. Accordingly, as growth proceeds, we find that the foreign market impends ever more closely as a constraint on the growth rate. In this sense, Japan's foreign trade dependence has progressively increased.

An important element of the mechanics of growth within the home market has been the competition for market shares among leading *keiretsu* (*zaibatsu* successor) firms. This gave rise to speculative investment in plant and equipment, causing productive capacity to expand massively in advance of home demand. The imports that were needed both at the investment and the operational stages of this new investment created periodic deficits in the balance of payments, at which time the government implemented tight money policies for the double purpose of restricting imports and encouraging exports. Thus the incentive of greater and easier profits at home than abroad, the machinery (including the credit system) by which speculative investment was made possible, and the rivalry

61

among oligopoly firms were the motor force both of Japan's domestic expansion and of the recessionary phenomenon of supply-oriented exports. It is of particular interest that during the peak of the domestic boom in 1964, only about 82 percent of the installed capacity of Japanese industry was being operated.

In many cases, firms had not completed the transition from a primitive accomplishment of import substitution to the attainment of world competitive standards. Such firms were obliged to compete in foreign markets simply on a price basis during times of recession. Their performance thus contributed a destabilizing, rather than stabilizing, element to Japan's export position, and by being inferior to world standards jeopardized its import liberalization program as well.

Increasing pressure on the supply side was accompanied by increased complementarity in the composition of Japanese trade. In the postwar period this was revealed by a steady increase in the role of manufactures among exports and by absolute and relative increases in the role of raw materials and food among imports. Increased complementarity was also shown by the fact that as compared with the increase in manufacturing output which it supports, the postwar expansion in the use of imported raw materials has been greater in Japan than the corresponding increase in the world at large. In geographical terms, as well as in terms of the commodity composition of trade, the degree of complementarity in Japan's foreign trade has increased during the postwar period.

The outlook for the liberalization program is immediately linked to the prospect for exports, which must be analyzed in terms of their composition and stability as well as in terms of volume. In these respects, Japan's recent performance leaves something to be desired. Ironically, in the long recession beginning in 1964 the level of exports was often identified as being one of the "bright spots" of the economy. According to my analysis, however, the high level of exports, resulting from excess capacity, and yielding very low profits, was a confirming rather than disconfirming indicator of the recession.

Part II concludes with a discussion of the capital accounts which have borne the burden of redressing the imbalance of Japan's commodity transactions during the period of rapid growth. The balance of payments includes a large component of short-term financing—much of it devoted to fixed capital investment—subject to periodic renewal. The short-term debt has hitherto been stable because the government has been very careful about the kind and the amount of foreign obligations eligible for validation. In case of prolonged economic difficulties, however, the terms for renewal may become highly unfavorable at the very time Japan's dependence on their renewal is at a peak.

---

7 · JAPAN'S MARKET SHARE IN HISTORICAL PERSPECTIVE

The Meiji Restoration of 1868 marked Japan's transition to the modern period. An essential ingredient of that transition was Japan's successful entry into international markets. Thus the contribution of foreign trade to Japan's development has furnished a "lesson" to other countries in a state of emergence. Likewise, in the aftermath of World War II, its own historical experience was a challenge to Japan to restore its economy by renewing external contacts. It is interesting to compare Japan's performance in achieving access to international markets following World War II with its performance after 1868.

In the recent period, there are considerable hazards in attempting to establish a trend line or logical law of growth connecting Japan's prewar and postwar experience. During the interregnum of the war, many established relationships were either disrupted or transformed. The stoppage of foreign trade entailed wholly uneconomic attempts at import substitution, with consequent effects on the postwar pattern of comparative advantage. Following the war, Japan found itself almost without foreign assets and the yen with no external value. All international transactions were controlled by the Occupation, whose objectives were not exclusively economic. A limited species of "private trade" was reintroduced near the close of the Occupation.

However, in plotting the course of Japan's postwar revival, and particularly the revival of its place in the world economy, as an alternative to a trend line, it is appropriate to relate simply the re-establishment of Japan's former level of income with the re-establishment of its former proportion of world trade. Of course, there is nothing "natural" about the prewar size of Japan's world market share. Moreover, while Japan's national income was being restored, the national income, as well as the trade of other countries, was likewise increasing. Nevertheless, if Japan's postwar role in world trade was disproportionately smaller than the corresponding size of its income would suggest, this affords further evidence that the role of the home market transcended the role of the foreign market in the process of revival. Figures for the comparison of Japan's income to world income in the prewar and postwar periods are not readily available. As a proxy, however, we might consider the relation between Japan's income and that of the United States: in 1937 it was less than seven percent, while in 1963 it was more than 10 percent.[1] On the other hand, as is seen below, even excluding prewar trade with Korea and Formosa from the calculation of her prewar total, Japan's share of world exports had barely recovered to the 1937 level by 1963.

With the limitations of the comparison in mind, a convenient way of contrasting the post-Meiji with the post-World War II experience is to look both backwards and forwards from the year 1937, which is often accepted as representative of a "normal" period in Japan's prewar

[1] United Nations, *National Income Statistics 1938-1948*; and United Nations, *Monthly Bulletin of Statistics*.

history. On the far side of 1937, our starting point will be 1899, approximating the date at which, according to Professor Horie, Japan entered the period of "take-off" into self-sustaining growth.[2] Also, these dates happen to coincide with the scheme of a recently published compilation of world trade statistics to which I would like to refer.[3]

After "starting over again" in the aftermath of World War II, Japan did not restore its real national income to the level of 1937 until 1952. Therefore, in terms of the magnitude of growth, 1899-1937 and 1937-52 are comparable periods. In order to use the full range of Maizels' data in analyzing the relation of exports to income, however, I will compare the period 1899-1937 with the extended period 1937-57.[4] This establishes a presumption that Japanese ex-

[2] Yasuzō Horie, "Business Enterprise and Capital Formation in the Initial Stages of Industrialization," in *The State and Economic Enterprise in Japan*, W. W. Lockwood, ed. (Princeton, 1965). For further discussion of the concept of "take-off" in connection with Japan, see Kenneth Berrill, "Historical Experience: The Problem of Economic 'Take-Off,'" in *Economic Development with Special Reference to East Asia*, edited by Kenneth Berrill, proceedings of a conference of the International Economic Association (London, 1964), chap. 7.

[3] Alfred Maizels, *Industrial Growth and World Trade* (Cambridge, Cambridge University Press, 1963). In accordance with the coverage of Japanese foreign trade statistics as officially compiled during the colonial period, Maizels has treated prewar exports to Korea and Formosa as "domestic trade" rather than as foreign trade. This has the effect of reducing Japan's apparent role in the prewar world economy. In 1937, for example, Japan's shipments to Korea and Formosa amounted to 31 percent of its exports to all other areas. If these shipments were included in the statistics discussed below, Japan's performance following World War II would appear to be even more unfavorable than shown here. Moreover, for the purpose of this analysis, and in accordance with usual practice, a strong case for considering Japan's prewar colonial trade as foreign trade could easily be made. In the first place, it would be appropriate on grounds of prewar and postwar geographical comparability. Second, in general, Japan's merchandise exports to Korea and Formosa required its imports therefrom. Clearly, if Japan had entirely satisfied its import requirements from alternative sources, an equivalent quantity of exports would have been generated. For Japan's prewar colonial trade, see *Chosen Bōeki Tōkei Nenhyo* [Annual Return of the Foreign Trade of Korea], Government-General of Korea; and *Taiwan Bōeki Tōkei Nenhyo* [Annual Return of the Foreign Trade of Formosa], Government-General of Formosa.

[4] In some cases, Maizels' data include 1959; in others, they end at 1955.

65

ports should have attained a relatively greater role in the world economy during the latter period than during the former one. As will be seen, however, we find the contrary to be true.

JAPAN'S SHARE OF TOTAL WORLD EXPORTS

At the turn of the twentieth century, Japan's share of world exports was 1 percent; by 1936-38 it was 4 percent.[5] Following World War II, however, Japan's share of world exports lagged considerably behind the restoration of its income. In 1957, after the prewar income level had already been restored, its exports were only 3 percent of the world total, barely increasing to 4 percent by 1963.[6] Of course, the difference between the prewar and postwar composition of Japan's grosss national expenditure had an effect on the role of trade as an income-creating agent. In 1937, for example, gross domestic investment constituted 22 percent of the gross national expenditure (GNE) as contrasted with 41 percent in 1962.[7] At the moment, however, I wish to obtain some perspective on Japan's performance in relation to that of its peers rather than to account for changes in the role of foreign trade as such.

As classified by Maizels, the leading industrial regions include: France, Germany, the United Kingdom, Other Western Europe, Canada, the United States, and Japan. In 1899, Japan accounted for 2 percent of the total exports of the group; by 1937 its share had increased to 8.5 percent. In 1957, however, five years after national income had been restored to its 1937 level, Japan's share of the exports

[5] League of Nations, *Industrialization and World Trade* (Geneva, 1945; reprinted by the United Nations, 1948), pp. 157, 159, and 167. Excludes Japan's exports to Korea and Formosa. In order to provide a basis for comparison with postwar statistics, if Sino-Soviet exports are excluded from world exports and Japan's exports to Korea and Formosa are included within Japanese foreign trade, Japan's proportion of total world exports in 1938 was 5.4 percent. United Nations, *Statistical Yearbook*, 1959.

[6] United Nations, *Monthly Bulletin of Statistics*. Excludes Sino-Soviet region.

[7] The Bank of Japan, *Economic Statistics of Japan*, 1963.

of the industrial nations amounted to only 4.6 percent.

Another way of illustrating the contrast between Japan's post-Meiji and post-World War II performance is to calculate the relative increase in its exports during each of these periods, respectively. In deflated units of value, Japan's total exports increased 127 percent between 1899 and 1913, which was greater than that of any other country in the industrial group. Between 1937 and 1957, however, the increase was only 7 percent, the lowest of any member of the same group. Making the corresponding calculation for these two periods for exports from each of the industrial nations to (a) all other industrial nations and (b) to other than industrial nations, we find almost identically corresponding results.

Historically, a decrease in Japan's dependence on foreign trade is shown by the fact that despite a relatively smaller role in world commerce, Japan's real national income was 49 percent greater in 1957 than in 1937, and 15 percent greater on a per capita basis. In the "contingent" sense, however, Japan's dependence has surely increased. For, as compared with the increase in output which it supports, the postwar expansion in Japan's use of imported raw materials appears to be relatively greater than the corresponding increase in the world at large.[8] Therefore, in attempting to keep pace with the progress of other advanced countries, Japan's export market is a clear constraint on the ultimate expansion of its domestic productive capacity and potential income. The domestically based expansion of Japan's national income following World War II was a one-time phenomenon, which if not succeeded by increased participation in the world economy can only frustrate its efforts to catch up with the living standards of the West.

As argued earlier, the per capita level of exports is one of the key determinants of the distance that separates Japan's living standard from that of its richer Western partners. In 1963 Japan's export level was only $57 per capita. Ac-

[8] See Chapter 9.

cording to this measure, then, it remains by far at the bottom of the list of the industrial nations with whose export performance its market share has been compared.[9]

JAPAN'S MARKET SHARE FOR MANUFACTURES

Manufacturing industry accounts for approximately one-third of Japan's national income, and over 90 percent of its exports consist of manufactured goods. In order to understand the aggregate export performance described above, therefore, we must consider separately Japan's exports in this category.

As might be expected, the picture almost exactly resembles the one just seen. When in 1952 Japan's national income had recovered its 1937 level, Japan's share of the total world market for manufactures remained considerably below the 1937 proportion. It was somewhere in the neighborhood of 4 percent, as compared with 6.9 percent in 1937. As expressed in an index of export volume, Japan's relative decline is also very clear. At the time Japan's national income was restored to its prewar level, the volume index of its exports as a percentage of the volume index for all major exporting countries (1929 = 100) was approximately only half the 1937 level, and by 1959 it was little more than two-thirds the 1937 level.[10]

The relative decline in Japan's postwar exports of manufactures which accompanied a substantial relative increase in its national income prompts us to inquire about the proportion of manufactures absorbed in the home market. The figures show that whereas in 1899 one quarter of Japan's manufacturing output was exported, by 1937 the proportion had increased to two-fifths, but declined again to one quarter in 1959.[11] It would be interesting to study whether the identity in these proportions during Japan's period of take-off and during its period of income-doubling is anything more than a coincidence.

[9] Second lowest in 1963 was Italy, with exports of $100 per capita. United Nations, *Monthly Bulletin of Statistics.*
[10] Alfred Maizels, *Industrial Growth*, p. 189.   [11] *Ibid.*, p. 223.

Next, we compare Japan's performance with that of its peers in a breakdown of the individual countries within the group of leading industrial nations. Again, the results are almost identical with those in which we compared Japan's total exports with the total exports of the industrial nations.[12] During the period in which it established international market entry, 1899-1913, Japan's exports of manufactured goods increased 151 percent—more than the relative increase of any other member of the group. In the period of war and reconstruction, however, 1937-57, Japan's relative increase of 31 percent was smaller than that of any other member of the group.

Repeating this comparison in a further breakdown of exports from each of the specified industrial nations to (a) all other industrial nations and (b) to other than industrial nations, the results again are almost identical, except that during 1937-57 both Canada and the United Kingdom had relatively lower rates of expansion of exports of manufactured goods to all other industrial nations than did Japan.

Finally, I would like to present some details of Japan's comparative market share in terms of particular categories of manufactured goods. As before, I refer to Japan's share as a member of the group of leading industrial nations.

In each of the categories shown, we find that Japan had a greater market share in 1937 than in 1899 and a smaller market share in 1959 than in 1937. However, it is also clear that Japan's market shares were rising between 1955 and 1959. More recent developments will be discussed below.

In historical perspective, we have found that after World War II the recovery of Japan's real national income both in total and in per capita terms occurred considerably sooner than the restoration of her prewar international market share; the latter was measured both as an aggregate and by individual commodity groups. This implies that regardless of the controversy concerning its status in Japan's

[12] France, Germany, the United Kingdom, Other Western Europe, Canada, the United States, and Japan.

Category	Japan's Share of Manufactured Goods Exports from Industrial Countries[a] (percent)			
	1899	1937	1955	1959[b]
Machinery	0.0	3.5	1.6	3.1
Transport equipment	0.0	3.5	2.4	n.a.
Chemicals	n.a.	4.1	2.4	3.0
Textiles and clothing	2.5[b]	21.8[b]	15.1[b]	18.9
Other manufactures[c]	1.0[b]	10.0[b]	4.9[b]	8.4

[a] France, Germany, the United Kingdom, Other Western Europe, Canada, the United States, and Japan
[b] Including India
[c] Including other metal goods
SOURCE: Maizels, *Industrial Growth*, pp. 490, 492, 496, 498, 500, 504.

growth prior to World War II, clearly the home market became the leading source of growth in the postwar period.

In terms of potential income, or in the contingent sense, on the other hand, Japan's dependence on exports became greater than ever before. The absolute volume of exports rose to new heights, and among enterprises which were highly export-oriented they assumed a critical role in the circular flow of Japan's economic life. Also, the greatly increased need for imports, together with the lag in Japan's recovery of its export market share, while at the same time its capacity for export production was enormously augmented, implies that the foreign trade sector is the key constraint to Japan's further economic growth.

8 · COMPETITIVE POWER

The dominant role of Japan's home market as the leading source of growth when compared with the export sector during the postwar period and the relative diminution of Japan's export share in the world economy during the 1950s, as compared with 1937, have been emphasized in the foregoing discussion. With these results in mind, we are in a better position to appraise the actual rate of increase in Japanese exports in recent years. Their rate of advance, of course, is more impressive than the level attained, especially as measured in terms of the per capita level of exports.

Before discussing the elements of competitive power which promote Japan's exports, however, it may be relevant to mention the income target for 1970 and the export target which is its chief determinant. These targets are specified in the *New Long-Range Economic Plan of Japan, 1961-70*, otherwise known as the National Income Doubling Plan. The plan (expressed in terms of fiscal year 1958 prices) aims at a gross national product of ¥26 trillion (or $72.2 billion) and exports of $9.32 billion in 1970.[1]

Thus the target requires that exports more than double during the period 1961-70. In terms of rates, the ten-year plan calls for average annual growth of 7.8 percent in GNP,

[1] Although its initial year, with regard to the calculation of "doubling," was 1960, the "base year" of the plan for specifying levels already achieved when the plan was published was the average for the Japanese fiscal years 1956-58. In order to designate it nominally as a "ten-year plan," however, and inasmuch as it was published in 1961, its printed version is entitled *New Long-Range Economic Plan of Japan, 1961-70*. When the plan was prepared, it was estimated that GNP would amount to ¥13 trillion in the initial year; therefore, "doubling" refers to the achievement of ¥26 trillion in 1970. However, actual GNP turned out to be higher than ¥13 trillion in the initial year, and thus doubling calls for a higher figure than the target. On a per capita basis (1960 prices), the GNP in 1970 is projected at $797, as compared with $436 in 1960. Consolidated Planning Bureau of the Economic Planning Agency, *Yushutsu Sankō Shiryō* [Reference Data for Exports], Sept. 23, 1963, p. 3.

as compared with an average annual growth of 10.0 percent in exports. As actually accomplished, the GNP has increased at the average rate of 10.2 percent annually during 1955-60; it is estimated that it will rise at the average rate of 8.0 percent during 1960-65, and 6.4 percent during 1965-70. Exports, on the other hand, have increased at the rate of 13.5 percent annually during 1958-62, as compared with an annual increase of 5.8 percent in world exports during the same period. Japan's competitive power will have to expand considerably in order to maintain the recent rate of growth in exports.

INGREDIENTS OF COMPETITIVE POWER

It is easier to specify the ingredients of competitive power than to evaluate their respective importance. In general, they include relative costs and prices, quality and consistency of performance, the degree of variety and novelty of the goods, the services accompanying them, the system of distribution by which they are marketed, promptness of delivery, and conditions of deferred payment. Traditionally, Japan has relied primarily on price competition in foreign markets, concentrating on a rather narrow and deep commodity front.[2] Recently, however, in the promotion of diversified durable consumer goods, quality and performance have been emphasized and efforts have been made to establish permanent marketing organizations abroad which advertise brand names and provide after-sales servicing. Hitherto, one reason for Japanese reluctance to invest in marketing activities abroad has been the fear that too much success would be attended by a change

[2] According to Dr. Osamu Shimomura, the elasticity of Japan's export volume in relation to total world GNP ranges between 3.0 and 3.5. Thus with world GNP rising at an average rate of 3 percent each year, Japanese exports would rise between 9 and 10.5 percent. (Osamu Shimomura, "Basic Problems of Economic Growth Policy," Indian Statistical Institute [Translation Series No. 37, Calcutta, 1961], cited by M. Bronfenbrenner in "Economic Miracles and Japan's Income-Doubling Plan," in W. W. Lockwood, ed., *State and Economic Enterprise in Japan*, p. 543.) As Bronfenbrenner points out, this estimate is highly optimistic.

in the rules of the game as a countermeasure by the importing country.[3] Incidentally, the effects of price competition may be hardest to evaluate in precisely those cases where it most greatly affects the elasticity of demand by foreigners for goods from Japan. For where Japan's goods are highly competitive with the home products of the importing country, very small changes in price may be associated with very large changes in quantities sold.

The costs which determine Japanese prices are in turn affected by both foreign and domestic factors. World commodity prices were favorable to Japan during the 1950s; they were favorable to its industrial competitors as well.[4] During 1963 and 1964, however, the prices of metals, food, and fibers stiffened considerably, tending to raise the import cost of Japanese output.

Domestically, costs have been reduced through technological advance and by capital expansion leading to economies of scale. However, while productivity has thereby been increased, wages have also risen and interest costs have been an increasing burden.[5] In particular, there has been a shrinkage in the wage differential between the light and heavy industries, which to some extent wipes out Japan's former competitive advantage in such products as textiles, furniture, and sundry goods.

Although Japan's competitive position has been impaired by rising labor costs, it has been broadened by diversification of the export list. Variety has been increased among traditional as well as modern products. A list of

3 Another reason is the general practice of exporting through "trading companies," which will be discussed below.

4 The correspondingly adverse terms of trade sustained by primary goods producers in Asia, however, resulted in a shrinkage in their income and thus in their demand for Japanese goods.

5 In general, increases in productivity have exceeded increases in wages. The index of productivity in manufacturing (1960 = 100) reached a level of 141 in 1964, while the index of wages in manufacturing (1960 = 100) rose to 136. Due to the rise in consumer prices during the interval, however, in 1964 the index of wages in real terms was at the much lower level of 119. Ministerial Secretariat of Labor Ministry, *Rōdō Tōkei Chōsa Geppō* [Monthly Labor Statistics and Research Bulletin], Feb. 1965.

24 export items which in 1953 accounted for only $21 million in export sales, were developed by 1961 to a level of $536 million, or 13 percent of total Japanese exports in that year.[6]

As mentioned above, the expansion of durable consumer goods exports such as cameras, television sets, and tape recorders has been promoted by the establishment of after-sales service agencies within customer countries. In the producer goods field, an outstanding example of technical innovation combined with short delivery schedules is the shipbuilding industry. For producer goods (other than ships) in general, however, Japan's principal market is the developing countries of Southeast Asia—these require special assistance in financing, something especially difficult for Japan to provide. When domestic demand is high, therefore, Japanese firms have little incentive to strive for exports to Southeast Asia.[7]

The heavy and chemical industries, of course, have benefited most from Japan's effort to increase its competitive power. Of particular interest, therefore, is the result of a recent study by the National Institute of Economic and Social Research, which shows that as compared with other major industrial countries, the performance of Japan's heavy and chemical industries in world trade during the interval 1954-55 to 1960-61 has been singularly poor.[8]

The study concerns world trade as represented by the exports of nine major industrial nations[9] in three major categories: machinery, transport equipment, and chemicals. The items in each of these categories were split into two

[6] Economic Planning Agency, *Economic Survey of Japan, 1961-1962*, p. 363. The new—so-called "star"—commodities included canned mandarin oranges, synthetic fabrics, radios, tape recorders, machine parts, motorbikes, organic chemicals, and construction machinery.

[7] However, when domestic demand is slack, Japanese financing, as well as Japanese commodities, seek out the developing economies—another example of supply-oriented exports.

[8] "Fast and Slow-Growing Products in World Trade," *National Institute Economic Review*, Aug. 1963.

[9] Belgium–Luxembourg, France, Italy, Japan, the Netherlands, Sweden, the United Kingdom, the United States, and Western Germany.

groups, those for which world trade increased relatively fast and those for which the increase was relatively slow. During the period studied, the proportion of Japan's exports classed as fast growing in the three categories as an aggregate was smaller than that of any other country specified. In individual categories, Japan's position was lower than that of any other country in both transport equipment and chemicals, but it was third highest in machinery. The reason for this was that Japan's exports of miscellaneous electric machinery (primarily radio equipment, including transistor radios) were successfully expanded in the fast-growing sector.[10]

Although Japan was at the bottom of the list in terms of its share of the increase in aggregate "fast-growing" exports, by virtue of the arithmetic of starting from a small base, its total exports nevertheless increased proportionately more than those of any of the other nine countries studied by the National Institute. This indicates that the competitive power of "new" items in Japan's export list, as compared with that of already established items, needs to be distinguished from the competitive power of those same "new" items, as compared with "fast-growing products in world trade." This is a sobering distinction, inasmuch as the optimistic view insists only on the fact that Japan's heavy and chemical industries—which are the principal source of the "new" items—have achieved substantially greater expansion in terms of the quantum index of exports than have the traditional light industries during the period analyzed by the National Institute. In terms of levels of

10 It is interesting to compare Japan's prewar and postwar share of the world market in manufactures other than textiles. In 1937, as a member of the group including the United States, the United Kingdom, France, Germany, and Canada, Japan's share of exports of specified manufactured goods (percentage for Japan shown in parentheses) was as follows: metals and engineering (4.5), chemicals (5.2), finished manufactured goods other than textiles (20.6). In 1959, Japan's share was: metals and engineering (5.5), chemicals (3.9), finished manufactured goods other than textiles (14.8). Calculated from data presented by Maizels, *Industrial Growth*, pp. 432, 477, 479, 483, 485, 487, 496.

achievement, despite their comparative success in relation to other Japanese exports, the international competitive power of the heavy and chemical industries, while improving, remains weak.

In further understanding the limits of Japan's competitive power it may help if we examine next the source of Japan's exports in terms of firm size and wage rates.

FIRM SIZE AND WAGE LEVEL

A common remark concerning Japan's dual economy has it that the small, low-wage enterprises produce for the home market while the large, efficient, high-wage firms produce for the foreign market. Statistically, this is far from true. Although the role of middle and small size enterprises has been declining in recent years, they still supply over half of Japan's industrial exports.[11] In 1956, the proportion was 59 percent, declining to 54 percent in 1962.[12]

In some categories, almost the entire supply of exports is produced by medium or small enterprises. In 1961, for example, 97 percent of clothing and other textile products, 94 of furniture and fittings, 98 of leather products, 99 of metal products, 80 of timber and wood products, and 89 percent of precision machines and tools other than weapons were produced by medium or small enterprises.[13] These figures, moreover, have a downward bias, inasmuch as they

[11] What is a "middle or small size enterprise"? According to the Middle and Small Enterprise Agency of the Ministry of International Trade and Industry, there are two alternative criteria: (1) in terms of the issued value of capital stock, a manufacturing company whose capital is less than ¥50 million; or a commercial or service company whose capital is less than ¥10 million; (2) in terms of employees, a manufacturing company with less than 300 workers; or a commercial or service company with less than 50 workers. In 1960, out of a total of 3,220,000 private enterprises, 3,200,000 (or 99.4 percent of the total) were classified as medium or small.

[12] Medium and Small Enterprise Agency, *Chūshōkigyō Hakusho, Shōwa Sanjū-hachi Nendo* [Medium and Small Enterprise White Paper], 1963, p. 51. The data were compiled by the Commercial and Industrial Economic Research Laboratory of Osaka.

[13] *Ibid.*, *Chūshōkigyō Tōkei Yoran* [Medium and Small Enterprise Statistical Bulletin], 1964, p. 288.

include only the direct exports of middle and small size companies; the value of output (either components or finished products) produced by such companies as subcontractors and then assembled for export by large companies is not included.

The statistical difficulties in evaluating the role of low wage output in Japanese exports are similar to those encountered in measuring the contribution of small and medium size enterprises. However, a one-time study made by the Economic Planning Agency provides a clear picture of the situation. According to the study, 75 percent of Japanese exports in 1958 were shipped by firms whose average annual wage was below the mean wage of all industry.[14]

Particularly interesting is the breakdown of wages in the distribution of Japanese exports to advanced, as compared with developing, countries. The same study finds that 90 percent of Japan's exports to advanced countries in 1958 were produced by enterprises paying less than the mean wage in all Japanese manufacturing. On the other hand, the proportion of Japan's exports to backward countries which were produced by enterprises paying less than the mean wage was approximately 60 percent. This is one aspect of the fact that the products of Japan's modern heavy and chemical industries find a better market in the backward countries than elsewhere.

Japan's heavy dependence on exports of its low-wage industries may also be illustrated from a somewhat different point of view with data for 1963. My method was to reclassify Japanese exports in terms of the spectrum of their wage costs. First I took the 30 commodities specified by the Ministry of International Trade and Industry as Japan's principal export commodities.[15] Collectively, they represent

14 Economic Planning Agency Investigation Bureau, Domestic Investigation Section, *Bōeki to Koyō no Kanren, Tōkei Shiryō* [Relation between Foreign Trade and Employment, Statistical Material], July 28, 1962, p. 18. The mean annual wage in manufacturing in 1958 was ¥253,932. *Year Book of Labor Statistics, 1962*, Ministry of Labor.

15 Ministry of International Trade and Industry, *Bōeki Tōkei Geppō* [Monthly Foreign Trade Statistics], May 1964.

two-thirds of Japan's total exports. I arrayed these commodities according to the average monthly cash earnings received by regular workers in the industries in which they are produced. Assuming that the distribution of wage rates among export commodities not represented on the list is the same as that for the principal commodities included, I estimate that only one-third of total Japanese exports are produced by industries whose wages are above average monthly cash earnings in all Japanese manufacturing.[16] This is evidently consistent with the results of the Economic Planning Agency study cited above, in which it was found that only 25 percent of Japanese exports in 1958 were produced by firms paying more than the average wage in manufacturing.[17]

Carrying this analysis a step further—and as an introduction to the following discussion of complementarity in Japanese trade—if we compare Japan's export performance during 1962 (admittedly an early date for the purpose of comparisons) with the targets projected for 1970, we see that the low wage products of light industry have approached their goal much more closely than the high wage products of the heavy and chemical industries. In 1962, light industry goods had achieved 66 percent of their 1970 targets, whereas heavy and chemical goods lagged at 44 percent.[18] The latter, however, could be placed in a more flattering light by the observation that between fiscal

[16] Average monthly cash earnings per regular employee in Japanese manufacturing enterprises engaging 30 workers or more was ¥30,204 in 1963. (Ministerial Secretariat of Labor Ministry, *Rōdō Tōkei Chōsa Geppō* [Monthly Labor Statistics and Research Bulletin], April 1964.) At the prevailing rate of exchange, this is the equivalent of $83.90 per month.

[17] Some additional data for 1963 in relation to 1958 are given in Economic Planning Agency, Investigation Bureau, *Keizai Geppō* [Monthly Report on Economy], May 29, 1963, p. 104. These show that the value of exports produced by industries in the intermediate wage brackets increased between 1958 and 1963 at a greater rate than those in either the lowest or the highest wage brackets.

[18] Economic Planning Agency, Consolidated Planning Bureau, *Yushutsu Sankō Shiryō* [Reference Data for Export], Sept. 23, 1963, p. 21. Different rates of growth were of course targeted for different industries.

years 1956-1958 and fiscal year 1962 heavy industry exports have increased at an average annual rate of 21.3 percent, as compared with an average rate of 11.8 percent in light industry.[19] These alternative calculations emphasize once more the importance of the distinction between comparison of levels as contrasted with the comparison of rates in evaluating recent Japanese progress.

It should be noted that there has been a shrinkage in the wage differential, especially for young workers, between large and small firms in recent years.[20] As mentioned above, in manufacturing at large, increases in productivity exceeded increases in wages during 1960-64; in the sector producing Japan's traditional labor-intensive exports, however, the tendency has been the other way.[21]

EXCESS CAPACITY AND SUPPLY-ORIENTED EXPORTS

It is useful to distinguish between the forces which drive exports, as contrasted with objective elements of competitive power as such. Excess capacity with regard to demand in the home market is a prime example of these forces and one which has been of increasing moment in Japan in recent years. As a defense against new competition expected to arise with import liberalization, producers have expanded plant capacity according to engineering estimates of optimal scale. In some modern industries, the size of equipment makes piecemeal moves

[19] *Ibid.*, p. 19.

[20] In fact, between 1954 and 1961 the discrepancy in wages paid to young workers by large, as contrasted with small, firms was actually reversed. In the latter year, for example, male employees less than 18 years old in manufacturing plants engaging 10 to 29 workers were paid ¥9,232 a month as compared with ¥8,297 in plants engaging 500-999 workers. Japan Labor Association, *Nippon Rōdō Keizai Tōkei* [Japanese Labor Economic Statistics], Bulletin No. 66, p. 47.

[21] "The rate of increase in wages of labor-intensive industries such as textiles, plywood, toys and sundry goods, which were mainly responsible for an increase in Japan's exports up to around 1957-1958, has largely exceeded the average wage increase of all industries and this has begun to exert an adverse influence on the nation's export competitive power." Economic Planning Board, *Economic Survey of Japan, 1962-1963*, p. 193.

towards efficient scale unfeasible; thus a firm may gamble on expansion beyond its own realized demand in the hope of expanding its market share. However, for prestige, as well as for the maintenance of their competitive cost positions and protection of their market shares, rival *keiretsu* groups may each simultaneously install new equipment of a similar type.[22] As an intermediate effect, the demand for capital goods stimulates investment for further investment, herein lies an essential mechanism of Japan's recent high growth rate. Eventually, however, as more and more plants reach the operational stage, they swamp the potentialities of the domestic market and export pressure is generated.

In an attempt to evaluate this phenomenon beyond the analysis of a previous chapter, I obtained the results of an unpublished survey, performed by the Ministry of International Trade and Industry, of the actual rate of operation of manufacturing plant capacity. Using these data, together with an "Index of Operating Ratio" (1960 = 100) which appears regularly in *Tsūsan Tōkei* [International Trade and Industry Statistics], edited by MITI, I have estimated the rates of operation of plant capacity in various categories of Japanese industry, as shown in Table 15. It is of particular interest that even during the fever pitch of the boom in 1964, Japanese industry at large was operating at approximately only 82.4 percent of installed capacity.

With the exception of textiles and clothing, by far the two most important export industries in the table below are iron and steel, and machinery.[23] Evidence consistent with the hypothesis of supply-oriented exports is found in the fact that the decline in the rate of operation of installed

[22] *Keiretsu* companies are "successor" companies, a euphemism for "New Zaibatsu."

[23] The weights attached to the various categories in MITI's "Index of Operating Ratio" are as follows: Total manufacturing industry, 100.0; iron and steel, 20.0; nonferrous metals, 4.7; machinery, 24.9; ceramics, 3.3; chemicals, 12.0; petroleum products, 3.5; coal products, 1.1; rubber products, 3.2; pulp and paper, 5.0; textiles and clothing, 22.3.

TABLE 15

Index of Rates of Operation, and Actual and Estimated Rates of Operation of Installed Capacity in Japanese Industries During Specified Years, 1960 to 1964

| | Index of rate of operation (1960 = 100) | | | Rate of operation | | | |
| | | | | Actual | | Estimated | |
	1962	1963	1964	1960	1962	1963	1964
Total manufacturing	94.7	95.1	101.5	81.2	76.9	77.2	82.4
Iron and steel	89.4	89.7	102.9	77.7	69.5	69.7	80.0
Nonferrous metals	88.1	91.1	99.9	87.5	77.1	79.7	87.4
Machinery	97.7	95.4	100.8	80.4	78.6	76.7	81.0
Ceramics	97.2	87.8	86.0	85.5	83.1	75.1	73.5
Chemicals	98.9	105.8	110.5	70.0	69.2	74.1	77.4
Petroleum products	82.7	84.2	87.4	93.1	77.0	78.4	81.4
Coal products	105.1	112.7	122.3	86.8	91.2	97.8	106.2
Rubber products	96.3	88.2	87.2	108.5	104.5	95.7	94.6
Pulp and paper	92.6	97.3	100.7	86.0	79.6	83.7	86.6
Textiles and clothing	98.0	100.8	106.1	80.6	79.0	81.2	85.5

SOURCE: The actual rates of operation in 1960 were based on an unpublished survey by the Ministry of International Trade and Industry. The estimated rates of actual operation in other years were calculated by combining the published index with the actual rates for 1960. The index as such appears regularly in *Tsūsan Tōkei* [International Trade and Industry Statistics] *MITI*.

capacity in these industries between 1960 and 1963 was accompanied by a rise in the quantum index of exports for metals and machinery. According to the index (1960 = 100), the figures for metals and machinery in 1963 were 200.6 and 192.0, respectively, as compared with the lesser figure of 143.5 for the quantum of total Japanese exports in that year.[24] This effect was accentuated in 1964, when, as compared with a figure of 177.8 for the quantum index of total exports, the figures for metals and machinery were 246.9 and 286.3, respectively.

The pressure of excess capacity on export volume may also be seen in the record of export prices. According to the foreign trade unit value index of export prices (1960 = 100), metals and machinery each declined to 82.8 in 1963, as compared with a figure of 93.7 for total Japanese export commodities.[25] In 1964, when the unit value index for total exports declined to 92.6, the figure for metals was 85.7, while that for machinery was 74.4. Thus in the key categories of metals and machinery, the evidence of both price and quantity movements in relation to increases in excess capacity seem to testify in favor of the hypothesis of supply-oriented exports.[26]

[24] Bank of Japan, *Economic Statistics of Japan, 1963*, p. 271.
[25] MITI, *Bōeki Tōkei Geppō* [Monthly Foreign Trade Statistics].
[26] The "Index of Operating Ratio" taken by itself can be misleading in the interpretation of this hypothesis, as may be seen in the case of chemicals. In 1963, the unit price of chemical exports was low and the export quantum was high; at the same time, the index shows a high operating ratio of 105.8 for chemicals in the same year. Unless it is known that in the base year the rate of operation of chemical plant capacity was at an unrepresentatively low level, as shown in Table 15 above, these figures would erroneously appear to be inconsistent with each other and with the hypothesis.

9 · COMPLEMENTARITY

In discussing Japan's market share and competitive power, I have emphasized its export performance. However, the market has two sides, and import demand is its other chief determinant. Taking account of imports and exports alike, further aspects of Japan's dependence may be expressed in terms of the complementary structure of its economy within a worldwide environment. As distinguished from the quantitative magnitude of total trade, the degree of complementarity reveals a *qualitative* dimension of Japan's foreign trade dependence. This dimension is of special interest in relation to Japan's transition towards a more liberal economy. Below, the condition of complementarity is discussed first with regard to the commodity composition of Japan's foreign trade and then from the point of view of its geographical pattern.

THE COMMODITY COMPOSITION OF TRADE

Imports

Beginning at the aggregate level, attention is drawn first to the relation between total imports and national income. Evidently, the relation is increasing, although in 1963 it still remained lower than its prewar level. It may be noted, however, that because of the steady decline in the price of Japan's imports between 1958 and 1962, the relation was rather larger when calculated in real terms, as distinguished from current values during that period. Using national income and import deflators based on 1958, the comparison is shown in Table 16. Apart from the relation between imports and national income as such, by 1963 imports in quantum terms were more than double their prewar volume.[1]

[1] In terms of current yen converted at prevailing average annual exchange rates, the dollar value of imports into Japan during 1963 was approximately seven times as great as the average value of imports during 1934-36. In terms of depreciated current yen, the increase was more than 700-fold.

TABLE 16

Relation of Japanese Imports to National Income in Nominal and in Real Terms During Selected Years, 1936 to 1962 and Estimated 1970 (percent)

Year	Based on current values	Based on deflated values
1936	23.5	—
1958	12.8	12.8
1959	14.1	15.4
1960	14.1	15.8
1961	15.3	18.2
1962	12.9	16.1
1970 (Income Doubling Plan)	—	17.5

SOURCES: The Bank of Japan, *Historical Statistics of Japanese Economy*, and *Keizai Shingi Kai* [Economic Deliberation Council], *Kokumin Shotoku Baizō Keikaku Chukan Kentō Hōkoku* [Interim Inquiry and Report on Income Doubling Plan], May 1, 1964, p. 458.

The increasing complementarity of Japan's foreign trade is evident from changes in the major categories of imports and exports over time (Table 17). Even before 1900 crude materials and food comprised more than half of Japan's total imports. Between 1936 and 1963, among the various categories of imports, by far the greatest absolute increase (almost 2 billion prewar yen) took place in raw materials and mineral fuels. Together with foodstuffs, these categories more than doubled in quantum terms in the interval; in relative importance, however, they declined from 89 percent of total imports in 1936 to 76 percent in 1963. The chief reason for this was the accompanying increase —almost six times—in imports of finished products, especially machinery and other producers' goods.[2] In the attempt to advance Japan's heavy and chemical industries to a "higher level," machines were often imported as proto-

[2] In 1963, machinery accounted for more than half of the imports of finished products. The increase by 1970 in imports of finished products is projected at a higher rate than that of any other commodities in the Income Doubling Plan.

84

TABLE 17

Japanese Imports and Exports by Economic Category During Selected Years, 1936 to 1963

Year	Total	Foodstuffs	Raw materials and mineral fuels	Finished products	Other
			IMPORTS		
			A: In percent		
1936	100.0	8.4	80.1a	10.6	0.9
1953	100.0	25.9	60.8b	13.2	0.1
1963	100.0	16.1	59.4c	24.3	0.2
		B: In million yen deflated by Wholesale Price Index (1934-36 = 1)			
1936	2,668	223	2,138a	284	23
1953	2,467	639	1,499	327	2
1963	6,812	1,100	4,044	1,653	16
		C: Quantum Index Based on (B)			
1936	100.0	100.0	100.0a	100.0	100.0
1953	92.5	286.5	70.1	115.1	8.7
1963	255.3	493.3	189.1	582.0	69.6
			EXPORTS		
			A: In percent		
1936	100.0	7.6	31.3a	58.0	3.1
1953	100.0	9.4	7.2	82.5	0.9
1963	100.0	5.3	3.9	90.2	0.6
		B: In million yen deflated by Wholesale Price Index (1934-36 = 1)			
1936	2,599	197	814a	1,509	80
1953	1,305	123	94	1,076	12
1963	5,513	293	214	4,976	31
		C: Quantum Index Based on (B)			
1936	100.0	100.0	100.0a	100.0	100.0
1953	50.2	62.4	11.5	71.3	15.0
1963	212.1	148.7	26.3	329.8	38.8

a Crude and fabricated basic materials.
b Mineral fuels accounted for 12.0 percent of total imports.
c Mineral fuels accounted for 18.0 percent of total imports.
SOURCE: Compiled and calculated from The Bank of Japan, *Economic Statistics of Japan*.

85

types on a one-time basis for the purpose of producing similar machines at home, as in the case of joint ventures for the procurement of technological know-how. Thus food and industrial raw materials obtained along the North-South axis and machinery obtained along the East-West axis each promoted the development of Japan's industrial processing activities.

Increased complementarity may be demonstrated not only by the absolute, as well as relative, increase in imports of food, industrial raw materials, and mineral fuels, but also by the change over time in the relation between raw material imports and manufacturing production. Between 1938 and 1959 the index of industrial production (1955 = 100) rose from 82.2 to 178.2, an increase of 117 percent. The quantum index of raw material imports (1953 = 100) increased from 110.8 in 1934-36 to 182.0 in 1959, an increase of 64 percent.[3] For the total of free world countries, however, the volume index of food and raw material exports (1953 = 100) changed from 99 in 1938 to 139 in 1959, an increase of only 40 percent; on the same base, world manufacturing production increased from 50 in 1938 to 131 in 1959, an increase of 162 percent, which exceeded the proportion of manufacturing increase in the case of Japan.[4] As compared with the increase in output which it supports, therefore, the postwar expansion in Japan's use of imported raw materials is evidently greater than the corresponding increase in the world at large.[5] From the point of view of the composition of imports, then, Japan's foreign trade dependence seems to have increased both in relation to its own prewar degree of dependence and also in relation to the average change in the degree of import dependence in other countries.

[3] The Bank of Japan, *Economic Statistics of Japan, 1960*, pp. 207, 244.
[4] United Nations, *Statistical Yearbook*, 1960, p. 402.
[5] Mineral fuels are excluded from this comparison. If they were included, the comparison would reflect even more adversely on Japan than indicated here.

86

Within the postwar period taken separately, these conclusions are supported by the results of input-output studies of the Japanese government, which reveal Japan's average propensity to import by key categories of final demand. In the data cited (Table 18), the volume of direct and indirect imports is shown in relation to total input requirements, without regard to types of commodity input as such. Between 1955 and 1962, there was a slight increase in the ratio of total imports to total demand, which is reflected in the rising ratio of imports to national income mentioned above. Of special interest, however, is the way the increase is distributed among the various categories of demand.

With two exceptions, the average propensity to import (API) increased in every category between 1955 and 1962. The more striking of the exceptions was the case of imports for inventory investment, which dropped drastically from 24 percent in 1961 to five percent in 1962. This accords with the well-known volatility of inventory investment, which is subject to psychological as well as financial and technological determinants.[6]

The second exception was the case of household consumption, which accounts for almost half of Japan's total import demand. In this category the API, which declined slightly after 1955, has had a tendency to rise since 1959, but it has been held in check by the low priority assigned to liberalization of consumer goods imports.[7] In addition,

[6] The proportion of total Japanese imports attributable to increased inventories in 1962 was 1.1 percent, as contrasted with 8.7 percent in the preceding year. MITI, *Tsūshō Hakusho Sōron, 1963* [International Trade White Paper, General Remarks, 1963], p. 133.

[7] It is noteworthy that in accordance with its complementary role, Japan processes almost all of its own consumer goods from the primary materials stage. Moreover, the ratio of imports of semi-finished goods of all descriptions, such as metal products and chemicals, is also extremely low. (Economic Planning Agency, *Economic Survey of Japan, 1962-1963,* p. 206.) In this connection, incidentally, some distinctions are necessary among the evidently conflicting statistics of various official agencies. According to the United Nations' *Economic Survey of Asia and the Far East, 1963,* p. 214, in 1962 45.4 percent of Japan's imports were materials to be used in the production of consumer goods, besides

TABLE 18

Average Propensity to Import (API): Ratio of Imports Directly or Indirectly Consumed in Relation to Total Inputs, by Category of Final Demand, 1955 and by Year, 1959 to 1962

(percent)

Year	Total demand	House-hold consump-tion	Government consump-tion	Inven-tory invest-ment	Private fixed capital formation	Government fixed capital formation	Exports	Special procure-ment
1955	9.2	9.0	4.5	16.2	9.7	6.5	14.1	7.4
1959	8.5	7.5	5.3	12.3	9.4	6.9	14.5	6.5
1960	9.8	7.7	5.2	16.7	12.9	10.7	15.6	9.3
1961	11.0	8.6	5.8	23.8	13.8	11.4	15.5	10.9
1962	10.0	8.8	5.7	5.0	12.9	10.7	14.7	10.7

SOURCES: MITI, *Tsūshō Hakusho Sōron, 1963* [International Trade White Paper, General Remarks, 1963], p. 133; *ibid., 1964*, p. 147.

consumer goods imports have been restrained by factors such as the shift to consumer durables and to services which have a relatively low dependence on imports, as well as by shifts from consumption of natural fiber to artificial fiber textiles. Indeed, for these reasons, during 1955-57, although total consumption expenditure was rising, foreign currency requirements for consumption showed a relative decline.[8]

On the other hand, if we take account of the trend in imports of food, the prospect for a decline in total consumer goods imports is less promising. The fact that Japan has reached a substantially self-sufficient position in the supply of rice is sometimes misconstrued as implying a reduction in the need for imported food in general. In 1963, for example, although the value of imported rice amounted to only $29 million, total food imports reached an all-time high of $1.089 billion, which was one and three quarters as much as during 1953.[9] From a long-term

---

which 12.5 percent of total imports were in the form of food for consumption and 2.4 percent for other consumption goods. This gives a total of 60.3 percent of total imports attributable to consumption. According to *Tsūshō Hakusho Sōron, 1963*, p. 133, however, the proportion of total imports attributable either directly or indirectly to *household consumption* in 1962 was only 45.8 percent. The difference presumably consists in the fact that in the ESAFE statistics "consumption" includes consumption by other than households, as for example feed and fodder for animals and raw materials consumed by industry.

[8] In 1955-57, consumption expenditure amounted to ¥4,802,000,000, ¥5,142,000,000 and ¥5,535,000,000 during each year, respectively, while foreign currency requirements for consumption (after adjustment for abnormal changes) amounted to 9.2 percent, 8.9 percent, and 8.4 percent of the total amounts expended on consumption in the corresponding years. (Economic Planning Agency, Economic Research Institute, *Consumption and Its Degree of Dependence on Imports in Japan*, Economic Bulletin No. 3, Oct. 1959, p. 43.) As a result of the factors mentioned, marginal dependency on imports tends to be lower than average dependency, yielding an elasticity of consumption demand for imports of less than one.

[9] The decline in imports of rice is due primarily to an increase in productivity of domestic rice production, together with a change in dietary habits in favor of dairy and other foods. In general, with the exception of labor-intensive specialties such as silk, mushroom, and strawberry production, Japanese agriculture is very weak in international competitive power. (Economic Planning Agency, *Kokusai Keizai*

point of view, moreover, it is notable that the proportion of foodstuffs in relation to total imports—16 percent in 1963— was twice as great as it had been during 1934-36.

Another element in the prospect for consumer goods imports is the fact that they tend to increase both cyclically and contracyclically. "[D]uring the three years after the trade liberalization program was implemented, there has been a gradual increase in imports of consumer goods, quite independent of the cyclical fluctuations of the econ- omy . . . and this increase is expected to quicken in the future."[10] However, this observation refers specifically to the category of finished consumer goods other than food, which, as mentioned above, represents only a small fraction of total imports into Japan.

Disaggregating further to the level of individual com- modities, there are various criteria for designating those worthy of special attention. For example, a principal im- port commodity may be specified in terms of its physical quantity, the relative importance of the import in relation to domestic supply of the same commodity, its role in ex- port production, its key importance (as a catalyst) without regard to its quantity or value, its role as a balancing agent in multilateral relations, or its role in the interplay between strong and weak currencies.

Some of the commodities imported in greatest volume are distinguished by the fact that the ratio of the value of their imports in relation to the sum of the value of pro- duction plus imports of the same commodities respec- tively exceeds 50 percent. Some items which fit this de-

---

Bunkakai Kentō Shiryō [Sono Jūni], Yunyū ni Kansuru Mondai-ten [Discussion Materials for International Economic Subcommittee No. 12, Problems of Imports], Sept. 23, 1963, p. 2.) In the case of rice, as well, "the productivity of agricultural labor in Japan is low by western standards." Food and Agriculture Organization of the United Nations, Possibilities of Increasing World Food Production, Basic Study No. 10 (Rome, 1963), p. 135.

[10] Economic Planning Agency, Economic Survey of Japan, 1962-1963, p. 22. During fiscal year 1962, while total imports declined 16 percent from the preceding year, consumer goods imports increased by 15 per- cent. Ibid., p. 47.

scription include the following (the ratio for 1962 is given in parentheses) : phosphate ore (100), bauxite (100), nickel (100), copra (100), raw cotton (100), wool (100), natural rubber (100), crude petroleum (98), iron ore (95), sugar (88), soy beans (79), maize (75), salt (75), wheat (61), coking coal (60), copper ore (59), skins (52). Collectively, these commodities accounted for more than half of the total value of Japanese imports during 1963. Clearly, the raw material requirements of the heavy and chemical industries, as well as those of natural fiber textiles, are well represented in the list. Concerning the former, since 1957 petroleum has exceeded raw cotton as the principal individual import commodity; and about half of the inputs of the iron and steel industry are imported. The huge import requirements of the rising heavy and chemical industries are concentrated in a relatively narrow list of commodities. Consequently, in the course of Japan's economic development since 1936 there has been a lesser tendency towards diversification of imports than of exports.

Exports

The composition of exports likewise emphasizes the complementary character of Japan's foreign trade. Over time, the relatively increasing importance of manufactured goods—including parts and components—in the export pattern is its most obvious aspect. The trend may be summarized by the fact that in 1936, exports of finished products represented less than two-thirds of total exports, whereas by 1963 the proportion had increased to over 90 percent.

The role of manufactured goods as a whole among Japanese exports, however, refers to complementarity only in its aggregate aspect. The next step is to investigate the distribution of complementarity within the manufactured goods category as such. By means of a coefficient which expresses the composition of manufactured exports in relation to the composition of total Japanese manufacturing output, an approach to the inner dimensions of export complementarity may be made.

The "index of disparity" (Table 19), as the coefficient is called, shows that both in prewar and in postwar years, the relation of exports to output has been higher for light than for heavy and chemical industry. Indeed, in 1960, the coefficient for light manufactures (1.5) was higher than it had been in 1928 (1.4). While light manufactures were increasing their ascendancy in this relation, in terms of the composition of output, light manufactures and heavy and chemical goods, in effect, changed places between 1928 and 1960: during the latter year light manufactures accounted for one-third of all manufacturing output while heavy and chemical goods accounted for two-thirds. Despite the reversal in their respective contributions to total output, however, the value of the index of disparity for heavy and chemical goods was only 0.8[11] in 1960, whereas for light manufactures in 1928—when they had accounted for the share of output represented by heavy and chemical goods in 1960—it had been 1.4. Therefore, the reversal of roles was incomplete.

This situation testifies to an imbalance in Japan's complementarity relations within the world economy. For while the rise of its roundabout heavy and chemical industries enhances the division of labor between Japan and other countries, these industries' failure to be correspondingly represented in the export pattern implies a new kind of bottleneck in the process of economic development.[12] It is thus the pattern as well as the quantity of exports which increasingly impose a constraint on the future

[11] Also, of course, this value was smaller than the corresponding value of the coefficient for other advanced industrial nations at the time.

[12] It was not until 1963 that heavy and chemical goods exports as much as equalled exports of light industry products from Japan (although by that year heavy and chemical goods output accounted for over two-thirds of total manufacturing output). In the years immediately ahead it may be difficult to increase or even maintain this export ratio because the government has decided to divert an increasing proportion of ship production to the Japanese merchant marine, in preference to exports.

TABLE 19

Composition of Manufactured Goods Production and Manufactured Goods Exports from Japan: Index of Disparity by Selected Years, 1928 to 1960

Manufactured goods	Composition of output^a A (percent)					Composition of exports^b B (percent)					Index of disparity B/A				
	1928	1935	1950	1955	1960	1928	1935	1950	1955	1960	1928	1935	1950	1955	1960
Total	100	100	100	100	100	100	100	100	100	100	1.0	1.0	1.0	1.0	1.0
Heavy and chemical:	35	53	50	52	68	7	18	33	42	51	0.2	0.4	0.7	0.8	0.8
Chemicals	15	20	15	14	11	3	4	2	5	5	0.2	0.2	0.1	0.4	0.5
Metals	9	19	19	21	23	2	7	20	22	14	0.2	0.4	1.1	1.0	0.6
Machinery	10	14	16	18	34	2	7	11	15	32	0.2	0.5	0.7	0.9	0.9
Light manufactures	65	47	50	48	32	93	82	67	58	49	1.4	1.7	1.3	1.2	1.5

^a In terms of value of shipments.
^b Excluding food.

SOURCE: H. Kanamori, *Exports of Manufactures and Industrial Development of Japan*, United Nations Conference on Trade and Development, E/CONF. 46/P/12, 9 March 1964, p. 68.

TABLE 20

Computation of Specialization Index for Japan by Selected Years, 1953 to 1961

Commodity group	1953	1958	1959	1960	1961
A. The commodity composition of world exports (percent)					
Total exports	100	100	100	100	100
Foods, raw materials and fuels	50	47	45	44	44
Light manufactured goods	20	19	17	16	17
Heavy and chemical goods:	28	33	37	38	39
chemicals	4.6	5.7	5.8	5.8	5.9
metals	6.1	6.7	9.9	10.7	10.2
machinery	17.5	20.8	21.2	21.8	22.6
Other	1	1	1	1	*
B. The commodity composition of exports from Japan (percent)					
Total exports	100	100	100	100	100
Foods, raw materials and fuels	17	12	12	11	11
Light manufactured goods	50	51	48	49	44
Heavy and chemical goods:	32	37	40	41	45
chemicals	4.9	4.9	4.8	4.2	4.5
metals	12.4	9.9	11.2	13.5	13.8
machinery	15.1	22.0	23.5	23.2	26.7
Other	*	*	1	*	*
C. B/A: Specialization index for Japan					
Foods, raw materials and fuels	0.4	0.3	0.3	0.3	0.2
Light manufactured goods	2.5	2.7	2.9	3.0	3.0
Heavy and chemical goods:	1.2	1.1	1.1	1.1	1.2
chemicals	1.1	0.9	0.8	0.7	0.8
metals	2.1	1.5	1.1	1.3	1.4
machinery	0.9	1.1	1.1	1.1	1.2
Other	*	0.1	0.9	*	*

* Less than one-half the unit.

SOURCE: *Exports of Manufactures and Industrial Development of Japan*, by H. Kanamori, United Nations Conference on Trade and Development, E/CONF. 46/P/12, 9 March 1964, pp. 58, 59, 61.

growth of income. In this sense, Japan's dependence has ostensibly increased.

The international, as contrasted with domestic, results of Japan's effort to "boost the industrial structure to a higher level" are further revealed by the so-called "index of specialization." The index is computed as the ratio of the share of a given commodity in the total exports of Japan to the share of the same commodity in total world trade. On this basis Japan's position as an exporter of heavy and chemical goods appears to have remained stationary because of the relatively greater progress of other countries during the past decade. In fact, between 1953 and 1961, while the index of Japan's specialization in heavy and chemical goods remained practically constant at a level of 1.2, its index for specialization in light manufactures actually increased from 2.5 to 3.0 (Table 20). This supports the analysis of a preceding section, in which the relative competitive position of Japan among its peers was discussed.

Dependence on export sales is highly variable for individual commodities within the major groups. The relation between exports and output for a list of 53 principal export commodities in 1963 ranged from two percent in the case of spun rayon yarn to over 90 percent in the case of barbed wire; the median ratio was 14.1 percent.[13]

Incidentally, the term "heavy industry" as used with reference to exports is a synthetic category which does not appear as such in either the *Yushutsunyū Tōkei Hinmoku Hyō* [Statistical Classification of Commodities for Japanese Foreign Trade] or the Standard Industrial Classification for Japan (the commodity code used by the Census of Manufactures).[14] However, a typical list of inclusions is that

[13] Ministry of International Trade and Industry, *Tsūshō Hakusho Sōron, 1964* [International Trade White Paper, General Remarks, 1964], pp. 270-71. All ratios were computed in terms of quantity. For corresponding ratios for 1934-36, see *Annotated Economic Statistics of Japan,* The Institute of Economic Research, Hitotsubashi University, Tokyo, 1961, p. 98 (the volume is in Japanese, the title in English).

[14] According to the Economic Planning Agency, heavy industry includes the metal, machinery, and chemical industries, all other manu-

specified by the MITI for purposes of its International Trade White Paper. Under "machinery," besides such weighty items as ships, we find the following: sewing machines, insulated wire, electric record players, radio receivers, electric fans, dry batteries, electric light bulbs, binoculars, cameras, lenses, and watches and clocks.[15] The above items account for a substantial proportion of the value of exports within the "heavy industry" category. Evidently the criteria for inclusion in this category are not unambiguous.[16]

THE GEOGRAPHICAL DISTRIBUTION OF TRADE

Japan's peculiar point of intersection between East-West complementarity on the one hand and North-South complementarity on the other, raises problems that have become acute in recent years. They arise from Japan's effort to complete its industrial transition at the same time it is implementing the import liberalization program. Joint pressures thus make it urgent for Japan to quickly resolve its role with regard to the international division of labor. These pressures have become more intense at the very moment foreign trade has become a larger and more sensitive ingredient of the Japanese growth rate.

Schematically, in its East-West orientation, Japan aspires to share in the horizontal division of labor among the advanced manufacturing nations of the North Atlantic

---

facturing being classified as light industry. The term "heavy chemicals," incidentally, refers simply to bulk chemicals, such as sulphuric acid.

[15] MITI, *Tsūshō Hakusho, 1964*, pp. 820ff. For purposes of foreign exchange transactions, a similar list of inclusions is given by The Bank of Japan in *Foreign Exchange Statistics Monthly*, January 1964, p. 105. It should also be noted that under Ministry of Finance Official Announcement 344, a substantial change was made in 1962 in the statistical inclusions of Japanese import and export commodities. Time series data for individual commodities overlapping the years 1961 and 1962 should be scrutinized with care.

[16] As mentioned above, a similar ambiguity occurs in the case of imports, where animal feeds and fodder are often included in the category "food."

region. In its North-South orientation, it endeavors to exchange manufactured goods for primary commodities with the developing nations of Southeast Asia. There is a difference in the type of manufactures marketable in each instance. To the advanced nations, along with traditional miscellaneous goods and textile products, Japan attempts to supply light manufactures; these consist primarily of durable consumer goods such as household electrical or electronic equipment. To the developing countries Japan offers heavy machinery and chemical goods. This dichotomy has its roots in the dual structure of Japan's domestic economy as well as in the contrasting character of its markets.

Ironically, however, it is precisely Japan's traditional export products, especially textiles, which threaten the declining industries of the advanced countries. Often the latter are protected specifically against Japan, which in this context ranks as a backward country, one which "dumps the output of its cheap labor," according to the protectionists. The "developing nations," whose labor may be cheaper than that of Japan, are sometimes admitted into the protected markets under rather less restrictive conditions.

In the markets of the developing countries themselves, Japan's heavy and chemical goods are subject to competition from the more technically advanced and financially strong firms of the North Atlantic region. The situation is complicated further by the fact that as a supplier of raw materials and food, North America is more important to Japan than all of Southeast Asia taken together.[17]

Thus the formal scheme of consistency in Japan's North-South and East-West complementarities is rather remote from their practical reconciliation. While Japan is in effect "backward" to the advanced countries which resist its "market disruption" at home but which compete with it in third markets, Japan is "advanced" in relation to the

17 Japan External Trade Organization, *Foreign Trade of Japan*, *1963*, cf. pp. 151 and 206.

developing countries of Southeast Asia, which likewise compete with Japan in third markets at the same time they call upon Japan for economic aid and demand unrestricted access to the Japanese domestic market.[18]

In one respect, which is not necessarily to Japan's advantage, its trade conforms precisely to the pattern characteristic of the advanced countries of the North Atlantic region. Since World War II, there has been a conspicuous tendency for trade among the latter to expand at a relatively greater rate than trade between them and the developing nations, as well as at a higher rate than trade among the developing nations themselves. During 1956-58, one-third of Japan's exports were shipped to advanced industrial countries and two-thirds to nonindustrial countries. By 1962 the proportions had become approximately equal.[19] Thus in its progress towards becoming an "advanced" nation, the proportion of Japan's trade with other advanced nations has likewise steadily increased while its trade with developing nations has tended to stagnate.[20]

The Role of Other Countries in the Trade of Japan

The regional distribution of Japan's trade may be observed both in the aspect of its importance to Japan and its role in the total trade of Japan's trade partners. First, from Japan's point of view, North America and Asia each account for roughly one-third of Japan's imports and exports, respectively (Table 21). However, as compared with the prewar period, trade with Asia has distinctly tended to decline while that with North America has tended to increase in relation to the total. Prewar exports to Asia, for example, were relatively twice as great as exports to North America, but by 1963 the former had de-

[18] See the recommendations of the United Nations Conference on Trade and Development, Geneva, 23 March to 15 June 1964.

[19] *Kokusai Keizai Bunkakai Kentō Jikō Sankō Shiryō* [Reference Material for Discussion on Items of International Economic Subcommittee], Economic Planning Agency, June 6, 1963, p. 13.

[20] *Foreign Trade of Japan, 1963*, Japan External Trade Organization, p. 15.

TABLE 21

Japan's Foreign Trade by Region, 1936 and by Year, 1956 to 1963
(billions of yen and percent)

Year	Total	Asia Total	South and Southeast Asia	Europe	North America Total	United States	South America	Africa	Oceania
	(billions of yen)			(percent)					
IMPORTS									
1936	3	38.5	16.8	11.8	34.1	30.6	4.1	3.9	7.6
1956	1,163	32.4	20.3	7.2	44.4	33.0	4.0	3.1	8.9
1957	1,542	28.8	16.2	9.4	46.3	37.8	2.9	2.4	10.2
1958	1,092	31.8	16.1	9.5	44.7	34.7	2.6	2.8	8.6
1959	1,296	31.7	18.2	10.9	41.4	30.9	3.0	3.6	9.4
1960	1,617	30.4	18.0	10.9	42.8	34.4	3.2	3.7	9.0
1961	2,092	26.2	14.7	12.5	44.5	35.8	4.4	3.3	9.1
1962	2,029	28.6	14.8	13.6	41.1	32.1	4.0	3.9	8.8
1963	2,425	30.6	14.8	12.6	39.9	30.8	4.1	3.9	8.8
EXPORTS									
1936	3	51.1	15.6	11.3	24.1	22.1	2.6	7.4	3.6
1956	900	40.9	26.6	10.0	26.3	21.7	5.4	15.7	1.7
1957	1,029	39.9	26.7	11.6	25.7	20.9	3.3	17.5	2.0
1958	1,036	36.8	23.1	12.1	29.9	23.7	4.0	14.4	2.8
1959	1,244	33.2	22.0	11.4	36.5	29.8	4.1	11.9	2.9
1960	1,460	36.0	24.9	13.2	33.2	26.7	4.4	8.7	4.5
1961	1,525	37.3	24.7	14.3	30.6	24.8	5.5	9.0	3.3
1962	1,770	34.0	21.8	17.2	33.7	23.5	4.6	6.8	3.7
1963	1,963	34.3	22.1	16.3	32.9	27.6	3.6	8.7	4.1

Note: Total column percent is 100.0 for all years.

SOURCES: Data for South and Southeast Asia: 1936: W. W. Lockwood, *The Economic Development of Japan*, *op.cit.*, p. 395. 1956, 1957: calculated by the writer. 1958-63: Mitsubishi Economic Research Institute, *Monthly Circular*, July 1964, p. 27. Other data from The Bank of Japan, *Economic Statistics of Japan*, 1963, pp. 257-58. The figures include Communist bloc trade as classified by continent.

clined to one-third of total exports while the latter had increased to that same proportion. Imports from Asia likewise declined in comparative terms—from 39 to 31 percent—while imports from North America increased from 34 to 40 percent during the same interval.

In a breakdown by country, the United States is by far Japan's most important individual trade partner. The same was true during the prewar period 1934-36, although in those days trade with China was of comparable importance. In the prewar days, however, Japan's major exports, especially to the United States, were textiles and sundry goods.[21] The present largely unprogressive state of Japan's complementarity relations with the United States may be expressed by the fact that in the era of heavy and chemical goods output this description still applies.[22]

In recent years Japan has been acclaimed for its success in introducing household electronic goods into the United States. This has been accepted as both evidence of innovative ability and competitive power on the part of Japan. The ascent of these "star" items, however, has already tapered off and their future is problematical. There are several reasons for this. In the first place, Japanese businessmen are reluctant to both innovate in technology and invest in market development abroad simultaneously. In the electronics industry, Sony is practically the only com-

[21] "As late as 1930 as much as 57 percent of all her exports to foreign countries and colonies were textiles. Another 13 percent were fish and agricultural products. The remainder were divided between minerals and metal goods, on the one hand, and cheap consumer wares made of wood, celluloid, paper, rubber, etc., on the other." W. W. Lockwood, *Economic Development of Japan*, p. 371.

[22] "Textiles and sundries constitute the principal items of export to the United States." Economic Planning Agency, *Economic Survey of Japan, 1962-1963*, p. 23. Moreover, "the rapid expansion of the Japanese exports in postwar years was due in a large measure to a sharp increase in the exports to the U.S. of labor-intensive commodities." (*Ibid.*, p. 192.) The latter include rubber manufactures, glass products, clothing, footwear, and light machinery such as office equipment, electrical appliances and optical instruments. However, steel mill products and iron and steel manufactures have also recently begun to grow at a rapid pace.

pany which has done so. Even in the Sony case, the innovation was one of application rather than of development: the transistor technique was developed in the United States as a military project; the Japanese innovation consisted in applying the technique to consumer products.

Second, Japanese technique in industrial electronics is poor and seems systematically to lag behind developments in the United States upon which it is already heavily dependent.[23] Up to 1964, the small amount of industrial electronics goods which Japan had exported were shipped almost exclusively to Asian countries under reparations agreements or official loan programs. Some Japanese makers produce low cost electronics products by importing used machinery which is obsolete in the United States or which has been relinquished by bankrupt firms. In Japanese industry, moreover, the tendency towards vertical integration requires that every company be a specialist in all techniques up and down the line; but in a highly sophisticated industry such as electronics this is very difficult to achieve. Therefore Japanese firms may suffer a progressively greater handicap as electronics technology becomes increasingly complex.

/ A third factor which darkens the export prospect in this field is the gradual decline of military expenditures for electronics production in the United States. Having been kept busy by military demand in the past, the American industry has been content to accept Japanese competition in the household goods field without mounting a maximum counteroffensive.\In the future, however, United States producers will not surrender any part of the American domestic market without a powerful struggle.\By the same token, they will become increasingly dangerous competitors against Japan in third markets as well. On the other hand, as an encouraging factor, there has been perceptible

[23] During the period 1949-62, according to the Foreign Exchange Department of The Bank of Japan, the industries principally responsible for induction of foreign know-how were communications apparatus (electronics) and chemicals.

progress by the Japanese electronics industry in the form of joint-venture activities designed to produce parts for export.

Following the United States, South and Southeast Asia as a unit comprises Japan's second leading trade partner.[24] Promise has been greater than performance in Japan's complementary relations with this region, however. The partnership is vexed by the fact that trade is unbalanced in Japan's favor and that it has increased at a lesser rate than Japanese trade in general. In the effort to industrialize, Southeast Asia has produced less and consumed relatively more of the primary commodities which it might offer to Japan. Thus its purchasing power is weak.[25]

Nevertheless, Southeast Asia has been Japan's chief market for heavy and chemical goods exports, and it is anticipated that by 1970 the developing countries as a group (in which Southeast Asia figures prominently) will take one-third of Japan's shipments in this category as compared with only one-fifth by advanced countries.[26] A breakdown of industrial as opposed to household products within the heavy and chemical goods category would show that Southeast Asia is an even more strategic market for Japan than these figures suggest.

[24] As used in Japanese government statistics, *Southeast Asia* includes South Viet-Nam, Thailand, the Federation of Malaya, Singapore, the Philippines, British North Borneo, Brunei, Sarawak, Indonesia, Netherlands New Guinea or West Irian, Cambodia, Laos and Portuguese Timor. *South Asia* includes Burma, India, Pakistan, Ceylon, the Maldive Islands, Portuguese India, Afghanistan, Nepal, and Bhutan. *Eastern Asia* includes the Republic of Korea, Ryukyu Islands, Hong Kong, China (Taiwan), the Bonin Islands, the Iwo Islands, and Macao. The designation *Eastern Europe, USSR, and China* includes Communist bloc areas. Statistical Standards Bureau, Administrative Management Agency, *Supplement to the Monthly Statistics of Japan: Explanatory Notes*, January 1964, p. 101.

[25] "In regard to Asian countries near Japan, only 36 percent of their increase in imports during the past five years was financed by the increase in exports. The remaining 64 percent had to be covered by foreign aid." *Economic Survey of Japan, 1962-1963*, Economic Planning Agency, p. 23.

[26] *Yushutsu Sankō Shiryō* [Reference Data for Exports], Economic Planning Agency, September 23, 1963, p. 21.

102

As already indicated, however, this market has been largely "bought" by grants, loans, or reparations. Japanese reparations deliveries reveal both an aspect of export promotion and an aspect of development assistance. The first is seen in the fact that reparations procurement is tied exclusively to Japanese goods; the second results from the circumstance that reparations are due entirely to less developed countries. In fulfilling its obligation, Japan has promoted the procurement of capital goods rather than consumer goods. In the short run this assists the industrialization of the recipients; in the long run it consolidates Japan's role as a supplier of replacement parts, new equipment, and technical advice. The total amount of agreed reparations approximates $1 billion, to be supplied over a period of 20 years following the inception of deliveries in December 1955.[27]

Until 1961, moreover, a considerable amount of Japan's heavy and chemical exports to Southeast Asia were shipped under the auspices of United States foreign aid programs, particularly the system of offshore procurement by which both the recipient and the seller (in this case, Japan) received the benefit of American aid expenditures.[28]

[27] The deliveries (in millions of dollars) are to the Philippines ($550), Indonesia ($223), Burma ($200), and Viet-Nam ($39). Reparations exports are included, together with ordinary commercial exports in the basic official record of Japanese foreign trade, the *Annual Return of the Foreign Trade of Japan*, published by the Ministry of Finance. For a breakdown of reparations exports, see the monthly publication, *Gaikoku Bōeki Gaikyo* [General Conditions in Foreign Trade] published by the Japan Customs Association. Since 1959 reparations exports have amounted to approximately $50 million annually.

[28] Prior to its termination at the procurement level (as of December 5, 1960), approximately 10 percent of Japan's shipments to Asia were financed by AID (subsuming former ICA and DLF) offshore procurement. Actual shipments under the AID program reached a peak of $147 million in 1960. In that year, 50 percent of Japan's shipments to Korea, 31 percent of shipments to Formosa, 60 percent of shipments to Viet-Nam, 24 percent of shipments to Pakistan, and 45 percent of shipments to Iran were financed by AID. These shipments are included, together with ordinary commercial shipments in the *Annual Return of the Foreign Trade of Japan*. For a breakdown of AID transactions, see *Bōeki Tōkei Geppō* [Monthly Foreign Trade Statistics] of the MITI.

Relations between Japan and South and Southeast Asia are conveniently summarized in United Nations statistics of the ECAFE region, which covers substantially the same area (plus the addition of Australia and New Zealand).[29] According to the recent study of change in these relations, 27 percent of Japan's total imports came from the developing countries of the ECAFE region in 1955; by 1961 the proportion had declined to 16 percent. During the same interval, on the other hand, Japan's imports from developed countries increased from 51 to 63 percent of the total. In the meantime, Japan had maintained its exports to the developing countries of the ECAFE region—in both years they received approximately one-third of Japan's total exports.[30] In view of the way in which this was accomplished, as described above, neither the past performance nor the imminent prospects for relations between Japan and the ECAFE region seem especially bright.

Aside from Asia and North America, Japan's trade is not highly concentrated by continent. Exports to West Europe, for example, have ranged approximately from 10 to 15 percent of total exports in both prewar and postwar periods. Japan's principal exports to Europe include canned and frozen fish, textiles, ships, and light machinery. Principal imports include machinery, instruments, chemical, and pharmaceutical products. Since Japan's accession to OECD it seems that some of the barriers which formerly hindered its relations with Western Europe may be removed.

[29] The ECAFE region includes Afghanistan, Australia, Brunei, Burma, Cambodia, Ceylon, China (Taiwan), Hong Kong, India, Indonesia, Iran, Japan, the Republic of Korea, Laos, Malaysia, New Zealand, Nepal, Pakistan, the Philippines, Thailand, the Republic of Viet-Nam, and Western Samoa. At its 36th session in 1963, the Economic and Social Council extended the geographical area of the region to include Australia, New Zealand and Western Samoa. The term *developing* ECAFE *region* refers to all members other than Australia, Japan, and New Zealand. United Nations, *Economic Survey of Asia and the Far East, 1963*, p. iv.
[30] United Nations Conference on Trade and Development, *Trade Between Developing ECAFE Countries and Centrally Planned Economies*, E/CONF.46/39, 27 January 1964, p. 13.

Until recently, Japan's trade with the Communist bloc has been marked by unpleasant vicissitudes and on the whole has been of almost trivial dimensions. In 1953, exports to Mainland China were valued at $5 million and those to the USSR were valued at less than $1 million. By 1963, however, exports to Mainland China amounted to $62 million and exports to the USSR $158 million. Indeed, by 1963, the USSR had risen to fourth on the list of Japan's leading export destinations (Table 22). The importance of exports to the Communist areas, moreover, is not to be judged in terms of volume alone, for they consist primarily of plant and equipment within the heavy and chemical goods category.[31]

Japan's exports to Mainland China likewise are concentrated in plant and equipment and fertilizer. The rupture in Mainland China's relations with the USSR have increased the importance of its access to Japanese heavy industry goods.[32] By the same token, the rupture has increased the availability to Japan of Chinese raw materials previously earmarked for the Soviet Union. Principally, these include coking coal and iron ore; Mainland China also supplies Japan with salt, soybeans, and corn. From a political as well as economic point of view, both Main-

[31] According to the Russo-Japanese Trade Agreement for 1964, the target for Japan was $142 million in exports and $130 million in imports. Japan's exports were to include freighters, tankers, chemical industrial equipment, cranes, machine tools, rolled steel materials, nitrogenous fertilizer, and liquid petroleum gas. Imports were to include scrap iron, lumber, coal, petroleum, and pig iron (these covered the bulk of Japan's imports from Russia in 1963). (The Bank of Japan, *Monthly Review*, February 1964, p. 6.) For a summary of agreements on trade and payments, as well as technical and financial assistance agreements between the centrally planned economies and Japan from 1950 to 1963, see *Trade Between Developing ECAFE Countries and Centrally Planned Economies*, Annex No. 2, pp. 64-70.

[32] Trade between Japan and Mainland China was suspended after the Nagasaki flag incident of 1958. Thereafter, the first long-term contract between the parties was signed in August 1964. It provided for shipments of fertilizer over a three-year period from the Japan Ammonium Sulphate Industrial Association to the China National Chemicals Import and Export Corporation.

TABLE 22
Japan's Leading Trade Partners During 1963
(millions of dollars)

Japanese imports: countries of origin		Japanese exports: countries of destination	
United States	$2,077	United States	$1,507
Australia	514	Hong Kong	246
Canada	319	Republic of Korea	160
Philippines	230	USSR	158
West Germany	220	Australia	158
Malaya	183	United Kingdom	156
Saudia Arabia	179	India	154
USSR	162	Philippines	150
United Kingdom	149	Ryukyus	136
Iran	138	Liberia	133

SOURCE: *Bōeki Tōkei Geppō* [Monthly Foreign Trade Statistics], Ministry of International Trade and Industry.

land China and the Soviet Union have keen motives for cultivating trade with Japan.[33]

The interesting potentialities of trade between Japan and the Communist countries concern not only their political implications but also the fact that if realized, the exchange of agricultural and industrial raw materials for capital goods would represent a type of complementarity in trade which Japan has not yet successfully achieved on a substantial scale with any other region and which would be a dynamic factor in the development of Japan as well as Mainland China and East Siberia. The chance that this potentiality may be realized, moreover, is enhanced by the relative decline which has steadily diminished the role of the ECAFE region in the structure of Japan's foreign trade.

[33] Japan's share of total free world exports to the Communist bloc was 0.4 percent in 1953, increasing to 4.3 percent in 1962. Japan's share of free world imports from the Communist bloc was 1.6 percent in 1953, increasing to 4.0 percent in 1962. *Yushutsu Sankō Shiryō* [Reference Data for Exports], Consolidated Planning Bureau of the Economic Planning Agency, September 23, 1963, p. 12.

The Role of Japan in the Trade of Other Countries

A helpful measure which expresses the place of Japan in the trade of other nations is known as the "coefficient of export intensity." The coefficient is calculated as the proportion of Japan's total exports to any specified region, divided by the region's proportion of total world imports. When these two proportions are identical, the coefficient equals unity. A coefficient of less than unity, as in the case of Japan's exports to Western Europe, indicates that the "intensity" of Japan's exports to that region is low in relation to the region's ability to import.[34] As evaluated for Japan's major regional trading partners, the results are as follows:

TABLE 23

Japan's Exports to Selected Regions: Coefficient of Export Intensity
During Selected Years, 1938 to 1960

Year	Western Europe	North America	East and Southeast Asia
1938	0.18	1.92	5.33
1948	0.25	1.54	4.93
1955	0.22	1.39	5.80
1960	0.27	1.83	4.29

SOURCE: Ministry of the International Trade and Industry, *Tsūshō Hakusho* [White Paper on International Trade], 1962.

According to the coefficient of intensity, both in prewar and postwar times the place of imports from Japan has been of relatively great importance in the trade of East and Southeast Asia, of lesser importance in the case of North America, and of relatively low importance in the case of Western Europe. The secular trend of the coefficient is

[34] The analogous formula for the intensity of Japan's imports from Western Europe would be:

$$\frac{\text{Japan's imports from W. Europe}}{\text{Japan's total imports}} \div \frac{\text{W. Europe's exports}}{\text{Total world exports}}$$

107

of particular interest: between 1938 and 1960, Japan's role as an exporter increased moderately in relations with North America while it distinctly declined in relations with South and Southeast Asia.[35]

This trend in the role of Japanese products in the trade structure of other regions should be considered together with the results of an analysis by the Economic Planning Agency concerning the change in Japan's exports which would result by repercussions arising from a change of one unit in Japan's imports. The effects are expressed in the form of coefficients for each of Japan's regional trade partners, respectively. According to the estimates, North America is least responsive to increases in Japan's imports (coefficient of 0.79). Sterling Asian countries and Other Asian countries have the highest coefficients (1.30 and 1.41 respectively). From the point of view of export promotion, therefore, "it would be more advantageous to Japan . . . to increase imports from less developed countries than from elsewhere."[36]

The tendency in actual practice, however, has been precisely the reverse, for the proportion (although not the absolute amount) of Japan's imports procured from the developing ECAFE countries has been declining. As mentioned above, in 1955, 27 percent of Japanese imports were received from those countries, while by 1961 the proportion had declined to 16 percent.[37] A further decline is in prospect. For according to estimates assembled by the United Nations, the share of the developing ECAFE region in Japan's imports in 1980 will range only from 7 to 10

[35] Persistence of the trend towards relative disengagement may be inferred from an estimate that in 1980 Japan will supply only nine percent of the imports of the developing ECAFE region, whereas in 1958-60 the proportion was 13 percent. Economic Commission for Asia and the Far East, *Economic Bulletin for Asia and the Far East*, December 1963, p. 29.

[36] Economic Planning Agency, *Economic Survey of Japan, 1962-1963*, p. 202. The analysis was based on data for 1960-61.

[37] United Nations, *Trade Between Developing ECAFE Countries and Centrally Planned Economies*, p. 13.

percent, given alternative low or high assumptions.[38] This may help account for the fact that in terms of the region's ability to import, Japan's exports to South and Southeast Asia have likewise been declining.

Japan's role in the trade of the United States, on the other hand, as well as the role of the United States in the trade of Japan, has been steadily increasing in recent years. In 1963 nine percent of U.S. imports were shipped from Japan, as compared with only two percent in 1953. During the same decade, the proportion of total United States exports shipped to Japan increased from four percent to eight percent.[39] Of course, the relative importance of the two partners in each other's trade is distinctly inverse; in 1963, for example, the United States was the destination of one-third of Japan's total exports.

This inverse relationship in trade with the United States leads to the observation that in general, on an individual country basis as distinguished from regional areas, if we consider either Japan's principal markets or its principal import sources, we find that the relative importance of trade with Japan in the total trade of countries having a *higher* per capita GNP than Japan is much *lower* than the relative importance which trade with them has for Japan. Conversely, the relative importance of trade with Japan to those

[38] United Nations, Economic Commission for Asia and the Far East, *Economic Bulletin for Asia and the Far East*, December 1963, p. 21. The expected doubling of Japan's imports of foodstuffs between 1959 and 1980 is likely to be concentrated on demand for processed food and "luxury" items not supplied by the ECAFE region. Japan's manufactured goods imports are expected to increase by about six times in the same interval, but it is also unlikely that these can be supplied by the region. Japan's principal promise as a market for the ECAFE region consists in her anticipated demand for more agricultural raw materials and crude petroleum.

[39] From the point of view of the United States, Japan is valued primarily as a customer for farm products—food, feed and fibers. Japan is the leading market for U.S. cotton, soybeans, hides, tallow, and powdered milk, besides being a major customer for wheat, feedgrains, and tobacco, as well as scrap iron, timber, wood pulp, chemicals, petroleum products, and coal. In the field of manufactured goods, Japan is an important market for industrial and office machines and transportation equipment.

countries having a *lower* per capita GNP than Japan is much *higher* than the relative importance of their trade with Japan within the overall volume of Japanese trade.

Not only does Japan's trade with developing areas play a relatively larger role in their economies than in its own, but this trade is also largely unbalanced in Japan's favor. Again, the converse is the case in Japan's trade with the United States.

---

10 · THE INTERNATIONAL ACCOUNTS

For a clear picture of a nation's international economic position, we need both an income statement and a balance sheet of its external accounts. Usually, we have only the balance of payments, which as a tool of economic analysis is essentially an income statement rather than a balance sheet. It reports the current volume of activity in foreign commodity trade and finance. The implications of this activity, however, can be understood only in relation to the total outstanding level of the nation's international assets and liabilities.

On the occasion of the IMF annual conference, held in Tokyo in September 1964, the Japanese government for the first time released a partial account of Japan's external assets and liabilities. Its reluctance to do so earlier can be appreciated from the high degree of Japan's dependence and vulnerability which the figures reveal.

EXTERNAL ASSETS AND LIABILITIES

One of the astonishing features of Japan's high postwar rate of economic growth is the manner in which it was achieved despite meager foreign exchange reserves. Of all the world's major trading nations, only England operates with a smaller ratio of gold and foreign exchange in relation to current payments than does Japan, and the English growth rate is far from comparable with that of Japan.[1] Qualitatively, Japan's reserve position is especially poor in view of the high degree of fluctuation in Japanese trade and payments.

The financial explanation of Japan's growth rate in the face of this handicap is borrowed capital. At the end of 1963 Japan's total external liabilities amounted to $7.5 billion; they exceeded its external assets by almost $2.5 billion. At the same time, its foreign currency reserves were only $2.2 billion. In the present stage of growth, characterized by rapid capital accumulation, Japan urgently needs stable long-term rather than short-term capital. However, in 1963 its short-term liabilities were more than three-fourths as large as its "ordinary" long-term liabilities.[2] Moreover, its short-term liabilities alone considerably exceeded its total foreign exchange reserves; even when offset by short-term assets the short-term debt was three-fourths as large as the foreign exchange reserves (Table 24).

In accordance with Japan's new reporting obligations as a member of OECD, figures concerning the external short-term assets and liabilities are now being regularly transmitted to that agency.[3] On the occasion of its first transmittal, the Ministry of Finance also released selected details of this report (Table 25). These give Japan's position as of a date six months later than the figures in Table 24.

Both Tables 24 and 25 exclude "impact" loans, which in the United States would be called term loans. In Ministry of Finance parlance, an impact loan is the liability of a private Japanese firm arising from a loan extended to it by

[1] Although Japan is a country with a high growth rate, however, in several respects it assumes characteristics of countries with a low rate of growth. In general, countries with a high growth rate have a favorable balance in current transactions and also have adequate foreign exchange reserves. In both these respects, Japan has the aspect of a low growth rate country.

[2] In 1965, approximately $1 billion of Japan's long-term liabilities were scheduled to come due. *The Japan Economic Journal*, January 12, 1965, p. 5.

[3] Japan became a full member of OECD on April 28, 1964.

TABLE 24

Japan's Outstanding External Assets and Liabilities as of December 1963
(millions of dollars)

Assets		Liabilities	
Total assets	4,978	Total liabilities	7,460
Long-term assets:	1,853	Long-term liabilities:	3,350
Deferred payment for exports		Stocks and corporate bonds	350
(including yen loans)	1,012	Foreign bonds	500
Direct investments	564	Loans (from the World Bank,	
Investments in international		U.S. commercial banks, and	
agencies	277	private sources)	1,300
		Loans for purchase of U.S.	
		surplus agricultural products	104
		Deferred payment for imports[a]	1,096
		"Special" long-term liabilities:	1,246
		Reparations	712
		GARIOA and EROA repayment[b]	534
Short-term assets:	942	Short-term liabilities:	2,559
Export usance facilities ex-		Import usance facilities ex-	
tended by Japanese banks	760	tended by foreign banks	1,328
Open account outstanding		Euro-dollar deposits	357
credit	82	Free yen deposits	304
Foreign currency held by for-		"Clean" loans	300
eign exchange banks	100	Other foreign currency	
		deposits	162
		Loan for the purchase of U.S.	
		raw cotton	56
		Petroleum standby credit	52
Foreign currency reserve:	2,183		
Gold bullion	289		
Foreign government short-term			
securities	700		
Time deposits with U.S. com-			
mercial banks	700		
Other foreign currency, includ-			
ing pound sterling deposits	189		
Drawable IMF credit		IMF standby credit	305
Gold tranche	180		
First credit tranche	125		

a Primarily loans from United States Export–Import Bank.
b Repayment for American aid supplied to Japan during the Occupation ("Government and Relief in Occupied Areas" and "Economic Rehabilitation in Occupied Areas").
SOURCE: *Nihon Keizai Shimbun* (in Japanese), March 13, 1964, p. 1.

TABLE 25

Balance of short-term assets and liabilities of Japanese banks and foreign banks recognized as exchange banks (including branch offices of foreign banks), as of June 30, 1964: (millions of dollars)

	Assets	Liabilities	Net Assets
Foreign currency base	2,191	2,635	— 444
Japanese currency base	0	578	— 578
Total	2,191	3,213	— 1,022

Of the above foreign currency base assets of $2.19 billion, about $1 billion was for trade credits, such as export usance. Out of the foreign currency base liabilities of $2.64 billion, $1.9 billion was for trade credits, such as import usance.

SOURCE: Ministry of Finance Press Release (in Japanese), October 21, 1964.

a foreign bank. An impact loan is not "tied" by project, nor must the proceeds be spent in any specified country. These loans are usually guaranteed by Japanese banks and therefore are without collateral.[4] The term of impact loans is either less than one year or three years or more, usually the latter. The hiatus is explained by the fact that short-term loans (less than one year) are subject to the Foreign Exchange and Foreign Trade Control Law (Law No. 228, December 1, 1949), whereas long-term loans (three years or more) are subject to the provisions of the Law Concerning Foreign Investment (Law No. 163, May 10, 1950). Formally, the government provides no machinery for validation of impact loans intermediate in term between one and three years. In practice, however, the Ministry of Finance validates 35-month or even 34-month loans as a "kind of three-year loan." Where the parties to a one-year loan agree to extend it for a period of two more years, the ministry will also validate the two-year extension as another kind of three-year loan.

[4] Foreign loans guaranteed by banks are not included in the statistics of loans extended by banks. Nevertheless, the contingent liability of the guarantees does constitute a source of potential vulnerability on the part of Japanese banks on the international level.

113

The Japanese currency base figures in Table 25 refer to the "free yen" account system which was established in July 1960 as a step towards foreign exchange liberalization. Free yen accounts—which are almost entirely time deposits—are accounts established by the deposit of designated foreign currencies in Japanese banks; withdrawal may likewise be made in foreign currency, but the accounts are denominated in yen.

Formally, banks cannot make loans against free yen deposits without permission from the Ministry of Finance (though such permission has never been sought). Nevertheless, the foreign exchange bank which receives dollar or pound sterling deposits will ordinarily sell these in the foreign exchange market for yen, which promptly lose their identity among the other yen assets of the bank. Evidently, therefore, the prohibition of the Ministry of Finance against loans made on the basis of free yen deposits is not actually effective. Due to the "tight money" situation in Japan, moreover, it is a well known practice for foreign parent companies to deposit dollars in Japanese banks on the understanding that the applications of their subsidiaries in Japan for yen loans will then be favorably considered. United States enterprises, in fact, are the source of most free yen deposits. The procedure has been refined to the point where it is possible for a Japanese resident to arrange, through the services of a broker, for a foreigner to make a dollar deposit as the basis for a domestic yen loan by the bank.[5]

The chronic "money shortage" of Japanese business thus has turned the free yen deposit system into an auxiliary source of funds for the domestic economy.[6] In addition to

[5] The foreign depositor receives not only the high rate of bank interest available in Japan, but also, it is said, an additional fee "under the table" from the Japanese borrower who arranged the transaction through the broker. This parallels the standard procedure on the entirely domestic banking level by which parties unknown to each other arrange for complementary deposits and loans in yen. The bank assists the parties by notifying the loan applicant when the supporting deposit has been received.

[6] The relatively few Japanese companies which can obtain govern-

its other obvious dangers is the practice among Japanese firms of applying funds so obtained to long-term uses, such as fixed investment. In general, of course, the application of short-term funds to fixed investment is a leading characteristic of the Japanese domestic financial system. When short-term foreign loans are used in a similar manner, however, Japan's vulnerability on the international level is much increased.

This situation is very ironic. For while in some instances contributing to increased vulnerability, the induction of foreign currency through free yen deposits redounds to the benefit of the foreign exchange reserves and helps explain why official reserves have increased in recent years despite deficits in the current account. Thus an element of weakness may masquerade as an element of strength in the statement of external assets and liabilities. The result is also interesting as an example of the difficulty of achieving one desirable object under a regime of foreign exchange control without simultaneously incurring some collateral disadvantage.

Foreign currency may also be deposited with the Japanese banking system in the form of Euro-dollar or other Euro-currency accounts. These, together with import usance and free yen accounts, represent the chief components of the short-term debt.[7] As of June 1964, the foreign currency base liabilities of Table 25 included, besides the $1.9 billion in trade credits mentioned above, $450 million in

---

ment approval for direct foreign loans in dollars, on the other hand, are able to borrow at a much lower interest rate than would be possible in terms of yen in the domestic market.

[7] "Usance" is credit extended by foreign banks (principally in the United States) for the finance of Japanese imports. Import usance facilities include three types of instruments: (1) bankers' acceptances; (2) bills for collection; and (3) "refinance." The procedure of refinance begins with the extension of credit by a Japanese foreign exchange bank to a Japanese importer. The bank then borrows from a foreign bank on the basis of its claim against the Japanese importer. With the foreign currency proceeds of its loan, the Japanese bank pays the foreign importer.

the form of Euro-dollar deposits, $200 million of other Euro-currency deposits, and $100 million in the form of "clean loans."[8]

I have noted the large size of the external short-term liabilities, the fact that they are used domestically in connection with long-term capital projects, and the markedly increasing instability of the Japanese economy despite its recent high rate of growth. In these circumstances, the degree of volatility of the foreign short-term loans is of critical importance. In principle, both the free yen and the Euro-dollar accounts are highly volatile. In practice, there is more deposit-and-withdrawal activity in the latter than in the former.[9] However, the level of total deposits in both categories seems to have been fairly stable and to be rising gradually. Does this reflect increasing confidence in the strength of the Japanese economy? In the case of the free yen deposits, as mentioned above, where a domestic borrower has been granted a yen loan subject to the deposit of foreign currency by a third party beforehand, the life of the loan is conditional upon the existence of the deposit; and since to a substantial extent the proceeds of these loans are sunk in long-term projects, this imparts a degree of apparent stability to the free yen deposits with which they are associated. A factor helping to stabilize the level of Euro-dollar deposits, on the other hand, is the fact that Japanese banks have offered premium rates of interest in London. It is profitable for the banks to do this because however high the rate to depositors in London, the rate to borrowers in Japan is higher still.

Besides the foreign exchange reserves, Japan's principal long-term external assets consist of deferred payments

[8] A "clean loan" is a liability of a Japanese foreign exchange bank to a foreign bank, without collateral. Clean loans usually have a term of six months.

[9] The high interest rate offered on Euro-dollar accounts induces short-term deposits such as that of the Russians, who in 1963 deposited the proceeds of their London gold market sales in Japanese accounts while their purchases of wheat from the United States and Canada were being negotiated. European banks are also major depositors.

116

for exports, mostly to Southeast Asian countries. At the end of 1963 these amounted to more than $1 billion; by September 1964 they had increased to $1.3 billion. Similarly, among short-term assets, the chief component of Table 25, as in Table 24, is usance credit extended by Japanese banks to foreign importers. These credits are conveyed in the form of "export bills."

On the liability side, an interesting fact emerges from Tables 24 and 25 in connection with usance credit. As of December 31, 1963, the outstanding amount of import usance credit received by Japan was $1.3 billion. As of June 30, 1964, outstanding import credits—primarily usance—amounted to $1.9 billion. These figures do not give much of a picture of the seasonal variation in outstanding usance credit; however, assuming that usance facilities on the average are extended for a period of about three months, they enable us to estimate the total amount of usance credit utilized by Japan in the course of a year. Adding, and multiplying the sum of the figures by two, gives a total of $6.4 billion, which may approximate the total amount of short-term import financing received by Japan during the year ending June 1964. Moreover, inasmuch as shippers' usance, as distinguished from bank usance, has not been included in the statistics, the estimate is distinctly low.[10] In addition to the short-term import credit, moreover, Japan also received a substantial amount of long-term import credit. Thus a very large proportion of imports into Japan—which during the year ending June 1964 amounted to $7.6 billion—has been financed by foreign loans.

The chief source of finance, as well as the chief source of goods, has been the United States. For example, as mentioned above, in June 1964 Japan's total outstanding short-

[10] Both Tables 24 and 25 exclude the liability of shippers' usance, which finances a substantial portion of Japanese imports. For example, the import of crude oil, which is Japan's principal import commodity, is financed in this manner through credits extended by parent oil companies abroad to their subsidiaries in Japan.

term banking liabilities amounted to $3.2 billion. At almost the same time, in May 1964, total short-term banking claims on Japan recorded in the United States amounted to $2.4 billion.[11]

The flow of short-term finance from the United States to Japan chiefly takes the form of acceptance credit. In May 1964, short-term claims in this category payable by Japan amounted to $1.5 billion.[12] It is significant that this figure accounted for two-thirds of the total amount of acceptance credit extended by the United States to all countries at that date.[13] The volume of United States bankers' acceptances in favor of Japan has increased tremendously since the end of 1959 when the outstanding amount was only $180 million.[14] It is evident that the United States finances far more of Japan's imports than simply those from the United States.

[11] United States Treasury Department, *Treasury Bulletin*, July 1964, p. 98. As expressed in terms of U.S. statistics, Japan's asset and liability position must be surveyed with caution. Japan's short-term assets with regard to the U.S. arise largely from its foreign exchange reserves which are on deposit in U.S. commercial banks or invested in short-term U.S. government obligations. From the point of view of U.S. statistics, the U.S. has short-term liabilities to Japan corresponding to these Japanese assets. To that extent, we must take care not to add U.S. reported liabilities to Japan to Japanese reported foreign exchange reserves in determining the offset to Japan's liabilities.

[12] This moreover excludes "refinance" by Japan in the New York money market, which amounted to approximately $200 million at the same date.

[13] *Treasury Bulletin*, July 1964. U.S. banks charge a commission of 1.5 percent for acceptance credits; in addition, there is an interest charge of 4 percent. The total cost to Japan of 5.5 percent is much less than would be incurred in most other foreign markets. *The Journal of Commerce*, Aug. 31, 1964, p. 14. It might also be observed that the acceptance business, in which banks sell their guaranty of the loan rather than their funds, is one of the banks' most lucrative activities. Consequently, U.S. banks are very anxious to provide this service to Japan.

[14] Long-term credit, on the other hand, has been a rather small component of total U.S. bank loans to Japan, although it has been increasing as a result of the Interest Equalization Tax. During the period Aug. 1962–July 1963, long-term loans extended by U.S. commercial banks to Japan amounted to $125.4 million, increasing to $279.0 million during Aug. 1963–July 1964. Ministry of Finance, Foreign Investment Section.

In support of their borrowing policy, Japanese authorities often say that bankers' acceptances are "self-liquidating" and that they therefore present no threat to Japan's foreign exchange reserves. The claim, however, is subject to some reservations. Imported raw materials financed by bankers' acceptances may or may not have been processed into goods actually sold as exports by the time obligations in the New York money market mature. To a considerable extent, the output financed in this way may never even have been intended for export, and thus Japan's foreign exchange position may be jeopardized. This is precisely what happened in 1961, when the threat was so grave that the Japanese government was obliged to borrow $325 million from a consortium of United States banks for the purpose, in effect, of funding the impending acceptance maturities into a one-year loan.

Besides the flow of physical commodities into Japan, a further basis for the extension of credit by United States banks to Japan are the deposits, mentioned above, of the foreign exchange reserves. Over one-third of Japan's foreign exchange reserves is on time deposit in United States banks.[15] Thus Japan's foreign exchange reserves play a multiple role: in their prime function, they compensate for short-term discrepancies between receipts and payments of foreign exchange; second, in the form of deposits in United States banks they serve as collateral for loans extended by those banks to Japanese banks and private firms; third, they earn interest.[16] Moreover, a residual quantity

[15] These are the "ministerial accounts." The extent to which the Japanese government's deposits with U.S. banks provides a basis for loans extended by those banks to Japan is subject to negotiation; it has never been formally established. In practice, the ratio of the ministerial accounts to the loans for which they serve as collateral is said to be approximately 30 percent.

[16] In the U.S., interest is paid on these accounts in accordance with provisions of the Federal Reserve Board's Regulation Q. As of July 17, 1963, the maximum interest payable on funds deposited for a period of from 90 days to six months was raised from 2.5 percent to 4 percent. Board of Governors of the Federal Reserve System, *Federal Reserve Bulletin*, May 1964.

of the foreign exchange reserves is deposited with some of the foreign exchange banks in Japan, where it serves as working capital in their daily transactions. The Japanese city banks have relatively little foreign exchange of their own. Thus small as they are in total amount, Japan's official foreign exchange reserves are still far from idle.[17]

Japan's external assets and liabilities are considerably affected by the role of the Japanese branches of foreign (mostly United States) commercial banks.[18] Although altogether the volume of business handled by branches of foreign banks amounts only to about one percent of the total banking business in Japan, their foreign exchange activities are more important than this figure would suggest. In particular, after World War II when the ability of Japanese banks to engage in international transactions had not yet been restored, the branches of foreign banks in Japan were a window to the world. In Japan, there is still neither a government bond market nor a discount market. Thus the branches of foreign banks facilitate Japan's access to the money markets of the United States and other countries. It is preeminently by this means, as mentioned above, that Japan's imports are financed, thus economizing on the foreign exchange reserves of the Japanese government. Second, some of the reserves of the Japanese government are conveniently placed on deposit with the branches of foreign banks in Tokyo, as well as in the head offices of those banks overseas. Third, the presence of the foreign branches forms a bulwark against emergencies, for in case of need the Japanese government

[17] An extremely small part of the reserves is held in the form of gold. At the end of 1963, the proportion was 13.2 percent, as can be calculated from Table 24. Some have asserted that in recent years Japan has "cooperated" with the United States in not converting more of its foreign exchange reserves into gold. In refraining from doing so, it has clearly acted in its own interest as well, for a higher proportion in gold would mean a smaller proportion in the form of working and earning assets.

[18] Branches in Japan of foreign banks are classified as residents of Japan. Their activities are reflected in Japan's international accounts in the same way as those of ordinary domestic banks.

could borrow from these branches at very short notice. Since the overseas head offices of the foreign banks in Japan are very anxious to maintain good relations with the Japanese government, their branches would provide every facility they could muster in the event that they were called upon. Branches of United States banks in Japan in turn benefit from the presence of the United States military forces. Dollar checks deposited by American troops in the American banks are sold by them for yen which they then can lend to their customers.

The branches of foreign banks in Japan act as "bankers' banks" by lending to Japanese commercial banks. In so doing, they are associated with one of the hidden elements of vulnerability mentioned above in the structure of Japan's external liabilities. For characteristically, the funds borrowed by Japanese banks from the foreign banks at short-term are reloaned by them to Japanese firms at long-term. Purely at the domestic level, it is a well known characteristic of the Japanese economy that the Bank of Japan supplies yen on ostensibly 90-day terms to the city banks, which the latter then relend at long-term to their customers.[19] Dangerous as this strategy is when based on short-term yen, it is far more dangerous when based on short-term dollars.

Another source of vulnerability on the international level lies in the short-term and long-term impact loans advanced to private Japanese firms by foreign lenders under the protection of guarantees provided by Japanese city banks. Substantially all loans received by these firms from abroad are guaranteed by the city banks; their outstanding total amount, however, is not disclosed by the Japanese government. To a substantial degree, the proceeds of these loans are used for domestic equipment investment; therefore the connection between the investment and prospective earnings in terms of foreign exchange may be rather remote. However, at maturity these loans represent a

---

[19] Frequently caught in the middle, as they are, the city banks are often obliged to resort to the call market. They are its chief customers.

charge on the foreign exchange resources of Japan. An adverse pattern of maturities could have embarrassing repercussions at some future date. For example, the bunching of bank loans with a maturity of slightly less than three years which took place in 1963 and 1964 as a reaction to the U.S. Interest Equalization Tax (IET) means that in 1966 and 1967 a considerable volume of loans will mature at about the same time.[20]

Fears concerning the potential impact of pressures such as these may have been unduly allayed by the success of Japanese authorities thus far in maintaining the apparent stability of the foreign exchange reserves. As shown below, however, this has been achieved largely by means of borrowing in excess of deficits in the current account. In the event of any future crisis of confidence, Japan's ability to borrow further would be crippled at precisely the moment when its need to borrow more would have become most urgent.

In case of pressure against the reserves, several alternatives stand open. First, Japan could invoke its standby credit with the IMF. Second, it could activate its swap arrangement with the Federal Reserve Bank of New York.[21] Third, the government could borrow from foreign commercial banks, as was done in 1961. Fourth, the government could issue bonds abroad. To a limited extent, the government could also buy foreign exchange from the Japanese commercial banks. This action, however, might

[20] Initially, bank loans were not subject to the tax, although there were clear indications that the exemption might be removed, especially for loans of three years or more. Therefore there was a rush to arrange loans with a term of slightly less than three years. In Feb. 1965, President Johnson announced that bank loans of more than one year would become subject to the IET but that new securities issued or guaranteed by the Japanese government in the United States would be exempt from the tax up to a limit of $100 million each year.

[21] The standby swap arrangement between The Bank of Japan and the Federal Reserve Bank of New York was established for the first time in Oct. 1963, in the amount of $150 million. It was drawn upon for the first time in April 1964 in connection with Japan's implementation of formal external convertibility of the yen.

unduly raise the price of foreign exchange in the market, which would oblige The Bank of Japan to support the yen by equalization operations. Consequently, the cost might be approximately as great as the benefit of buying foreign exchange from the banks.

THE BALANCE OF PAYMENTS

As distinguished from the statement of total outstanding assets and liabilities, the balance of payments summarizes activity during a specified period. The current account (transactions of a recurrent nature between residents and nonresidents in goods, services, and transfer payments) is expressed in terms of gross transactions on a credit-debit basis. Capital items, however, are expressed in terms of net changes in assets and liabilities during the period under consideration.[22]

In order to gain some perspective on Japan's recent balance of payments situation, I will introduce first a summary of its historical experience.

Japan's Prewar Balance of Payments[23]

Material on Japan's balance of payments in the prewar period exists since 1902. Although the organization of the

[22] Increases in assets or decreases in liabilities represent an outflow of capital (debit); decreases in assets or increases in liabilities represent an inflow of capital (credit). Changes in valuation, arising, for example, from fluctuation in the price of securities, or revaluation of assets or liabilities due to variations in the rate of exchange, are not transactions and thus are excluded from the balance of payments.

[23] Two of the major economic reports referring to Japan's international economic affairs issued annually by the Japanese government are the *Nenji Keizai Hōkoku* [Annual Economic Report] of the Economic Planning Agency and the *Tsūshō Hakusho* [International Trade White Paper] of the Ministry of International Trade and Industry. The former is also published in an English version (*Economic Survey of Japan*) issued by the EPA, while the latter appears in a partly translated version (*Foreign Trade of Japan*) issued by JETRO (Japan External Trade Organization). The *Tsūshō Hakusho* emphasizes a different theme each year; in 1964, the theme was the balance of payments, including a useful summary of the transition in the structure of the balance of payments in the prewar period. The present subsection, which is not included in the JETRO version, is translated from the 1964

123

statistics differs from that of the IMF method employed for current data, there will not be much error if they are used as a basis for rough approximation.

The prewar transition in the balance of payments can be divided into five periods: 1902-13, 1914-20, 1921-28, 1929-36, and 1937-45. The fifth period, being subject to wartime controls, was an abnormal one; therefore it may be excluded from our consideration.

The First Period: 1902-13. The first balance of payments period corresponds to the period of the Russo-Japanese War. Except for 1909, the balance of payments was marked by excess imports. Excessive imports were especially large in 1904 and 1905 because of military requirements due to the war; and imports of iron, non-ferrous metals, and machinery increased remarkably. After the war, although cotton yarn and cotton textiles came to be exported in addition to silk (which was Japan's main export), the increase in imports exceeded that of exports since the development of the spinning industry increased imports of fiber raw materials such as raw cotton and wool, and the deficit increased from 1910 to 1913.

The invisibles account was basically in equilibrium, but because of an increase in government expenditure during 1904 and 1905, a small deficit is shown for the period as a whole. Looking at the factors increasing receipts and payments in the invisibles account in this period, we see that transportation and revenue from investment made the principal contribution to increased receipts, and remittances of investment income made the principal contribution to the increase in payments. The increase in transportation receipts was due to the increase in Japanese shipping capacity after the war. With the aid of the government's policy of encouragement to ocean lines, including subsidies, the rate of shipment of foreign trade commodities in Japanese vessels increased from 37 percent in 1903

---

volume, pp. 193-200. The translation was done by the writer with the assistance of Yoko Yamamoto.

to 49 percent in 1913. The increase in receipts of revenue from investment was due to active investment abroad in the former colonies, including China, which was designed to exploit foreign markets in order to make up for the narrow home market while Japanese domestic industry was being developed. The increase in remittances of revenue from investment was due to the increase in interest paid as a result of borrowing for expenditures in the Russo-Japanese War and for the large inflow of capital after the war. Next, the capital account showed large excess receipts. This tendency was especially remarkable from 1903 to 1906, for the government depended on the issuance of bonds abroad for much of the war expenditures. Beginning with the issue in 1904 of British currency bonds at six percent interest, bonds issued abroad during the war reached a total of about 800 million yen. After the war, national bonds were issued to retire outstanding debts, as well as British currency Tokyo City bonds at five percent interest, British currency Osaka City bonds at five percent interest, British currency bonds of the Hokkaido Coal Mine Railways at five percent, and bonds for public enterprises such as gas and water service. Consequently, the capital account showed excess receipts all through this period despite active Japanese exports of capital in the postwar years.

The Second Period: 1914-20. The second period corresponds to the years of World War I. Japanese exports increased rapidly, owing to the decline in the supply capacity of European exporting countries such as England and Germany. The growth in Japan's exports of industrial products was especially remarkable. This increase owed not a little to the rise in export prices as well as to the increase in the quantity exported. In this period, in addition to the traditional textile industry, the so-called heavy and chemical industries, including machinery, made rapid progress. Accordingly, imports of metallic raw materials increased in addition to the traditional fibers. The increase in exports, however, exceeded the increase in imports, giving rise to large excess receipts. Invisibles also showed a large surplus, mainly because of the transportation account. This was engendered by development of the Japanese merchant marine and the increase in freight tonnage caused by the worldwide ship shortage. The ratio of Japan's foreign commerce carried in Japanese ships rapidly increased in this period from 58 percent in 1914 to 72 percent in 1920, reaching as high as 88 percent in 1918.

The capital account incurred excess payments because Japanese subscriptions to foreign government bonds, such as British Exchequer bonds, as well as local bonds and corporation bonds and stocks of foreign countries, reached a considerable value; besides, there were redemptions and repurchases of bonds issued abroad by Japan.

The Third Period: 1921-28. This was a period of suffering for the Japanese economy, beginning with the reaction to the boom after World War I, continuing with the Great Earthquake in the Kanto Prefectures in 1923, followed by the financial crisis of 1927. Exports did not increase because of such factors as the postwar recession abroad, the rise of prices in Japan, the recovery of productive capacity in the advanced countries, and the movement to expel Japanese commodities from China. Imports, on the other hand, increased markedly as a result of the Great Earthquake. Therefore the balance of trade in this period registered the largest deficit prior to World War II. Although the invisibles account remained in surplus, the size of the surplus was considerably smaller than it had been in the preceding period, due to the decrease in transportation receipts and the increase in payments of revenue from investment.

The capital account registered a small surplus of receipts due to the issue of United States currency bonds at six and a half percent interest and British currency bonds at six percent interest in 1919 and 1920 and the issue of foreign currency bonds by the cities of Tokyo and Yokohama thereafter.

The Fourth Period: 1929-36. This period includes the

interval between the world panic beginning with the stock market collapse in New York and the advent of the quasi-wartime system in Japan.

Japan lifted the gold embargo in 1930 in an effort to reduce prices through industrial rationalization, to expand exports, and to achieve equilibrium in the balance of payments. However, because of the fact that the gold embargo was removed at the former high parity rate and at the peak of the world panic, Japan suffered from a stagnation of exports, increase in imports, and hence a deficit in the balance of merchandise trade and a large outflow of gold. Consequently, the export of gold was again embargoed in 1931. At this point, the Japanese exchange rate fell markedly, which, together with the rationalization of industries due to the subsequent deflationary policy, brought about the expansion of Japanese exports and recovery of equilibrium in the trade balance. The balance of trade during this period as a whole was slightly in deficit. The invisibles account still showed a surplus despite an increase in payments for transportation and government transactions. Therefore the current account showed a slight surplus. However, the capital account registered a deficit owing to the flight of capital abroad and to investment abroad as Japan advanced into Manchuria.

Characteristics of the Prewar Balance of Payments. Although in the prewar, as in the postwar period, equilibrium was not achieved easily in the balance of payments, from the foregoing account we find some contrasts in the characteristics of the two periods.

In the first place, before World War II the invisibles account always showed a surplus, except in the first period when government expenditures increased abnormally as a result of the outbreak of the Russo-Japanese War. Transportation accounted for a large proportion of the excess receipts among invisibles. Although precise figures for the transportation account are not available since payments for freight were not reported separately as a part of total commodity transactions, it is thought to have been in surplus as judged from the quantity of trade and the ratio of shipments carried by Japanese ships in the prewar period. This contrasts sharply with the large deficit in the postwar transportation account. In the prewar period, excess receipts in the invisibles account were not based on special factors such as aid or special procurement, as were seen in the postwar period; moreover, they showed a basically stable transition and contributed substantially to the maintenance of equilibrium in the balance of payments.

The second distinction concerns the large growth of exports in relation to production in the prewar as contrasted with the postwar period. The growth in exports was especially remarkable in the second and fourth periods when the balance of merchandise trade showed a surplus. Dependency on exports was also much larger than during the postwar period. The significance of exports in the economy in the prewar period seems to have been greater than during the postwar period.[24]

Third, the prewar balance of payments was comparatively stable. Although there was a deficit in the current account in the first and third periods, there was a large surplus in the second period and a modest surplus in the fourth. During the period as a whole, the prewar balance of payments is judged to be rather strong as contrasted with the deteriorating trend of the current account in the postwar period. Considering that in the prewar period Japan maintained a high rate of economic growth as compared with advanced countries in the world (although it was not so high as in the postwar period), that the structure of the economy was simultaneously improved, and that equilibrium in the balance of payments was achieved under a system of free international transactions, Japan's balance of payments in the prewar period can be said to have been rather stable as compared with the postwar period.[25]

[24] As argued elsewhere in this volume, this official view of the matter by the Japanese government is much too simple.

[25] It should be noted, however, that in the first period Japan's prewar borrowing exceeded its postwar borrowing, and in the fourth

Recent Trends in the Balance of Payments

The Basic Balance. Recent trends in Japan's balance of payments may be summarized in terms of changes in the basic balance. The basic balance consists of the net balance of goods and services, debt service on investment, and the net balance of government aid and long-term capital movements.

Despite the fact that the basic balance excludes the short-term elements of Japan's international transactions, which are highly unstable, it has been marked by extreme fluctuations and extraordinary deficits in recent years. Deficits were especially large in 1957, 1961, and 1963. While the deficit of $315 million in 1963 was considerably less than the deficit of $990 million in 1961, the 1963 relapse in the basic balance occurred after only two years of surplus, as compared with an interval of three years which intervened between each of the preceding deficits. This acceleration in the tempo of fluctuation was perhaps more ominous than the actual size of the deficit itself. On all three occasions, the basic balance revealed a failure on the part of long-term capital receipts to outweigh the unfavorable effect of transactions in goods and services. The latter, in turn, was primarily the result of Japan's unfavorable balance of merchandise trade with the United States.

Deficits in the basic balance are financed by an inflow of short-term capital. As shown in Table 26, in most years this inflow has exceeded the amount of the deficit in the basic balance; in some years there was an inflow despite the absence of a deficit. Consequently, the difference between the inflow and the basic deficit would take the form of an increment to official capital. Thus in 1963, when the inflow of private short-term capital (including errors and omissions) amounted to $561.1 million as against a deficit of $314.9 million, foreign assets in the amount of $246.2 million were

---

period equilibrium in the balance of payments was achieved only at the expense of a drastic depreciation in the exchange rate.

TABLE 26

Japan's Basic Balance and Its Financing, by Year, 1956 to 1964
(millions of dollars)

Calendar year	BASIC BALANCE				FINANCING OF THE BASIC BALANCE	
	Net goods, services and private transfer payments[a]	Net private long-term capital	Net central government transfer payments[b]	Total	Net private short-term capital[c]	Net official capital[a]
1956	−26.2	−60.9	16.2	−70.9	126.6	−55.7
1957	−554.6	−10.9	−63.1	−628.6	82.5	546.1
1958	498.8	40.4	−193.2	346.0	−7.7	−338.3
1959	431.7	−20.4	−2.7	408.6	93.3	−501.9
1960	223.7	−83.2	−47.2	93.3	410.6	−503.9
1961	−883.5	−41.2	−65.7	−990.4	591.8	398.6
1962	36.1	147.6	−74.3	109.4	127.4	−236.8
1963	−693.8	507.3	−128.4	−314.9	561.1	−246.2
1964 (Jan.-June)	−803.0	116.0	−33.0	−720.0	566.0	154.0

a Includes "special procurement" receipts for goods and services provided to U.S. military forces stationed in Japan.
b Includes "miscellaneous capital."
c Refers to nonmonetary sector and commercial banks. Includes net errors and omissions.

d Includes Treasury and Bank of Japan capital and gold.

SOURCE: Compiled from International Monetary Fund, *Balance of Payments Yearbook*, various issues. Data for January-June 1964 from The Bank of Japan.

TABLE 27

Basic Balance and Financing of Japan's International Transactions with the United States and Canada, by Year, 1956 to 1963
(millions of dollars)

Calendar year	BASIC BALANCE				FINANCING OF THE BASIC BALANCE	
	Net goods, services and private transfer payments[a]	Net private long-term capital	Net central government transfer payments[b]	Total	Net private short-term capital[c]	Net official capital[a]
1956	73.8	−43.4	52.8	83.2	153.3	−236.5
1957	−290.3	16.5	37.0	−236.8	−155.5	392.3
1958	144.9	57.1	9.5	211.6	−19.0	−192.6
1959	243.7	50.0	32.7	326.4	−76.8	−249.6
1960	−66.1	23.9	−5.6	−47.8	533.3	−485.5
1961	−564.0	186.9	−2.1	−379.2	−124.7	503.9
1962	−78.8	342.2	12.6	276.0	18.9	−294.9
1963	−537.6	547.0	−6.6	2.8	243.8	−246.6

a Includes "special procurement" receipts for goods and services provided to U.S. military forces stationed in Japan.
b Includes "miscellaneous capital."
c Refers to nonmonetary sector and commercial banks.

Includes net errors and omissions.
d Includes Treasury and Bank of Japan capital and gold.

SOURCE: The Bank of Japan.

acquired by The Bank of Japan from the commercial banks.

The inflow of short-term capital far exceeded the inflow of long-term capital during the decade ending in 1963 because the Japanese government during that period maintained a rather restrictive policy with regard to the inflow of long-term capital. On balance, while there was a net inflow of private short-term capital, there was a net outflow of private long-term capital in most years prior to 1962. As already mentioned, the conversion of short-term liabilities into long-term assets is one of the chief aspects of Japan's vulnerability on the international level. In this instance, however, the claims by Japan are based primarily on shipments either of final products or investment goods made in Japan. Therefore, except to the extent that these embody imported raw materials, the immediate impact on Japan of the long-term capital outflow is registered in terms of yen rather than foreign exchange.[26]

Recently the policy of the Japanese government has changed in favor of stabilizing Japan's debt position by increasing the proportion of long-term debt in relation to total obligations. In effect, this means that Japan is now placing greater emphasis than before on wiping out the deficit in the basic balance. As can be seen from Table 26, however, in this respect the recent situation leaves much to be desired. Moreover, with regard to long-term loans, the underlying situation is even worse than appears in Table 26, for the "long-term" classification in that table in accordance with standard government practice includes all loans with a term of longer than one year. Prior to and following enactment of the United States Interest Equalization Tax, many loans with a term of between one and

[26] Direct investment and export financing account for the greater part of Japan's long-term capital exports. The Balance of Payments Section of the Ministry of Finance reported that as of Sept. 30, 1964, the total of Japan's direct private investment amounted to $629 million, of which $115 million was invested in Southeast Asia. In addition, on the same date, the total of outstanding deferred payments for exports amounted to $1,344 million, of which $483 million was the amount of credit extended to Southeast Asia.

three years were arranged between Japanese banks and the branches of United States banks in Japan. Properly, however, they should be segregated as intermediate term rather than long-term loans.[27]

The relative size of Japan's long-term, as contrasted with short-term, indebtedness has an immediate bearing on the problem of secular as contrasted with cyclical deterioration in the balance of payments. In recent years, as discussed below, secular deterioration has become a pronounced feature of the invisibles account. A coincidence of the cyclical and secular deterioration is of course greatly to be feared; however, often in the past, for specific purposes and on specific occasions, the Japanese authorities have been able to invoke powerful controls in order to avert a crisis. A conspicuous occasion on which the economy made apparently smooth passage over rocky terrain was in April 1964 when Japan's accession to IMF Article 8 together with Japan's admission to full membership in OECD exposed the yen to formal external convertibility. Despite the fact that the basic balance was in substantial deficit at the time, the transition was accomplished with only minor evident damage to the foreign exchange reserves.[28] It would seem, however, that the process of progressive liberalization will hereafter undermine the basis for implementation of some of the controls upon which the authorities have relied in the past.

As remarked above, recently the pace of cyclical deterioration in the balance of payments seems to have been accelerated. During the decade ending in 1964, Japan experienced four recessions, 1954, 1957-58, 1961-62, and 1963-64. Whereas the interval between each of the first three recessions was a period of approximately three years, the interval between the third and the fourth was less than

27 The Japanese government publishes no breakdown of the volume of outstanding loans by length of term. Informally, however, it is possible to obtain such a breakdown at the stage of licenses granted for foreign loans.

28 As mentioned above, this may be partly attributed to Japan's use of its swap facilities with the Federal Reserve Bank of New York.

two years. In each case, stringency in the balance of payments was the critical factor that touched off the recession. This fact, incidentally, should be noted by those who argue that the role of foreign trade has diminished in the postwar as compared with the prewar period. Moreover, in each case, also, especially the first three, the stringency evolved despite the government's exercise of direct foreign exchange controls.

In the matter of cyclical versus secular balance of payments deterioration, the 1964 White Paper of the MITI makes a trenchant comment. It states that casual observation creates the impression that, subject to domestic and foreign business cycles, excess payments alternate with excess receipts in the current account. However, it continues, long-term observation reveals that the current account and the basic balance, as well, have steadily tended to deteriorate, the general turning point from surplus to deficit having taken place at about 1955.[29]

The structural problem has several facets. In the merchandise category, as we observed above, it is difficult for exports to keep pace with the import needs of the heavy and chemical industries for machinery and for increasing amounts of raw materials from abroad, as well as the increasing demand for manufactured consumer goods imports. At this point, however, I should like to discuss the structural difficulties of the invisibles account.

Deterioration in the invisibles account is attributable to more than a few of its items. In order to analyze the situation, therefore, it is helpful to separate invisible expenditures into two classes—autonomous and induced. Autonomous invisibles are those that change without regard to the level of trade or capital flow; they include tourist expenses, government expenditures (such as expenses of the diplomatic corps and contributions to international organizations), private donations, personal remittances, copyright and patent fees, rent on fixed assets, and film rentals. Conspicuous increases have occurred in patent and copy-

29 MITI, *Tsūshō Hakusho, 1964*, p. 174.

right fees due to the induction of foreign technology into Japan during the postwar period.

By far the most important of the autonomous items is Special Procurement, which refers to purchases of goods and services by the United States armed forces in Japan. These purchases became a major source of revenue to Japan at the outbreak of the Korean War in June 1950; thus they overlapped and effectively replaced the contribution to Japan's growth rate which hitherto had been provided by the American Aid program.[30] To some extent, the contribution of Special Procurement transactions has been disguised by the fact that they are not subject to customs inspection and therefore do not enter the foreign trade merchandise statistics of either the buying or selling nation. From Japan's point of view, however, they constitute what might be called "high-powered exports," for they yield foreign exchange receipts for (a) merchandise sales which in the normal course of events would not be consummated and (b) for services which ordinarily are not internationally traded and which, moreover, use up a minimum of resources other than labor.[31]

Until recently, the Special Procurement component of invisibles (including AID offshore procurement in behalf of Southeast Asia) performed the function of placing that account in surplus, as well as offsetting the deficit in Japan's merchandise trade. In accordance with dollar-saving measures introduced by the United States, however, these expenditures have been reduced since 1960.[32] From a peak

30 For an analysis of the imputed contribution of American Aid and Special Procurement expenditures to Japan's national income, see Leon Hollerman, "Japan's Foreign Trade Dependence and the Five-Year Economic Plan," *The Review of Economics and Statistics*, Nov. 1958.

31 Analogously, American Aid imports during the period 1946-52 constituted "high-powered imports," for they required no payment in terms of current exports. Ironically, American Aid imports, which were included among visible transactions, were responsible for the apparently "unfavorable" balance of Japanese merchandise trade during those years.

32 Also the Japanese government has assumed the burden of some of the labor cost incurred by U.S. armed forces in Japan.

of $824 million in 1952, Special Procurement expenditures declined to approximately $310 million in 1964, which still provides a substantial contribution to the Japanese balance of payments.[33] Notwithstanding, the net balance of autonomous invisibles changed from a surplus prior to 1957 to a steadily deepening deficit thereafter.

As distinguished from autonomous invisibles, induced invisibles arise as a consequence of concomitant or antecedent merchandise or capital transactions. Here the structural difficulty is the fact that induced invisible expenditures have a tendency to increase as the volume of trade increases. Items of this kind include transportation expenses, insurance, proceeds from investment, advertising fees, communications expenses, management fees, agency charges, and securities dealer commissions. Induced invisibles have been steadily in deficit throughout the postwar period and are the chief component of the total invisibles deficit.

In turn, the principal component of the induced invisibles deficit is the cost of transportation, which itself is composed of several elements, namely the quantity of Japanese merchandise imports and exports, the ratio of shipment in Japanese ships, and the unit cost of freight. Concerning the quantity of shipments, there is a wide discrepancy in the volume of import freight as compared with export freight. This is due, of course, to the bulky character of raw materials and food which comprise the greater part of imports, whereas exports chiefly include finished prod-

[33] MITI, *Tsūshō Hakusho, 1964*, p. 170, erroneously reports the cumulative total of Special Procurement expenditures from their inception through 1963 as $3.7 billion. The correct figure is $7.2 billion. It might also be noted that the *Tsūshō Hakusho* (p. 184) erroneously attributes the entire Japanese reparations burden to the invisibles account. Reparations payments are delivered by Japan almost entirely in the form of machinery and other merchandise; in the reports of the Customs Bureau of the Ministry of Finance these are not separately identified by individual commodity but are simply combined with regular commercial exports. Only reparations in cash, which form a very minor part of total reparations, are actually included among invisibles by the Ministry of Finance.

136

ucts. Consequently, the ratio of tonnage in relation to value is much higher for imports than for exports.[34] In recent years, moreover, the discrepancy between the freight cost of imports as compared with exports has increased because of the progressively expanding needs of Japanese industry for such imports as iron ore, petroleum and coal: these have a much greater weight per unit of value than the traditional raw material imports such as natural fiber. Furthermore, as a result of Japan's effort to diversify its sources of supply, these bulky commodities have tended to come from more remote sources, thus increasing the disproportion in the cost of import freight.

While the freight cost of imports has been rising, the proportion of imports carried in Japanese ships has been declining. This has been due partly to the lack of specialized bulk carriers in the Japanese merchant fleet, and partly to the Ship American policy of the United States, which is Japan's principal supplier, as well as to similar preferences given by other countries to their national shipping lines. Another contributing factor is the nature of import contracts, of which 65 percent are on a cif or c&f basis; in such cases, Japanese buyers have no right to designate the vessels used to fulfill the contracts.[35]

For various reasons, petroleum plays a special role in the invisibles deficit. The quantity of petroleum imported into Japan in recent years has greatly exceeded the level consistent with the Income Doubling Plan. At the same time,

[34] Maizels made an estimate of the ratio of freight and insurance in relation to the FOB value of total merchandise imports for each of 16 countries in 1955. The highest bracket, 19-21 percent, included only two countries, Japan and Peru. Maizels, *Industrial Growth and World Trade* (Cambridge: Cambridge University Press, 1963), p. 529.

[35] *Tsūshō Hakusho, 1964*, p. 189. Nevertheless, in 1963 the monthly average of total import tonnage carried in Japanese ships was 45.7 percent; the corresponding figure for exports was 44.6 percent. Economic Planning Agency, *Japanese Economic Statistics*, Oct. 1964. According to the Income Doubling Plan, it is projected that by 1970, as the result of a major shipbuilding program, the proportion of total imports and exports carried in Japanese vessels will be increased to 62.2 percent.

the building of specialized tankers for petroleum transportation has lagged behind schedule.[36]

In this connection, the bunker fuel situation is interesting. During the postwar period, most of the bunker fuel supplied to foreign ships at Japanese ports has been released from stores of foreign refined oil held in bond. Since technically these stocks of oil were never "imported," their sale to foreign ships as bunker fuel is not considered a domestic transaction. This enables the shipping companies to make payment by remittance from their head offices abroad to the foreign head offices of the oil refining companies. Consequently, besides receiving no customs duties, the Japanese economy likewise receives no foreign exchange as a result of the sale of these supplies. In the small proportion of cases in which foreign ships buy bunker fuel which has been refined in Japan, remittance must be made to the Japanese seller; but even in these cases the equivalent of a drawback arrangement allows the buyer to avoid payment of customs duties.

Capital movements are another source of the invisibles deficit. Not only does the volume of foreign investment in Japan exceed the volume of Japanese investment abroad, but the rate of return on the former considerably exceeds the rate of return on the latter.[37] In this matter, the MITI observes that whereas foreign investment comes to Japan simply in search of "revenue," Japanese foreign investment largely takes the form either of credit extended in con-

[36] Economic Planning Agency, *Kokusai Keizai Bunkakai Kentō Shiryō* (*Sono Jūsan*), *Bōeki Gai Shūshi ni Kansuru Mondai-ten* [Discussion Materials for International Economic Subcommittee, No. 13, Problems of the Invisible Balance], Sept. 23, 1963.

[37] If the time series of investment returns to foreigners is plotted in relation to long-term capital investment in Japan and the result compared with the time series of investment income received by Japan in relation to Japanese long-term investment abroad, we find that the former has a sharper slope than the latter. (*Tsūshō Hakusho, 1964*, p. 193.) This comparison, however, takes account only of repatriated earnings. Nonrepatriated earnings may be either reinvested or taken out in the form of favorable terms of merchandise trade. Incidentally, the interest rate on Japan's capital exports is generally higher than the interest rate on Japan's borrowings.

nection with the export of machinery or ventures designed to assure the supply of specifically needed raw material imports.[38] It could probably be agreed that while "revenue" provides motivation to the capital supplier in both instances, the demand conditions for investment in Japan are different from those in Southeast Asia. From a balance of payments point of view, incidentally, Japanese investment in foreign sources of raw material supply might be described as "paying for imports twice": once in the form of the investment proper and once again for its output of commodities.

In summary, the basic balance is subject to both cyclical and secular difficulties. Typically, during a domestic boom, imports increase rapidly but exports fail to increase as much. Induced variations in the invisibles account arise principally from fluctuations in merchandise imports; the joint effect of these variations reinforces the cyclical instability of the balance of payments. Increases in merchandise imports, moreover, tend to increase invisible expenses by more than the amount of invisible receipts which would accrue from an equal increase in merchandise exports. Thus the deterioration in the invisibles sector is not entirely of a cyclical nature and would not be corrected in the near future even if merchandise trade were balanced. The autonomous items of the invisibles account simultaneously show a strong adverse secular tendency. It is dangerous to depend on a surplus in the short-term capital account to fill the resulting gap, for short-term capital is itself subject to sharp cyclical fluctuations.

Consequently it is within the realm of the basic balance itself that the structural problems of the current account must be solved. There are two main approaches: first, by attaining a surplus of merchandise exports, and second, by increasing the role of long-term as contrasted with short-term capital inflow.

Japan needs long-term capital from abroad for various interrelated reasons. In the first place, it cannot raise the

[38] *Ibid.*, p. 192.

technical quality of its productive plant to Western standards by means of domestic capital alone. Nor, second, can it maintain the recent absolute level of investment, and thus the recent rate of growth, by means of domestic capital alone. Third, foreign, long-term capital in some measure acts as a counterweight to the unstable elements in the balance of payments.

For these reasons, together with the fact that the United States preeminently has been Japan's chief source of long-term capital, promulgation of the U.S. Interest Equalization Tax was the occasion of a very unpleasant shock to Japan.[39] The purpose of the act was to protect the United States balance of payments by discouraging the outflow of long-term portfolio capital. Subject to tax were all United States purchases of foreign stocks and bonds from nonresident foreigners except those issued by less developed countries or Canada. Securities with a maturity of less than three years were excluded from the provisions of the act. Direct investment and commercial bank loans were also exempt from the tax, as were Export–Import Bank financing and credit extended directly by U.S. producers to their foreign customers. The tax on equities was the same as for bonds of the longest maturity. From the United States point of view, the protection afforded by the tax took the form of raising the net cost of foreign borrowing in the United States by one percent.[40]

From a Japanese point of view, it was singularly ironic

[39] Public Law 88-563, 88th Congress, H.R. 8000, Sept. 2, 1964. Although the act embodying the tax was signed by the President on Sept. 2, 1964, it took effect with regard to transactions made after July 18, 1963 when plans for the tax were first announced. As enacted in its initial form, it was to remain effective until Dec. 31, 1965. This was later extended for an additional period of two years.

[40] As observed by the London *Economist*, however, to attract investors the yield offered by foreign borrowers in New York must in any case be 1½ to 3 percent higher than the yield on top-grade American company bonds. In addition, the borrower must pay commissions and legal fees which amount to 0.2 to 0.4 percent on overseas loans. *Economist*, Aug. 8, 1964, p. 566.

that protection of the United States balance of payments through the Interest Equalization Tax was being implemented at the same time that Japan, by accepting the obligations of IMF Article 8 and full membership in OECD, was increasing the vulnerability of its own balance of payments. The exemptions, moreover, appeared to be both discriminatory and unrealistic. They were discriminatory inasmuch as Canada was by far the chief borrower and the only other substantial individual borrower from the United States besides Japan. They were unrealistic because the exemption of commercial bank loans opened a wide avenue for the escape of United States capital. In the exemption of direct investment, moreover, the act was particularly unrealistic since large firms (such as automobile companies with subsidiaries in Western Europe) were causing enormous sums to leave the United States without penalty.

As of July 1964, the way in which the market responded to the effects of the Interest Equalization Tax suggests that the tax redounded to Japan's disadvantage while contributing very little to the improvement of the United States balance of payments. This conclusion may be drawn from Table 28, which contrasts the validation of foreign investment in Japan during the year prior to the effective date of the tax with that during the year thereafter. The table shows that the collapse of foreign investment in Japanese stocks was practically offset by an increase of over $150 million in loans from U.S. commercial banks.[41] This shortened further the already undesirably short pattern of maturities of Japanese foreign debt obli-

[41] The opposite anticipations of the Japanese financial community prior to the advent of the tax had been expressed as follows: "The total amount of capital which we hope to raise, off hand, either in the form of dollar bonds or in American Depositary Receipts, is around $150 to $200 million per annum—a figure roughly corresponding to 10 percent of the annual new issues in Japan." Tsunao Okumura, Chairman, the Nomura Securities Co., Ltd., and Chairman, Foreign Capital Committee, Federation of Economic Organizations, *The Japan Times*, July 31, 1964, p. B-6.

TABLE 28

Long-Term Foreign Investment in Japan, Validated by the Ministry of Finance,
August 1962 to July 1964
(millions of dollars)

Type of investment	Before the Interest Equalization Tax: August 1962- July 1963	After the Interest Equalization Tax: August 1963- July 1964
Total	917.8	906.2
1. Stocks (portfolio investment)	237.6	92.8
Purchased in Japan	115.9	51.2
American Depositary Receipts	63.3	11.8a
2. Direct investment	58.5	29.9
3. Bank loans	403.3	572.8
World Bank	0.0	125.0
U.S. Export–Import Bank	134.5	22.3
U.S. commercial banksb	125.4	279.0
Otherc	143.5	146.5
4. Bonds (denominated in foreign currency)	218.4	210.7
In U.S. market	193.4	20.0
In European markets	25.0	190.7

a Includes London Depositary Receipts.

b Includes loans of branches in Japan of U.S. banks. Regardless of the fact that it is a "resident," under the provisions of Japanese law a branch of a U.S. bank in Japan is a "foreign investor" to the extent that it makes dollar loans; therefore these loans require validation by the Ministry of Finance. The figures chiefly reflect impact loans.

c Includes loans from European commercial banks and loans arranged through the foreign parent companies of joint ventures in Japan. The former are chiefly impact loans, the latter are chiefly tied loans.

SOURCE: Ministry of Finance, Foreign Investment Section.

gations. At the same time, efforts were made to float new bond issues in European capital markets.[42]

Reduction of the total amount of lending to Japan in the first year of the Interest Equalization Tax was of very little benefit to the United States balance of payments, first because the absolute amount of the reduction was

[42] These efforts were attended by some early success, as shown in Table 28, but the narrowness of the European capital markets became sharply evident after July 1964.

142

small, and second because U.S. merchandise exports to Japan are in considerable measure supported by the flow of finance in the same direction. Specifically, it is estimated that due to a "feedback" effect (defined as the cumulative result of Japanese imports from the United States and imports of third countries from the United States due to their increased ability to import as a consequence of their exports to Japan), each dollar of increased United States spending in Japan results in a respending of $.55 in the United States.[43]

The balance of payments rationale of the Interest Equalization Tax also seems weak in view of the typical rejoinders made by American officials in response to Japanese complaints. For example, it is remarked that the cost of borrowing in the United States remains lower despite the tax than the cost of borrowing in Japan. And in lieu of portfolio investment, Japan is urged to welcome equity capital, which is not subject to the tax.

On the other hand, the Japanese response is in some respects odd. For reasons of its own, the Ministry of Finance in the first year of the tax restrained Japanese firms which despite the extra burden were anxious to issue bonds in the United States. Especially interesting is the well established reluctance of the Japanese government to admit equity capital from abroad. This matter is discussed below.

Instability in the Balance of Payments. As of 1964, symptoms of increasing instability in the balance of payments were revealed both by the fluctuations in the current account and by the manner in which Japan's foreign capital requirements were being financed. Concerning the former, prior to 1961 some substantial surpluses, as well as deficits, were recorded on alternate swings of the current account; during recent years, however, the current ac-

---

[43] Whitney Hicks, "A Matrix for Estimating the Foreign Exchange Cost of Foreign Assistance," AID Memorandum (August 31, 1962, processed), as amended by a letter dated October 20, 1962: as quoted by Walter S. Salant, *et al.*, in *The United States Balance of Payments in 1968* (Washington: The Brookings Institution, 1963), p. 276.

count has been marked by violent fluctuations almost entirely in the red.[44]

This performance was accompanied by a qualitative deterioration in the balance of payments as seen in the expanded role of short-term capital. During the first half of 1964 the inflow of private short-term capital actually exceeded the inflow of long-term capital.[45] The procedures of the Japanese banking system enhance the destabilizing effect of this disproportion, for as indicated above, in the *use* of funds it is difficult to distinguish long-term from short-term capital in Japan. In the case of foreign as well as domestic capital, short-term loans often become embodied in fixed assets rather than in working balances. Consequently, the degree of potential instability of the banking system on both the domestic and the international planes has progressively increased. In the extended recession of 1964-66, the policy of relying on foreign short-term capital in the degree to which Japan has become accustomed constituted a clear and present danger to its economy. For example, during the first five months of the Japanese fiscal year 1965, the capital outflow amounted to $345 million as contrasted with a net inflow of $205 million during the same period of the previous year. Of the outflow, more than 80 percent consisted of short-term capital.[46]

[44] In 1961, for example, the deficit on current account was $884 million, changing to a small surplus of $36 million in 1962, followed by a deficit of $694 million in 1963. During the first half of 1964, a record deficit of $803 million was registered on current account. Incidentally, 64 percent of the current account deficit in 1961 and 77 percent of the deficit in 1963 were attributable to Japan's relations with the United States.

[45] Private short-term capital includes chiefly nonproject ("impact") loans and trade credits received by nonbanking institutions (such as shippers' usance extended by foreign oil companies for the import of petroleum by their subsidiaries in Japan).

[46] At the end of March 1965, the dollar assets of the Japanese Government and banks in the United States amounted to $2,776 million. At the same time, Japan's short-term dollar liabilities to U.S. banks were $2,842 million, apart from long-term liabilities to U.S. banks of $468 million. *The Balance of Payments Statistics*, Hearings Before the Subcommittee on Economic Statistics of the Joint Economic Committee, 89th Congress, First Session, Part 3, June 9, 1965, p. 288.

Ingredients of the instability in the Japanese balance of payments may be further analyzed with the aid of new statistics provided by The Bank of Japan. The bank recently compiled time series for 37 types of foreign exchange and payments transactions; these were then seasonally adjusted and broken down by the U.S. Bureau of the Census method.[47] The data are in monthly form, and as first published most series cover an eleven-year period from January 1953 to December 1963. I have selected 32 of these indicators for the present analysis.

Ordinarily it would be preferable to analyze the data in terms of cyclical fluctuations. Since World War II, however, the number of complete cycles in Japan has been too few for this purpose.[48]

Accordingly, I have surveyed the time series data on an annual basis, making use of the fact that The Bank of Japan has separated the trend-cycle component (TC) of each series, thus excluding fluctuations due to seasonal and irregular causes. Changes in the degree of instability over a period of time due to basic economic forces are thus clearly revealed in the TC data.

As a first step in the analysis of these fluctuations, I have calculated the average deviation of monthly fluctuations in the TC component during 1963 as compared with the aver-

[47] Method II.X-10. The Bank of Japan, Statistics Department, *Basic Data for Economic Analysis*, Tokyo, May 1964.

[48] According to the Economic Planning Agency, the periodization is as follows:

Reference Cycle Dates in Postwar Japan

Business cycle	Trough	Peak	Trough
1		June 1951	October 1951
2	October 1951	January 1954	September 1954
3	September 1954	June 1957	April 1958
4	April 1958	n.a.	n.a.

SOURCE: Economic Planning Agency, Economic Research Institute, *Sengo Keiki Junkan no Keiryō-Bunseki* [Econometric Analysis in Postwar Japan], No. 12, December 1963, p. 5.

As of December 1964, the peak of the fourth cycle had not as yet been identified by the EPA. Therefore, two complete cycles are dated, only one of which falls within the scope of The Bank of Japan statistics.

145

age deviation during 1953. From graphic observation, these periods appear to lie in comparable phases of the business cycle. My calculations show that for 26 of the indicators there was a remarkable increase in the average deviation of the TC component in 1963 as compared with 1953.[49] The median increase was 197 percent. In only six of the 32 cases analyzed did the average deviation of the TC component of monthly data indicate a decline.[50]

Altogether, the high and increasing degree of variability through time seen in these indicator series is consistent with the evidence observed above of increasing instability in the balance of payments. It is particularly interesting that the degree of variability in exports of products of the new heavy and chemical industries (especially machinery) has greatly increased during the past decade, while for products of the traditional industries (such as food and textiles) the degree of variability in exports has decreased.

Some Statistical Matters: (1) Balance of Payments Statistics versus Foreign Exchange Statistics. A considerable amount of confusion has been caused in the analysis of Japan's recent balance of payments because two independent and mutually exclusive sets of statistics are often misconstrued as interchangeable. These are known respectively as the

[49] The cases were as follows (the percent of increase is shown in parentheses): exports certified (367); imports licensed (252); letters of credit received (88); total exports (511); exports of chemicals (343); exports of nonmetallic minerals (152); exports of metals (136); exports of machinery (1444); other exports (124); exports to Asia (93); exports to Southeast Asia (112); exports to North America (127); total imports (138); imports of food (136); imports of metal ores (648); imports of other raw materials (809); imports of mineral fuels (614); imports of chemicals (410); imports of machinery (13); other imports (540); receipts of foreign exchange, current transactions (406); receipts of foreign exchange, visible trade (140); payments of foreign exchange, current transactions (241); payments of foreign exchange, visible trade (90). For the following indicators, the comparison was between data for 1963 and data for 1956: quantum index of exports (369); quantum index of imports (98).

[50] These cases were the following (the percent of decrease is shown in parentheses): letters of credit opened (27); exports of food (5); exports of textiles (41); exports to Europe (3); exports to South America (36); imports of textile materials (49).

Foreign Exchange Statistics and the *Statistics Based on the* IMF *Method.* The former was originally designed as part of the system for implementing Japan's foreign exchange control system, while the latter is prescribed in accordance with Japan's reporting obligations as a member of the IMF. The foreign exchange statistics, which are compiled as a sum of the receipts and payments reported by Japanese banks authorized to deal in foreign exchange, are available monthly with a lag of less than a month following the transactions to which they refer. Japan's official balance of payments statistics, however, prepared according to the rules of the IMF *Balance of Payments Manual*, are available only quarterly, with a lag of three months or more following the quarter to which they refer.

The practice of quoting the balance of foreign exchange in the guise of the balance of payments dates from April 1960 when the foreign exchange statistics were revised to distinguish current transactions from capital transactions; also as of the same date, short-term capital transactions were included for the first time.[51] However, the foreign exchange statistics differ in coverage, valuation, and timing from the IMF version of the balance of payments.

As indicated by their name, the foreign exchange statistics are purely a financial record; their chief source is documents for transactions accompanied by a settlement in foreign exchange. Thus the foreign exchange statistics exclude imports received without accompanying drafts drawn on Japan, transactions on a consignment basis, reparations in kind, grants, and transactions arranged on an inconvertible yen basis. Invisibles are accounted for in terms of reports of foreign exchange holdings. Similarly, the value of exports is expressed as the total of bills negotiated; imports are valued at whatever amount the shipping documents show has been authorized by the foreign exchange banks. Consequently, depending upon what arrangements

51 Administrative Management Agency, Statistical Standards Bureau, *Nippon Tōkei Geppō, Shiryō Kaisetsu Hen* [Supplement to the Monthly Statistics of Japan, Explanatory Notes], Jan. 1964, p. 106.

have been made by the drawee, the cost of freight, the cost of insurance, or both, may or may not be included in the value of imports or exports. However, in the freight and insurance account, the report of receipts and payments is a precise record of the foreign exchange actually received or disbursed.

Statistics prepared for the purpose of Japan's reports to the IMF, on the other hand, are a complete record of economic transactions carried on between residents and non-residents of Japan, including transactions not accompanied by a movement of foreign exchange. All commodity imports and exports are expressed uniformly on an estimated FOB basis. The record of receipts and payments for freight and insurance is likewise estimated. The figures are entered in accordance with the principles of double entry bookkeeping.

For example, in the case of deferred payment for exports, the FOB value of the goods is entered in the current account category at the time the goods are physically cleared through customs, and the unpaid value of the goods is entered in the long-term capital account as a credit associated with the deferred payment. In the foreign exchange statistics, however, only a single entry would appear in this instance, showing the amount of payment whenever received, regardless of when the goods had been shipped.

In the case of a long-term loan to Japan, the foreign exchange statistics would include only a receipt entry in the long-term capital account. In the IMF version, however, the amount of the loan would be entered as an increase in long-term liabilities (credit) and simultaneously as an increase in short-term assets (debit).

Thus, while in the foreign exchange statistics the balance of current receipts and payments, plus the balance of capital receipts and payments, equals the increase or decrease in the foreign exchange reserves, in the IMF version the balance of current receipts and payments plus the balance of capital receipts and payments equals zero.

In the category of current transactions, the extent of the

discrepancy between the two versions is indicated in Table 29. In the category of invisibles transactions, as shown in Table 30, the contrast is even more striking. For whereas much attention has recently been drawn to the invisibles deficit as presented in terms of foreign exchange statistics,

TABLE 29

Japan's Net Current Transactions in Two Versions, IMF Base versus Foreign Exchange Statistics Base, by Year, 1957 to 1963
(millions of dollars)

Calendar year	IMF version	Foreign exchange statistics version
1957	—620	—384
1958	264	511
1959	361	339
1960	143	111
1961	—982	—1,085
1962	—49	98
1963	—779	—572

SOURCES: IMF version from *Monthly Statistics of Japan*, Bureau of Statistics, Office of the Prime Minister, October 1964, p. 76. Foreign exchange statistics from *Economic Statistics of Japan*, 1963, Statistics Department, The Bank of Japan, p. 273.

the deficit according to the IMF version is considerably greater.

(2) *Errors and Omissions.* Within the IMF version proper of the balance of payments, another matter of considerable interest concerns the magnitude of errors and omissions at the worldwide level as contrasted with their magnitude in Japan's relations with individual regions. During recent years, the relatively small net magnitude of errors and omissions at the global level has concealed extraordinary regional discrepancies, particularly in the case of the United States and Canada.[52] In 1961 errors and

[52] Errors and omissions of substantial magnitude are likewise found in the OECD and Soviet regions, as well as in "All Other Countries." Collectively, these more or less offset the discrepancies in the case of the United States and Canada.

TABLE 30

Japan's Net Invisibles Transactions in Two Versions, IMF Base versus Foreign Exchange Statistics Base, by Year, 1957 to 1964
(millions of dollars)

Calendar year	IMF version[a]	Foreign exchange statistics version[b]
1957	—225	169
1958	—111	139
1959	—4	68
1960	—128	—36
1961	—425	—153
1962	—451	—204
1963	—614	—365
1964 (Jan.-Sept.)	—701	—334

[a] Includes reparations and war debt payments averaging $75.3 million annually during 1957-63.

[b] Includes reparations and war debt payments in cash only.

SOURCES: IMF version from *Balance of Payments Yearbook*, International Monetary Fund, various issues. Foreign exchange statistics from *Economic Statistics of Japan*, 1963, The Bank of Japan, and *Economic Statistics Monthly*, The Bank of Japan, various issues.

TABLE 31

Errors and Omissions in Relation to Net Short-Term Capital Flow: Japan's Total Balance of Payments and the Balance of Payments with the United States and Canada, by Year, 1960 to 1963[a]
(millions of dollars)

Calendar year	TOTAL BALANCE OF PAYMENTS		BALANCE OF PAYMENTS WITH UNITED STATES AND CANADA	
	Net short-term capital[b]	Net errors and omissions	Net short-term capital[b]	Net errors and omissions
1960	378.1	32.6	369.3	163.8
1961	572.8	19.0	486.3	—611.0
1962	121.7	5.7	49.3	—30.3
1963	516.6	44.5	424.9	—181.1

[a] The regional breakdown prepared by The Bank of Japan for its report to the IMF does not show the United States and Canada separately. However, Canada's share is small, especially in the flow of capital and services.

[b] Excluding errors and omissions.

SOURCE: The Bank of Japan.

TABLE 32

Japanese Imports and Exports Transacted Without Letters of Credit,
by Year, 1958 to 1963

Calendar year	(PERCENT OF TOTAL FOREIGN EXCHANGE RECEIVED FOR IMPORTS OR EXPORTS)	
	Imports without letters of credit	Exports without letters of credit
1958	21.5	17.0
1959	25.8	15.3
1960	30.9	13.3
1961	34.1	15.8
1962	39.3	15.9
1963	41.5	17.8
1964 (p)	49.0	19.0

SOURCE: The Bank of Japan, Statistics Department.

omissions in Japan's balance of payments with these countries far outweighed the total short-term capital flow between them and Japan. The figures are shown in Table 31.

The Bank of Japan has no ready explanation for this phenomenon. A possible clue, however, lies in the item "multilateral settlements." This item refers to transactions in which the country of origin of a commodity is not the country which receives payment; correspondingly, the country of destination may be different from the country that renders payment.[53] Where the foreign commerce of a country, such as Japan, is subject to commodity quotas on imports and exports, as well as a degree of foreign exchange control, there is a likelihood—for legitimate as well as illegitimate reasons—that such transactions will play a greater rather than a lesser role. In any event, due to the complexity of these transactions, they have not been separately compiled or analyzed by The Bank of Japan; instead, they are included in "Errors and Omissions."[54]

[53] For an analysis of the substantial share of such transactions in world trade, see Robert M. Lichtenberg, *The Role of Middleman Transactions in World Trade*, National Bureau of Economic Research Occasional Paper, No. 64.

[54] The official balance of payments report of The Bank of Japan is

It is difficult to determine, therefore, what part of the reported errors and omissions in transactions between the United States and Canada arise from multilateral settlements as distinguished from "simple" errors and omissions. The Japanese reporting system for long-term capital flow does not permit of much error and thus it is appropriate that the "simple" errors and omissions should be classified with short-term capital, according to conventional practice. As presently reported, however, the short-term capital category contains more than "simple" errors and omissions; thus a further breakdown of the category is clearly necessary.

(3) *Letters of Credit as a Foreign Trade Indicator.* The lines of communication and confidence established between Japan and its suppliers prior to World War II made it unnecessary, with minor exceptions, for Japanese imports to be financed by means of letters of credit. This network of commercial contacts, however, was one of the casualties of the war, and beginning with the era of "blind trade" conducted under the auspices of the Occupation, a high proportion of both Japanese imports and exports has been negotiated by means of letters of credit.

In these circumstances, compilation of the letters of credit by The Bank of Japan has formed a basis for estimating future imports and exports. According to government regulations, imports must be paid for within four months of customs clearance of the merchandise; exports must be paid for within six months following customs clearance (or within five months after the sight bill has been presented to the payer).[55] The maturities of letters of credit

---

somewhat misleading on this point. For example, note that in the *Balance of Payments of Japan*, 1963, p. 57, the entry for "Multilateral Settlements" on line 21 is merely a series of dashes. This implies that there were no multilateral settlements during 1963, which, however, is not the case.

[55] The limitation on the period permitted for payment on imports enables the government to enforce, if need be, a tight money policy. The limitation on the period permitted for payment on exports is to

fall within these time limits. Since the letter of credit data are expressed in terms of foreign exchange, The Bank of Japan's estimates of future imports and exports refer to anticipated receipts and payments of foreign exchange rather than to the value of imports and exports on a customs clearance basis. Receipts and payments are estimated for one month in advance, the error of estimate being three percent.[56]

In recent years, however, the proportion of imports financed by letters of credit has declined sharply, and thus the value of the import indicator has been impaired. The proportion of total exports subject to letters of credit, however, has remained steady, as shown in Table 32.

The decline in the proportion of imports financed by letters of credit is explained by institutional changes in Japanese foreign trade. One such change is the increased importance of import financing arranged through non-banking channels. For example, petroleum, which has come to be Japan's leading import, is financed by suppliers' credit, as mentioned above.

Another reason for the decline of the import letter of credit is the increased strength and steadily expanding role of trading companies. These are a unique Japanese institution whose functions include production, distribution, and finance, and which are engaged in both domestic and international trade. They completely dominate Japan's imports of staple food and bulky raw materials. In the former case, they act as agents for the Japanese government's Food Agency, which administers the government's monopoly of staple food imports. These are paid for in cash. In handling other products, the trading companies often deal with the ever-widening network of their own subsidiaries or branches abroad; in this event it is unneces-

prevent flight of capital. It is the duty of the foreign exchange banks to implement these regulations.

[56] Estimates of future foreign exchange receipts and payments are made according to the method of distributed lags. See L. M. Koyck, *Distributed Lags and Investment Analysis* (Amsterdam: North-Holland Publishing Company, 1952).

sary to incur the extra expense of opening letters of credit, since the parties "trust each other."

If the proportion of imports financed by letters of credit continues to decline, future imports could still be estimated from the statistics of import licenses. These licenses, which are valid for a period of six months, are issued by the foreign exchange banks acting as agents for the government. Although in most cases they are issued as a mere formality, substantially all Japanese imports are subject to license, which provides an alternative basis for forecasting.

PART III: POLICIES

In Part I we observed various structural difficulties in the relation between production and foreign trade. These were emphasized in Part II by evidence that in the process of import substitution Japan's modern industries had not generally attained the level of world competitive standards. We also found that a counterpart to the structural defects in the capital composition of enterprises was the excessive role of short-term capital in the balance of payments. At the advent of the import liberalization policy—which is discussed in Part III—there were doubts about Japan's competitive power against foreign products at home as well as abroad. From a Japanese point of view, incidentally, the liberalization program is asymmetrical with the "voluntary controls" which Japan imposes on its own exports. Moreover, the timing of the policy was awkward since formally a high degree of liberalization was introduced in 1964 at the very outset of a recession markedly structural rather than cyclical in nature, one which proved to be the most persistent and intractable recession in Japan's postwar experience up to that time.

In referring to these events, Part III is concerned with the institutional environment within which the liberalization policy was adopted and with the countermeasures which were devised to reduce its impact on the Japanese economy. Although the policy was adopted as part of a grand political and economic strategy for Japan's advancement into the ranks of the "most advanced" nations, it was implanted in an uncongenial environment. For historically, the tradition of Japanese government paternalism and intervention is wide and deep. It culminated in an entire generation of absolutism during the period of Japan's military adventures. But the institutions and personnel that survived that generation are the executors of the liberalization program. Being accustomed to control, the government was confident that despite liberalization it could continue to master the key determinants of economic life in Japan.

155

Although formal controls were progressively dismantled in accordance with the assumption by Japan of new obligations under GATT, IMF, and the OECD, there remained a host of informal controls, collectively classified as "administrative guidance," by means of which a large part of the Japanese government's influence is exercised. Indeed, the void created by removal of direct controls provided a new opportunity for the expansion of indirect controls, and their role has steadily increased since the inception of the liberalization program. There is some variation in attitudes towards liberalization and also marked rivalry among Japanese ministries for spheres of influence; in general, however, their conflicts are not mutually offsetting insofar as liberalization is concerned. Moreover, while domestically there are frequent struggles between government and business with regard to economic policy, on the international level there is a high degree of collaboration between government and business in confronting the foreigner. This may be seen in the field of export promotion, as well as in government cooperation with import associations and renegotiation by the MITI of private contracts for the induction of foreign capital or technology.

Government collaboration with business, however, is essentially collaboration with big business. Each, for reasons of its own, has fostered the recent trend towards economic concentration in Japan. Liberalization has provided the oligopoly groups with an occasion in which to overwhelm weaker firms, while the government, in the name of "strengthening of enterprises," has sponsored mergers, cartels, and "agreed specialization." The government has had an additional objective, however, namely that of creating more favorable conditions for the implementation of informal controls. These can be more effectively invoked in an environment of the few rather than the many. Government influence has been powerfully enhanced during the long recession beginning in 1964, for the reliance of business on government during this period weakened its power of resistance to government

156

pressure and advice. The recession, as well as the liberalization program, incidentally, provided leading oligopoly firms with an opportunity for expanding their empires. The concentration movement thus reveals a contradictory element in government policy, for on the one hand the government purports to justify its resistance to foreign equity investment in Japan on the ground that such investment threatens the existence of small Japanese firms; but on the other hand it systematically sacrifices these same firms in favor of the interests of domestic oligopolies.

Mergers have likewise been instigated by the city banks, which have sought to strengthen their chief customers or to shore up the assets of their weaker ones. Moreover, increased concentration in Japanese industry is paralleled by increased concentration in the conduct of Japan's foreign trade. Trading companies are becoming larger and fewer, and the finance of foreign trade is largely in the hands of a few leading banks. This means that competition among Japanese buyers is being steadily reduced at the very time liberalization implies that the area of competition has been widened.

After imports have actually arrived, a further bottleneck arises in the form of closely held and rigidly restricted facilities for the distribution of goods within Japan. Thus while "anyone can import," not anyone can dispose of merchandise through domestic channels. As distinguished from commodity imports, imports of capital and technology are restricted by highly visible and explicit government intervention. In some respects, the inauguration of liberalization was associated—via new procedural requirements—with a greater degree of restriction than had existed prior to liberalization.

In the absence of procedural barriers, the escalation of economic concentration, the "agreed specialization," administrative guidance, and other restrictive devices—in the event of "pure" liberalization, that is—what level would by now have been attained by imports into Japan? This would be an empty as well as a very difficult evaluation, for no Japanese government could tolerate a flow of imports that would jeopardize its ability to manage the foreign exchange reserves. As a minimum, that amount of restriction has been and will continue to be imposed on imports which is consistent with maintaining the integrity of the reserves.

---

11 · THE ENVIRONMENT OF LIBERALIZATION, A[1]

Since the time of Meiji, Japan's economic system has been marked by a special relation between government and business, particularly large business. The government has participated in business decisions by means of its subsidies, licenses, loans, and franchises. Because of the high degree of centralization in both government and business, as well as the network of allegiances in the "master-servant" relationship, the difference between direct and indirect controls in Japan is difficult to distinguish. Traditionally, government bureaucracy has outranked business bureaucracy, and the law the former administers is in many respects vague. Thus almost more important than the law itself is the manner in which it is administered. The outsider cannot evaluate the degree of government control merely by reading the laws. Informal verbal requests from ministry officials in Tokyo can be fully as effective as direct controls would be in Western Europe or the United States. On the other hand, the exercise of influence is not entirely one way. Collaboration between the government and private firms, and a means by which business may influence government, is found in the system whereby important government officials enter private firms either at or before their rather early retire-

[1] Undocumented assertions in this and the following chapters are based on statements made to the writer by responsible business, banking and government officials who for one reason or another prefer to remain unidentified.

ment age.[2] An important means of communication between business and government also exists in the form of institutes, trade associations and research groups of one kind or another, which have a quasi-official status, are staffed chiefly by former government officials and are supported partly by government and partly by private funds.

The ministries chiefly concerned with the regulation of business are the Ministry of International Trade and Industry and the Ministry of Finance. The former controls licensing procedures for all major kinds of business activity, especially those in the field of foreign commerce. The strength and comprehensiveness of this control can best be understood in the perspective of Japan's wartime and postwar experience: after 1936 international movements of funds and commodities were completely controlled and remained so until well after the Occupation was terminated. But controls tend to be perpetuated by the institutions and careers which are based upon them. The officials who exercise Japan's economic controls are conscientious, idealistic, and technically competent to a high degree. In defending what they conceive to be the best interests of Japan, they review, for example, the tiniest details of contracts providing for the import of capital or technology. In doing so, they are not necessarily anti-business, nor even xenophobic; however, they are highly jealous of their prerogatives and especially of their power position in relation to the officials of other ministries. Since the law which they enforce may be merely a statement of broad principles, their interpretation of the law is crucial; thus their jurisdiction is wide and ill-defined. MITI officials supervise business largely by means of making "suggestions." If the suggestions are ignored by the parties to a transaction, strong reprisals may follow; simply and effectively, this may take the form of delays in official action on the many applications which a business must file

2 A former personnel director of the Ministry of Finance remarked to me that he had spent most of his time in that post attempting to place retiring staff of the ministry in private jobs.

for permission to proceed with even routine operations. An antagonized official need not necessarily perform the slowdown himself, for this can readily be accomplished by his colleagues with whom a particular business firm must also deal. Especially in cases involving foreign commerce, the activities of a firm which has antagonized MITI can easily be brought to a complete standstill in a perfectly legal and apparently innocent manner.

The authority of the Ministry of Finance is exercised through monetary and fiscal policy, especially the former. Control of money and credit, as implemented by The Bank of Japan, reaches down actively or potentially into the heart of every major business enterprise, for by a procedure known as "window guidance" (madoguchi shido), the individual loans of Japanese commercial banks are subject to scrutiny by The Bank of Japan.[3] The strategic use of monetary control has important implications for Japan's long-term economic plan. In the plan proper, there is no common program for the banking and industrial communities; nor, indeed, does the plan itself specify any formal machinery for the implementation of its provisions. However, banking and industry can in effect be yoked in harness by consensus at the policy-making levels of the various ministries and The Bank of Japan.[4]

If "the government" of Japan were actually a highly coordinated set of agencies, its powers could be applied with overwhelming force. Instead, partly as a result of sheer ambition for status and partly as a reflection of divergent interests within the society itself, there is intense rivalry and jealousy among the ruling agencies and their person-

[3] The Bank of Japan, "Window Operation," *Special Paper No. 6,* Sept. 1961.

[4] In the years immediately preceding the formal advent of the liberalization policy, the trend of government control has been described as follows: "The Government has further successively strengthened its controlling hand over the past several years by various pieces of legislation that have given it legal power to intervene directly in the affairs of particular industries, even to the extent of determining prices, volume of output and even types of product to be turned out." *The Japan Stock Journal,* Nov. 9, 1964, p. 8.

nel.[5] In competing for power, they tend to neutralize one another's authority to some extent. It is this offsetting effect, rather than the absence of specific powers of internal control, and also "rule by personalities" as opposed to "rule by law," which provides the degrees of freedom in Japan's peculiar species of enterprise economy. An additional degree of freedom arises from the powerful influence exerted by big business on the political party in control. Indeed, it is often difficult to identify which is the master and which the servant, for they exchange roles from time to time in various situations.

The era of liberalization has sharpened the power struggle among the ministries by dissolving or shifting some of their former jurisdictions. In general, if they are in favor of liberalization at all, ministries advocate liberalization of activities other than those in which they are entrenched. The Ministry of Foreign Affairs, for example, is in favor of relinquishment by MITI of controls over foreign commerce. The Ministry of Finance is in favor of liberalization of commodity trade, but it favors retention of controls on monetary affairs. MITI is reluctant to liberalize imports because it feels responsible for protecting Japan's young heavy-and-chemical industries against predatory foreign competition.[6] The Ministry of Agriculture and Forestry

[5] See *Kyōkan Kyōgō Jimu no Kaikaku ni Kansuru Iken* [Opinions Regarding a Revision of Overlapping and Conflicting Administrative Procedures Among Ministries], *Rinji Gyōsei Chōsakai* [Temporary Administrative Improvement Research Council], Sept. 1964, pp. 61-87. At the advent of liberalization, a new conflict arose concerning the representation of various ministries in the international agencies—such as the specialized committees of OECD—to which Japan was then admitted. For example, MITI claimed that the Foreign Ministry was incompetent to conduct international economic negotiations, while the latter stoutly resisted any encroachment by MITI on its traditional territory.

[6] In a communication from the U.S. Embassy in Tokyo to the U.S. Department of State, a comment was expressed concerning a pamphlet issued by the Japanese Foreign Office on Aug. 31, 1962. The communication observed, "With rather unusual candor, the pamphlet acknowledges that Japan's own slow pace of liberalization is partially responsible for current policies applied by Western European countries toward Japan." *Airgram* from United States Embassy, Tokyo to U.S.

is deeply protectionist; where the beleaguered interests of agriculture are concerned, it is opposed to liberalization perhaps more than any other ministry.

GOVERNMENT INTERVENTION IN THE MARKET MECHANISM

The Japanese government has an ambivalent attitude towards economic competition. Import liberalization—which implies import competition—has been accepted in principle as the price of permission by other countries for the expansion of Japanese exports. From a domestic point of view, import competition has also been advocated as a means of accelerating the rationalization and modernization of Japanese industry. At the same time, however, competition—especially "excessive competition" (*katō kyōsō*) —is regarded as wasteful, and the government has taken steps to counteract it.

Typically, what is known as excessive competition results from the fact that labor is an overhead cost rather than a variable cost in Japan. Permanent staff cannot be laid off in slack times, thus so long as variable costs are met (on this point Japanese accounting practices are unreliable), the loss of producing for sale at less than full cost may be less than the loss of not producing at all. Thus firms are induced to produce for inventory if not for sale, hoping that a buyer will come along in due course. When inventories and the cost of maintaining inventories become too high, prices tumble and cutthroat selling activities ensue.

A similar effect results from the system of distribution of bank credit. In general, small firms cannot obtain bank credit without either a guarantee provided by a large firm or by presenting a letter of credit for exports to a foreign buyer. When credit is tight, large firms may not be willing to sponsor the loans of the small companies. This leaves only the alternative of obtaining a letter of credit for ex-

---

Department of State, Sept. 14, 1962. The views of MITI on this question would be distinctly different from those of the Foreign Office.

ports, which can be discounted to provide working capital for the firm. If a small firm has high fixed expenses, it may be faced with the choice of producing for export at a loss or going out of business altogether. This also occasions excessive competition and distress selling.

Since size is respected in Japan, large firms, in the effort to become ever larger and to increase their respective market shares, may also engage in "excessive competition." It is in this context, rather than in the case of small-firm competition, that government intervention occurs. The following is a report of intervention in the oil industry:

Hajime Fukuda, Minister of International Trade and Industry, gravely concerned over recent underselling of oil products, has issued a stern warning to industrial leaders against undue competition among themselves.

Minister Fukuda invited the presidents of Nippon Oil, Toa Oil, Mitsubishi Oil and other refining and agent companies to the ministry and strongly requested them to abide by the production adjustment and standard price. . . .

Fukuda issued the direct warning because the market for oil products has been falling sharply since late last year in the face of keen industrial competition for greater market shares. The competition has gone so far as to considerably deteriorate their business and may ultimately affect the stable supply of oil products unless properly adjusted at present. . . .

. . . If the industry fails to restore the market by self-discipline, the Government may revise the Oil Industry Law and regulate production and sales. It may also take administrative steps to allow dealers to conclude business agreements to tone down sales competition.

Mainichi, April 3, 1964, p. 4.

In their overseas ventures, rivalry among business firms has also been checked by MITI, which has endeavored

163

rationally to regulate the advance of Japanese enterprises into overseas markets in the form of joint ventures with local capitalists. . . .

MITI started action in this direction some time ago to forestall intensified competition among Japanese enterprises planning to advance into overseas markets with similar production projects.

MITI feared that if such competition were allowed to continue, over-production would eventually result and the very existence of such joint ventures would be jeopardized.

On the basis of guidance being given by MITI for regulation of such competitive overseas joint ventures, there has been a rising move among Japanese enterprises to cooperate in unifying planned joint ventures and adjusting the variety of products involved.

Nihon Keizai Shimbun, International Weekly Edition, July 28, 1964, p. 1.

A typical business view of the same problem is expressed in the following report of a speech given by Kazutaka Kikawada, Director of the *Keizai Doyukai* (Japan Committee for Economic Development) which is generally regarded as the most progressive of the large business organizations:

Kikawada pointed out that it is necessary to eliminate competition among enterprises to increase market shares and to expand equipment. . . . He said that businessmen should compete to the extent permitted by business circles as a whole. If enterprises compete regardless of their responsibility to society, government intervention is inevitable, he argued. . . .

He pointed out that the lack of self-control is due mainly to the inefficient functioning of economic organizations. This means reorganization of economic

164

organizations is needed. The Committee has maintained that a policy board of business circles is necessary to materialize orderly competition.

Mainichi, April 15, 1964, p. 4.

Even socialists in Japan—as distinguished from socialists in the United States—are in favor of less rather than more competition in business. They regard the consolidation of large firms as a desirable first step in facilitating their transfer to government ownership.

As indicated in the statements quoted here, candid details of government intervention in business affairs are commonly reported in the Japanese press. Sometimes intervention is occasioned by short run micro-economic problems such as financial emergencies in individual firms, sometimes by short run macro-economic problems such as in the balance of payments; sometimes intervention is related to long run objectives such as plans for change in the structure of industry. Preparations for import liberalization have been marked by many interventions in the market mechanism. When Makoto Usami was installed as Governor of The Bank of Japan at the end of 1964, the task facing him was described as follows:

Problems requiring immediate attention include reduction or holding down of production, holding up prices, reducing heavy inventories, providing funds for hard-pressed firms and financing general adjustment of industry. Beyond these lie longer-range problems such as holding down plant expansion, selective capital outlays to improve efficiency and reduce costs rather than to increase capacity for its own sake, encouraging firms to merge or form working groups where present units are too small or inefficient, curbing cutthroat tactics in favor of more orderly competition, and getting firms to build up their equity capital and reduce their debts.

The Japan Stock Journal, Feb. 1, 1965, p. 8.

Rivalry for larger market shares has given rise to intense investment activity which is one of the chief ingredients of Japan's impressive growth rate. However, it may also lead to unsound or unbalanced growth. The government has therefore attempted to suppress market-share rivalry by encouraging mergers and by enforcing outright limitations on the amount of permitted investment. Ironically, in the process of encouraging mergers, the government increases the number of situations from which it cannot afford to remain aloof in the event of impending bankruptcy. Giant firms thus tend to feel immune from the possibility of becoming financially overcommitted.

Government control of investment takes place both at the industry and company level. During fiscal year 1964, out of an estimated total private investment of $11.9 billion in plant and equipment in Japan, the value of investment of 13 major industries under the control of MITI amounted to $4.5 billion.[7] The framework of this investment is supervised by the Industrial Fund Division of the Industrial Structure Council, a consultative organ to the ministry. Among other purposes, control of investment is a key aspect of the process by which the government has attempted to prepare the ground for import liberalization. Thus in its decisions for the year, the committee approved a large increase in the investment plans of the "Big Two" automobile makers (Toyota and Nissan) with a view to increasing their international competitive power. The investment plans of minor motor car manufacturers, however, were drastically curtailed "in view of the supply-demand situation."

Technically, the recommendation of the Council lacks legal binding force and is supposed to represent merely MITI's "administrative goal." In view of the fact that many

[7] The industries include electric power, coal, nonferrous metals, iron and steel, petroleum refining, petrochemicals, ammonium sulphate, synthetic fibers, automobiles, electric machinery, electronics, paper and pulp, and cement. *Nihon Keizai Shimbun,* International Weekly Edition, June 9, 1964, p. 5.

enterprises were greatly dissatisfied with the Council's recommended cutback of their investment programs, the degree of its effectiveness may perhaps be inferred by a review of the investment plans of those enterprises as revised in the light of the Council's recommendations. According to a study of this made for the fiscal year 1964, four industries (cement, oil refining, paper pulp, and ammonium sulphate) had failed to reduce their investment plans to the recommended level and were still subject to further action by MITI; for the supervised industries as a whole, however, the revised plans for new plant and equipment exceeded the recommendations by only five percent. Therefore the Council concluded that its recommendations had been substantially observed.[8] This example, of course, concerns only domestic investment. Where Japanese investment abroad is at issue, as well as foreign investment within Japan, the control of government ministries in even the smallest particulars is paramount.

The methods employed in government control are a combination of the carrot and the stick.[9] Industries nominated by MITI as "key industries" may receive special government financial help.[10] Hardship cases also receive special assistance. The chief industries in the list of 13 under MITI's investment control mentioned above were included as well in a list of industries designated for "selective financing."[11] On an even broader scale, the stock market

[8] *Yomiuri*, Nov. 19, 1964, p. 6.

[9] It has been remarked that "MITI, under Mr. Sakurauchi, has become acutely sensitive to charges from business leaders that it engages in extra-legal, heavy-handed interference in the management of individual industries and firms." *Asahi Evening News*, Jan. 20, 1965.

[10] Four such industries—petrochemical, special steel, ferro-alloys, and passenger cars—were designated to receive the benefit of low interest loans from the Japan Development Bank in fiscal year 1965. *The Japan Stock Journal*, Sept. 2, 1964, p. 2.

[11] "MITI has a list of 10 industries which it considers as hardship cases in need of government financing and direction. These are steel, special steels, cement, oil refining, synthetic textiles, cotton spinning, electrical manufacturing, machine tools, cameras, and specialty trading firms. . . . Business executives suspect, however, that MITI is planning to use credit as an instrument of detailed control over management

as a whole received the benefit of a series of remarkable measures of support when it fell into difficulties during 1963-65.[12] Not only industries, however, but also individual firms are marked for special attention.[13]

In addition to superseding the market mechanism by direct and indirect intervention, the Japanese government has also ingeniously *used* the market mechanism as an adjunct to intervention in ways calculated to achieve specific planning objectives. An important example of this can be seen in the case of the import of capital into Japan. If, for example, a Japanese bank could acquire an unlimited amount of dollars from abroad and exchange these for yen in the foreign exchange market, it could effectively frustrate the efforts of the government to restrict the domestic money supply, especially during periods of "tight money." However, the Ministry of Finance does not directly limit the amount of dollars which a Japanese bank

which would go beyond the proper bounds of administrative policy direction." *Asahi Evening News*, Jan. 8, 1965, p. 7.

[12] In July 1963, Japanese life insurance firms were asked by the Ministry of Finance to start buying on the stock exchange, and twelve Tokyo banks were asked to increase their loans to the Japan Securities Credit Corporation, which supplies credit to securities firms for their margin trading. (*The Financial Times*, London, July 24, 1963.) When this proved insufficient, the government in Jan. 1964 arranged with 14 major commercial banks and four leading securities companies to form the Nippon Kyodo Securities Company, for the further purchase of stocks. The Bank of Japan extended huge loans to Nippon Kyodo, making it in effect a government corporation. (*Mainichi*, Dec. 6, 1964.) For reasons not readily apparent, still another agency, the Japan Securities Holding Association, was formed by The Bank of Japan in January 1965, also to buy and hold stocks. (*The Japan Stock Journal*, Jan. 18, 1965.) It should be noticed that these measures of support to the stock market overlapped the opposite policy of tight money which the government applied in 1964 to other sectors of the economy.

[13] For example, it was reported that "the Development Bank will loan Teikoku Oil ¥1,500,000,000, expedite ¥2,500,000,000 more in loans from the city banks, and arrange a deferment on its debt payments." (*Asahi Evening News*, June 24, 1964, p. 7.) For statistics concerning the role of government finance in private fixed investment, see the table, "New Supply of Industrial Equipment Funds," in *Economic Statistics of Japan*, The Bank of Japan.

may acquire from abroad. Instead, it requires that the foreign exchange position of the bank must be "square."[14] This means that the sum of the bank's spot plus forward dollar liabilities must equal the sum of its spot plus forward dollar assets. Suppose, for instance, that the branch of the Chase Manhattan Bank in Tokyo receives dollars from its parent bank in New York for lending in Tokyo. If the branch in Tokyo were able to lend these dollars to a Japanese firm, its spot position would remain square because the dollar liability to its New York office would be offset by a dollar asset in the form of the loan extended to the Japanese borrower. However, Japanese residents cannot legally use dollars for domestic transactions; therefore, Chase Manhattan must convert the dollars to yen in the Japanese foreign exchange market in order to make loans within Japan.[15] The sale by the bank of dollars for yen, however, makes its spot dollar position "oversold"; that is, its spot dollar liabilities now exceed its spot dollar assets. In order to acquire sufficient dollars to cover its liability to New York, Chase Manhattan in Tokyo must buy forward dollar exchange. Having done so, the sum of its spot and forward assets in dollars will equal the sum of its spot and forward liabilities in dollars, which fulfills the square position requirement.[16]

Now the difference in the interest rate between dollar

14 In practice, the Ministry provides for a certain amount of leeway by interpreting this as "almost square."

15 If Chase wanted to make a transaction in dollars with a non-resident within Japan, it would have to obtain a license from the Ministry of Finance.

16 After World War II, Japanese commercial banks were not authorized to hold foreign exchange of their own until the treaty of peace came into effect in April 1952. At that time, their cash position was placed under the control of the Ministry of Finance. As of Jan. 1, 1955, their spot position was placed under control as well. (The spot position includes, for example, export bills subject to collection, but these are not included in the cash position.) As of Sept. 1, 1960, the overall (spot plus forward) position of the commercial banks was placed under governmental control.

loans and yen loans is, say, about 3.5 percent. This is the extent of the premium on forward dollars which Chase can afford to pay in buying forward dollars in order to maintain the square position. However, if a large volume of dollars were to enter Japan for the purpose of taking advantage of the differential in rates between dollar and yen loans, the premium on forward dollars would soon be bid up beyond 3.5 percent, which would wipe out the incremental profit on yen loans. Thus the Ministry of Finance, by requiring that banks maintain a square foreign exchange position, in effect limits the inflow of foreign capital partly by exchange control and partly by use of the market mechanism.

THE MEDIUM-TERM ECONOMIC PLAN, 1964-1968

Because the growth rate of GNP projected in the *Income Doubling Plan, FY1961-1970* was exceeded by the actual rate during the early years of its period of reference, and to correct "imbalances" in the economy, such as the rise in consumer prices, the plan was revised by a so-called *Medium-Term Economic Plan, FY1964-1968*, which was published in January 1965. The new plan calls for achievement of the "income-doubling" target two years earlier than its predecessor. In its various published versions, Japan's economic plan has called for successive increases in the growth rate of the GNP. The *New Long-Range Economic Plan of Japan, FY1958-1962* projected (in FY1956 prices) a rate of 6.5 percent per annum, the Income Doubling Plan projected (in FY1958 prices) a rate of 7.8 percent per annum, and the Intermediate Term Plan (in FY1960 prices) calls for a rate of 8.1 percent per annum. The projected rate of 8.1 percent, however, represents a decline from the GNP growth rate of 10.7 percent per annum (in FY1960 prices) actually achieved during the period 1961-63.

This relative decline is projected most strikingly in the field of private and government investment. As compared with 1953-63, when the average annual rate of growth in gross private investment in producers' durables was 19.8 percent per annum, the annual rate during 1963-68 is projected at 9.9 percent. Similarly, the rate of increase in government capital expenditures is scheduled to decline from the observed rate of 14.5 percent per annum during 1953-63 to 8.7 percent during 1963-68. In explaining the reason for these projected declines, the plan states, "This slower growth rate is envisaged mainly because measures to curb expansion of demand are deemed inevitable for maintaining the balance of payments in equilibrium and consumer prices stable."[17] In these words, the plan identifies the balance of payments as a prime bottleneck in the growth rate. Concerning the requirement for price stability, the plan provides for an average annual increase of 2.5 percent in consumer prices while it assumes that the wholesale price level will remain practically constant.

By "equilibrium in the balance of payments," the plan means that both the current account and the long-term capital account must be balanced by 1968. Fulfillment of the plan, therefore, requires that the projected deficit of $1 billion in the invisibles account will have to be offset by an equivalent surplus of merchandise exports. This in turn is dependent upon several factors. First, it is assumed that during the period of the plan world trade will expand at a rate of 6.1 percent per annum, and second, that simultaneously Japan's exports will expand at more than double the average world rate.

According to the plan, the shift from light industry to heavy and chemical industry will proceed further: in FY1961 heavy industry accounted for 61.0 percent of total manufacturing; by FY1968 it should account for 68.3 percent. During the same interval, large firms will increase their share from 53.0 percent of total value added in manufacturing to 58.0 percent.

In describing the role of the government, the plan states (p. 29) that, on the one hand, the government will

17 *Medium-Term Economic Plan, FY1964-1968*, Economic Deliberation Council, Tokyo, Jan. 1965, p. 17.

TABLE 33

Selected Japanese Economic Indicators: 1963 Performance and 1968 Projections

Indicator	Unit	FY1963	FY1968	Projected increase per annum: FY1963-1968
				(percent)
Population	thousands	96,187	100,700	0.9
Gross national product	billion 1960 yen	19,767	29,210	8.1
Index of industrial production	CY1960 = 100	149.5	239.3	9.9
National income per capita	U.S. dollars	526	830	7.6
Personal consumption	billion 1960 yen	9,767	13,901	7.3
Private investment in producers durables	billion 1960 yen	4,100	6,596	9.9
Government capital expenditures	billion 1960 yen	2,499	3,800	8.7
Government current expenditures	billion 1960 yen	1,794	2,650	8.1
Exports (Customs clearance base)	million U.S. dollars	5,460	10,064	12.3
Imports (Customs clearance base)	million U.S. dollars	7,247	10,747	8.2

SOURCE: *Medium-Term Economic Plan, FY1964-1968*, January 1965.

implement its provisions by "current activities and capital outlay . . . in such fields as are deemed improper to be entrusted to the market mechanism," and on the other by "arrangement" of the environment within which "sound development of enterprises can be expected through free, fair and orderly competition on their own responsibility . . . but it is also important to advise, guide and supervise private sectors with administrative aims, if it is deemed necessary." However (p. 44), "the activities of individual enterprises and persons, which are supposed to be freely decided, must not violate the bounds of laws, regulations or social customs."

Modernization of the industrial structure, it is hoped, will be accomplished primarily through the price mechanism. "Actually, however, the market mechanism in the domestic economy does not necessarily work well and, in addition, international division of labor based upon the principle of comparative advantage does not necessarily bring the development of advantageous industry because of difference of income elasticity of demand by industry from the long-term viewpoint" (p. 48). Accordingly, it is the task of government to provide the necessary correctives.

In discussing Japan's achievements prior to its own period of reference, the plan states (p. 3), "It cannot be overlooked that the continuation of restrictions on trade and exchange has enabled the government to protect and nurture domestic industries." In the future as well, it will be the government's policy to foster designated strategic industries in positive ways. Industries to be fostered include automobiles, large-scale machine tools, industrial machinery, large-scale electronic computers, special steel, and petrochemicals (p. 48). These are industries for whose products the income elasticity of demand is high but in which Japan at present lacks strong international competitive power.

Even prior to import liberalization, the government's use of monetary policy has constituted one of the chief instruments by which its control of the economy was accomplished. With the advent of liberalization, it can be assumed that this instrument will become more important than ever before. We have seen some examples of the way in which the government may place special financial resources at the disposal of business. I turn now to a review of some recent experience in which the alternative option of "tight money" has been exercised.

TIGHT MONEY POLICY

As mentioned above, one of the chief ingredients of Japan's high rate of growth in recent years has been the high proportion of gross national product devoted to investment. Gross domestic capital formation in 1951 was 32 percent of the GNP; in 1963 it was 38 percent, roughly two-thirds of which was private. In addition to the intensity of investment, the way in which it is financed makes money especially tight, for the ratio of self-financed investment is low. As of September 1963, the net worth of Japan's main manufacturing corporations amounted to only 29 percent of their total liabilities—a sharp relative decline from 1955 when the ratio had been 40 percent.[18] Borrowed capital has been supplied mostly by the commercial banks, which extend long-term loans for fixed assets as well as working capital funds. The stock market was the source of only 10 percent of new industrial funds in 1963.[19] Consequently, the business community is highly vulnerable to increases in the interest rate.

The commercial banks themselves are also in a vulnerable position, for their loans and discounts have been approximately equal to their total deposits in every year since 1950. This is known as the "overloan" situation.[20]

[18] The Bank of Japan, *Outline of Japanese Economy and Finance*, Tokyo, 1964, p. 47.
[19] The Japan Development Bank, *Facts and Figures on the Japanese Economy*, Tokyo, 1964, p. 150.
[20] As defined by The Bank of Japan, the overloan indicator is the ratio of loans and bills discounted in relation to the sum of deposits, debenture issues, and owned capital. This indicator has exceeded 100 percent for city banks in most years since 1950; for local banks it has

Second, they are vulnerable by virtue of the illiquidity of a large part of their loans, although to some extent this is mitigated by the fact that about half of their deposits are time deposits, mostly for longer than one year. Consumer credit is also in its infancy in Japan, which contributes to the liquidity of firms. Altogether, however, industry is largely dominated by the banks, and they in turn are held on a short leash by The Bank of Japan, to which they are heavily indebted.

Animating the investment boom which has been expanding more or less steadily since the Korean War is a headlong pursuit of increased market shares on the part of Japanese firms. At some stages of Japan's recent development this boom has simply reflected the temper of management, while at others it has been inspired by the rival empire building of a handful of leading banks. The latter, of course, have a leading voice in the policies of their heavily indebted clients among whom are the *keiretsu* firms which dominate Japanese industry. However generated, the investment boom by a similar series of steps has led on several occasions during the past decade to balance of payments crises, in which the tight money policy has been applied.

Leading to such a crisis, in the first place, in the process of expansion, manufacturers (or more often, the trading companies that distribute their output in foreign as well as domestic markets) find that sales are easier and the profit rate higher in the domestic than in the foreign market. Thus in the upswing of the domestic cycle, while imports of both raw materials and finished goods are rising, prices likewise rise, international competitiveness falters, and exports characteristically lag. As noted above, the immediate financing of merchandise imports does not place a great financial burden on Japan inasmuch as a large proportion of her imports are financed through the New York money market. However, when imports persistently

---

remained fairly constant at about 80 percent. The Bank of Japan, *Outline of Japanese Economy and Finance*, 1964, p. 33.

exceed exports, the eventual adverse balance of settlements, in the absence of offsetting net capital imports, results in a drain of foreign exchange reserves. The discrepancy between imports and exports cannot be allowed to get out of hand because Japan's entire foreign exchange reserve is the equivalent of only three or four months imports. This is the process by which balance of payments difficulties constitute the principal bottleneck to the growth rate.

The force of this process is shown by the fact that even when—prior to Japan's adoption of the "open-door system" (*kaihō keizai*) in 1964—imports had been closely regulated by the foreign exchange control budget, they nevertheless from time to time became excessive in relation to exports. It then devolved upon monetary policy to act as an adjunct measure in inhibiting imports, restraining prices, and stimulating exports. It may be useful to briefly outline the tight money measures before describing the episodes in which they were applied.

The first step in tight money therapy usually takes the form of restriction of the credit line of the city banks at The Bank of Japan. This is the "window guidance" (*madoguchi shido*) mentioned above. Since the city banks are always in debt to The Bank of Japan, any proposed credit expansion has to be justified in their quarterly loan requests. The Bank of Japan checks the proposed loan programs of the banks against the loan programs submitted by various trade associations in behalf of their members, the latter programs having already been approved by the government.

The second step occurs when The Bank of Japan, with the concurrence of the Ministry of Finance, raises the discount rate. It is evident that because of step one, the tight money situation will already have been communicated to the public in the form of reduced availability of credit. At this point, the increase in the cost of borrowing may be almost irrelevant for many would-be borrowers.

In contrast with the situation in the United States, where the level of free reserves—the amount of reserves over and above required reserves—is an interesting figure to watch, in Japan there are no free reserves. Moreover, change in the ratio of required reserves against deposits is a minor element of monetary policy in Japan inasmuch as the ratio is very low.[21]

Recourse to "open market" operations is also quite limited since government securities are subscribed for in private negotiations between The Bank of Japan and other banks; in effect, the transactions are not "open" and there is no "market." The amount of government securities (as distinguished from government-guaranteed securities) held either by the banks or by the nonbanking public, is very small.

In response to the restrictive policies of The Bank of Japan, commercial banks have heavily utilized the device of compensating balances. When making advances to customers, banks usually require that a portion of the advance must be left on deposit despite the fact that the customer is paying interest on the entire amount of the loan. Small businesses are the principal victims of this practice, whose incidence varies inversely with the bargaining power of the customer. Compensating balances may amount to as much as 30 percent on loans, only a part of which may be allowed to earn interest while on deposit. The effective interest rate, therefore, may easily be twice as much as the nominal rate. Besides being profitable, compensating balances improve the banks' statistical position by increasing both loans and deposits simultaneously.[22]

[21] Nevertheless, when in a token measure of relaxation the rate for reserves against demand deposits held by banks with more than ¥20 billion in deposits was reduced from 3.0 percent to 1.5 percent on Dec. 16, 1964, the move was criticized by the IMF as "untimely." *Japan Times*, Jan. 17, 1965.

[22] In another context, the device of compensating balances is also commonly used to evade the prohibition by the Ministry of Finance of borrowing by Japanese from foreigners at rates higher than 5.5 percent. (Higher rates might convey the implication that Japan is a backward country.) For example, when Japanese firms borrow from United States banks, it is usually arranged between the parties that a compensating balance—amounting from 10 to 20 percent of the loan—will be maintained by the borrower. The Ministry of Finance

Increases in deposit requirements associated with the opening of letters of credit for imports are another countermeasure employed by the banks, which in effect increase bank liquidity while restricting imports. The deposit ratio varies by commodity, higher rates being imposed against "less desirable" imports. The device, therefore, is of interest for commercial policy as well as for monetary policy. Export finance, incidentally, is always exempt from tight money restrictions.

As a means of buoying up the balance of payments, tight money of course is a much more blunt instrument than foreign exchange control, for its desirable effects are achieved at the cost of slowing down the growth rate of the entire economy. Nevertheless, as the foreign exchange control system is progressively dismantled, the role of monetary measures increases.

Between April 1952—the effective date of the peace treaty—and 1965, the Japanese authorities invoked tight money policies on four principal occasions. The first was following a balance of payments crisis in 1953. Tight money measures were applied in October of that year, with visible results within three months.[23] The pressure applied on this occasion was perhaps less onerous, and the response faster, than on any subsequent similar occasion. The second balance of payments crisis occurred following a cyclical climb in 1956, reinforced at the end of the year by the Suez affair. Speculative imports increased, foreign exchange reserves declined, wholesale prices rose, and the

---

is fully aware of this practice, but takes no action against it. In the case of foreign borrowing by Japanese banks, an alternative device is used by those banks having branches abroad. A Japanese bank with offices in New York, for example, may offer a U.S. bank having a branch in Tokyo a premium of say 2.5 percent over the permissible 5.5 percent. The Tokyo branch of the U.S. bank will extend a loan in dollars to the Japanese bank in Tokyo at 5.5 percent, and the 2.5 percent premium will be paid in New York by the branch of the Japanese bank. In its accounting, the latter may charge the expenditure to "office expenses."

[23] Economic Planning Agency, *Economic Survey of Japan, 1954-1955*, p. 50.

money supply was swollen: in Japan this condition of the economy is described as "overheated" (*kanetsu*). Tight money measures were applied in March and May 1957. Within six months, the current account of the balance of payments began to recover.

A boom in private investment which started in 1959 was enhanced by promulgation of the Income Doubling Plan in 1960. Again increases occurred in producers' imports of raw materials, in wholesale prices and in the money supply, while the foreign exchange reserves began to drop. Tight money measures were applied in July and September of 1961. Whether the period of adjustment was longer or shorter than in 1957-58 depends upon the indicator used. The degree of correction was smaller because monetary policy was less restrictive, partly (in contrast with the previous recession) as a result of the performance of exports in a favorable world environment. In particular, imports declined less than on the previous occasion.

Moreover, another balance of payments crisis occurred within a year—this marked a striking deterioration of the length of the interval between episodes, for previous crises had been separated in time by either three or four years. It was necessary at the end of 1963 to reimpose tight money measures which had been withdrawn in the fall of 1962. The Bank of Japan again restricted its supply of credit to the city banks, and in December 1963 the minimum reserve requirements for demand deposits (but not for savings deposits) were raised. In January 1964 The Bank of Japan requested the city banks to confine their advances in the first and second quarters to 90 percent and 88 percent respectively of the credit extended by them in the corresponding quarters of the preceding year. In March 1964 The Bank of Japan raised its rediscount rate from 5.84 percent to 6.57 percent; also the advance deposit required for imports of producers' goods was increased from one to five percent and the deposit required for imports of consumer goods was increased from five percent to 35 percent. On this occasion the scale and complexity of the adjustment to be made was much greater than ever before, and factors adverse to the adjustment were stronger. In addition to the fact that the interval between tight money episodes had shortened, statistical evidence of its effectiveness was also much slower in appearing. Since large firms had built up a liquidity cushion, money did not become really tight until the latter part of 1964. According to The Bank of Japan's series of seasonally adjusted economic indicators, for example, between December 1963 and December 1964, total money supply increased 12.8 percent, loans and bills discounted outstanding (of all banks) increased 15.6 percent, and imports increased 9.1 percent. Industrial production (mining and manufacturing) increased 10.2 percent, although 1964 was known as a year of "expansion without profit." Wholesale prices, however—which affect the competitive strength of exports—remained steady.[24]

Of particular interest during the tight money experience of 1963-65 are the statistics of exports in relation to the statistics for total shipments and inventories. In mining and manufacturing, producers' shipments increased 8.3 percent while inventories of finished goods increased by 20.7 percent. For reasons discussed above (especially the high and increasing ratio of fixed to total costs of production), firms were evidently impelled to produce for inventory at a greater rate than during previous periods of comparative slack, and the piling up of inventories stimulated efforts to increase exports. Exports were also impelled by the need to increase liquidity, for exports result in early cash settlement whereas it is often difficult to collect payments for merchandise sold in the domestic market during periods of tight money. The episode well illustrates, there-

---

[24] The fact that wholesale prices remained stable while consumer prices rose steadily may be partly attributed to the availability of credit on relatively easy terms to large firms whose costs are a principal determinant of wholesale prices. Small firms (including retail and service establishments), which chiefly populate the consumer goods sector, bore the weight of relatively adverse credit terms, while their efficiency was also lower than that of large manufacturing firms.

fore, the mechanism of supply-oriented exports. Exports increased at a greater rate than during any previous tight money period: the increase was 22.6 percent between December 1963 and December 1964, while imports increased only 9.1 percent in the same interval.[25]

It is interesting that productive activity actually increased in the midst of the tight money episode. To some extent this was made possible by the availability to large firms (but not to small) of foreign capital. In part, also, expansion of output was accomplished by an increase in commercial credit as distinguished from bank credit, and also by the device of "accommodation bills" (*yūzū tegata*). The latter is a bill or note issued by one firm to another *without* having received goods or services therefrom. Thus it is a method by which firms can redistribute their credit among one another. Most important of all was the "qualitative credit control" by which banks channeled available funds into those major enterprises to whose support they were already heavily committed.[26] In some cases, banks are in effect industrial entrepreneurs through their overwhelming financial control of their clients; often they participate in management by the selection of members of boards of directors. In other cases banks appear to be the creatures of their own customers, which influence the banks' lending policies through stock ownership. To a substantial extent, moreover, the banks have systematically flouted the loan ceilings of The Bank of Japan through a system of "hidden loans" and "hidden deposits." These

[25] Of course, some traditional industries, which produce almost exclusively for the domestic market, as well as industries which have a low price elasticity of export demand, have no alternative but to absorb the brunt of the credit squeeze. It may also be observed that to some extent, requisite stock levels of imported raw materials were lower during the 1963-65 tight money episode than during former episodes because of the greater ease of replenishment due to import liberalization. The stability of international raw material prices and some improved techniques of stock management also contributed to this effect.

[26] For statistics showing the amount of bank credit provided to small and medium size firms as contrasted with large firms, see Economic Planning Agency, *Economic Survey of Japan, 1963-1964*, p. 314.

are loans and deposits which do not appear in the monthly statements of the banks and are not reported to The Bank of Japan. The practice began to assume substantial proportions in June 1957. Among other devices, the evasion was accomplished by "making loans within the month period, or making loans that were paid off on the last day of the month with a check which was not collected until the first of the following month, at which time another loan covering the check was granted."[27] The existence of hidden loans is well known to The Bank of Japan, for they have been the subject of studies.[28]

Even the favored firms, however, were not fully accommodated at the banks. To obtain marginal supplies of funds, many of Japan's leading corporations issue promissory notes (*tegata*) which are sold through brokers; in 1964 these were commonly marketed at interest rates in the range of 13 to 18 percent per annum.[29] Lesser firms, of course, have had to pay much more.

During all periods of tight money, or any other kind of business hardship, a substantial part of the pressure on large firms is passed backwards to the small and medium size firms which act as their suppliers and subcontractors. Indeed, the process by which the "efficient modern sector" has exploited the "backward sector" in this respect is one of the most remarkable aspects of Japan's dual economy. Thus the parent firm not only gets preferred treatment from the bank, but it is also sheltered by its "family," while in sunny weather, ironically, it is the family which is referred to as being "under the umbrella" of the parent firm.

In an ordinary recession, the parent firm—which is staffed mostly by permanent life-contract personnel—re-

[27] Hugh T. Patrick, *Monetary Policy and Central Banking in Contemporary Japan* (University of Bombay, 1962), p. 154.

[28] See The Bank of Japan, *Monthly Economic Review*, May 1964.

[29] For example, see prospectuses of Nichigai Investment Consultation, Inc., which offer the promissory notes of C. Itoh Co., Marubeni-Iida, Toyo Menka, Sony, and Mitsui Bussan at interest rates within the range specified above.

duces its orders to the subcontractor. The latter is staffed largely by temporary workers, who are then discharged. In the past, this system has been the principal source of flexibility available to the parent firm, corresponding to the process of worker layoff in the United States. During a period of tight money, parent firms also gain flexibility by paying their suppliers with notes instead of cash, and they progressively extend the term of the notes. In the case of merchandise handled by trading companies, a similar process occurs. A foreign importer, for example, makes out a letter of credit in favor of the Japanese trading company in order to finance the production of goods he has ordered. The trading company discounts the letter of credit at the bank for about 80 percent of its face value. Because of the fact that this is a transaction financing exports from Japan, the rate for discount is lower than the rates of other transactions.[30] However, the trading company does not pass on this advantage to its supplier. Instead, it lends money to the actual manufacturer at perhaps two percent a month (24 percent a year); this is one of the usual sources of profit of trading firms. Captive suppliers—which produce solely or chiefly for particular parent companies— have to accept these practices on pain of losing the business of the parent, which would cut them off from credit, raw materials and possibly even plant and equipment that had been borrowed from the parent firm.[31] These practices

[30] In January 1965 The Bank of Japan's discount rate on export trade bills was 4.02 percent as compared with 6.21 percent on commercial bills. The Bank of Japan, *Economic Statistics Monthly*, Jan. 1965.

[31] A small minority of manufacturers export on their own account. In hard times they often face the alternative of exporting at a loss or going out of business. During a period of tight money a letter of credit supporting an export order is their only means of obtaining a bank loan. Even then, they are exposed to a squeeze by the banks which in tight money periods reduce the proportion of the face value of letters of credit which they are willing to discount in the form of loans. Nevertheless, very low prices are then offered to foreign buyers in order to obtain export orders. With the proceeds of the discounted letter of credit, a firm can carry on various kinds of transactions—not necessarily connected with supplying the order which the letter of credit was supposed to finance—and thus make an incidental profit.

give rise to the phenomenon of *kuroji tōsan* ("black ink bankruptcy") among the smaller firms, that is, bankruptcy caused by failure to collect bills. One of the first impressive signs of the impact of the tight money policy of 1963-65 was the increase in dishonored bills and the wave of bankruptcies among small and medium size enterprises beginning about ten months after the implementation of the policy. Indeed, one of the principal effects of the tight money policy—even if not an announced government objective—has been the liquidation or merger of small firms: this accords with the explicit goal of Japan's long-term economic plan, namely to "liquidate the dual economy." It has been argued that the resources released in this manner can be reallocated with relative ease during a period of comparatively high growth such as Japan has enjoyed even in the midst of tight money recessions, so that social distress caused by bankruptcy is minimal.

By its very nature, the impact of tight money reaches deep into the roots of the economy before yielding an antidote to balance of payments difficulties. Moreover, its ability to produce the antidote does not look as promising as it has in the past. This is seen, for example, as indicated above, in the progressively delayed response of the economy during successive episodes in which the policy was applied. Also, because of the increasing role of the deficit in invisibles, the nature of Japan's balance of payments difficulties—in whose name the tight money policy is always invoked—is developing a strong secular as distinguished from cyclical character: this change renders the tight money policy less appropriate. Consumer expenditures—helped by rising wages—are becoming a larger component of total spending; but since consumer credit is not well established, consumer spending is responsive relatively little to monetary policy. The nature of imports—a steadily larger role being taken by finished goods such as foods and mineral fuels—is also changing in a way which renders tight money less effective as a means of imposing import restraint. Furthermore, as Japan's exports become absolutely larger as well as relatively larger in relation to total world exports, it will require progressively sharper tight money measures to achieve a given percentage increase in exports.

At the same time, as the dual economy is gradually liquidated and the degree of vertical integration of industry is increased, it will become more and more difficult for the advanced modern sector to shift the burden of restrictive monetary measures to the backward sector, for less of this sector will remain in existence. It might be inferred consequently that in this respect the effect of tight money might instead be greater in the future than it has been in the past. If so, the question follows whether it would then be politically feasible to enforce it.

In any event, as dissociated from exchange control under the regime of an increasingly open economy, the task of monetary policy in safeguarding the balance of payments will become steadily more complex. The authorities may then resort to a greater use of direct monetary measures such as "selective financing" of "key" or, as the case may be, "depressed" industries and firms—devices which are already very well known in Japan.

---

12 · THE ENVIRONMENT OF LIBERALIZATION, B

As analyzed in Chapter 1, a basic distinction between Japan and other nations with a higher level of per capita GNP is its low level of per capita exports. In recent years, the value of Japan's per capita exports has been approximately one-fifth that of West Germany, one-fourth that of England, and one-half that of the United States. Besides its role in long-term economic development, the transition to an open economy increases the importance of export promotion as a means of defending the short-term balance of payments position. In the past, however, Japanese export pressure has often evoked import resistance on the part of other nations. As a newcomer in the ranks of heavy-and-chemical industry exporters, Japan is confronted by the superior competitive power of Western countries; on the other hand, it is being displaced from many of its traditional markets by the increasing competitive power of developing countries. Among Japan's other tasks in the great transition of the 1960s, Japan will have to work its way out of this economic encirclement.

EXPORT SUBSIDIES AND EXPORT FINANCE

In the early postwar period, methods of export promotion were easily devised in the form of subsidies based on the foreign exchange control system. As that system was gradually dismantled, visible subsidies were also abandoned.[1] Government facilities such as export finance then began to assume greater importance.

The link system was an early device based on foreign exchange control. It was used in various ways, but always with the purpose of promoting exports of commodities in which Japan's comparative advantage was low or to induce manufacturers to export despite the possibility of quick sales at high profit in the domestic market. Import licenses for needed raw materials were therefore allocated to processors on the basis of their export performance. Imports of raw cotton and raw wool, for example, were allocated in this way. As an alternative, exporters might also be rewarded with licenses to import scarce commodities other than those used in their own output but which could easily be sold at a high profit. For example, exporters of ships were rewarded with licenses for the import of sugar or bananas.

[1] Through the exercise of procedural and other bureaucratic prerogatives, they were replaced to a considerable extent by invisible subsidies in the form of "favors." This practice was elevated into a formal principle in connection with the program for designation of "export-contributing enterprises." A Cabinet meeting on April 9, 1965 arrived at the "understanding" that such firms would be given special consideration in the expediting of their administrative contacts. *Official Trade Bulletin*, April 1965, No. 1, p. 4.

The rewards of the link system were negotiated case by case. Often, the system was responsible for the fact that producers were willing to sell at sacrifice prices in the foreign market for the sake of the profits they could make at home in the processing of a retained portion (perhaps "spoiled," or otherwise diverted) of the import allocation. Link systems of one kind or another were gradually curtailed during the course of the 1950s.

The retention quota system was a procedure by which exporters were allowed to retain a portion of the foreign exchange that had been earned by their export shipments. Holders of export retention certificates could obtain licenses for travel, advertising, or office expenses abroad. Some imports were also allocated exclusively to holders of the retention certificates.[2] The retention percentage was revised at various times within a range of from three to 15 percent. In 1960 this system was abolished.

Another method of promoting exports was by means of credit availability and preferential interest rates on loans for the financing of export production. We have already noted that The Bank of Japan's discount rate on export trade bills is lower than that on other commercial bills. Still lower are the rates on both short-term and long-term loans by the Japan Export–Import Bank, which are established to conform with those available from competing institutions in other countries.

The Export–Import Bank, Japan's chief foreign trade financing institution, was established under Law No. 268 of 1950. At the end of March 1964 its outstanding loans—which are mainly for capital goods—amounted to one billion dollars, 75 percent in the form of export credits, 13 percent for foreign loans, 11 percent for investments

---

[2] Total bidding for import allocations always exceeded the amount of the allocation available. Therefore individual bidders would apply for a much larger quota than they expected to receive. In order to do this, would-be importers borrowed retention certificates from other holders thereof who did not plan to participate in a particular bidding. This was done—through power of attorney—despite the fact that the certificates were technically "non-transferable."

credits (including loans for Japanese joint ventures abroad), and only one percent for imports. Of the outstanding export credits, 51 percent was for the finance of exports of vessels. By area, the bank's loans were distributed as follows (percentage figures are given in parentheses): Southeast Asia (30); Europe (24); Central and South America (21); Africa (14); West Asia (5); East Asia (3); and North America (3).[3] The Export–Import Bank is the source of about three-fourths of all long-term Japanese capital outflow.

A basic similarity between the American and Japanese Export–Import Banks is that the chief function of both is to promote the private exports of their respective countries. However, there are five notable differences between the Export–Import Bank of Japan and the United States Export–Import Bank. First, in Japan the bank obtains all of its resources from the Japanese government (60 percent of its funds are borrowed from postal savings), whereas the United States bank borrows from the money market. Second, the United States bank makes a profit, whereas the Japanese bank does not (it borrows from the government at a higher rate than it charges on loans to customers). But the Japanese bank pays no dividend to the government for its capital contribution. Third, in financing exports the Japanese bank has hitherto provided credit only to Japanese suppliers (except in the case of India and Pakistan, which have received tied loans for purchases in Japan, and two tiny yen loans to Paraguay and Viet-Nam); the United States bank for the most part provides credit directly to the foreign importer. Fourth, the Japanese bank does not deal in export insurance (it is handled by MITI[4]), whereas the United States bank provides insurance as well as finance. Finally, the United States bank does not extend loans to

[3] The Export–Import Bank of Japan, *The Export–Import Bank of Japan: Its Object and Functions*, Tokyo, Aug. 1964.
[4] See *Export Insurance Law* (Law No. 67, March 31, 1950), Export Insurance Section, Trade Promotion Division, International Trade Bureau, MITI, April 1961.

finance the process of production for export, as is the case in Japan.[5]

New methods for the expansion of Export–Import Bank credit are frequently proposed. Beginning with fiscal year 1965, the bank planned to extend credits to banks in other countries in order to provide a means of finance on which their nationals could draw in purchasing goods from Japan.[6] Similarly, innovations are often made in the means by which Japan's competitive power is reinforced by credit from The Bank of Japan. In June 1964 The Bank of Japan began to finance production for export of canned goods even before export orders were secured; it was proposed by the MITI that this procedure should be expanded to include industrial products.[7] In order to strengthen Japan's competitive power, MITI also urged The Bank of Japan to extend credit on a "selective basis" to eleven "key industries" (among which were iron and steel, automobiles, electrical machinery, petroleum refining, cement, and synthetic fibers) in order to assist them during the process of liberalization.[8]

TAX INCENTIVES

Prior to April 1964, when in accordance with its new obligations as a full member of OECD and as a signatory to GATT Article XVI (4) the tax laws were revised, export incentives had also been offered by subsidies through the tax system. The first tax subsidy for exports was adopted in 1953 (revised in 1957), under which profits earned as a result of export sales were partially exempt from direct taxes. These allowances were calculated as a percentage of export sales. Manufacturing companies were allowed to deduct three percent (five percent in the case of plant or capital goods exports) of their proceeds from direct ex-

---

[5] The production credit component cannot be distinguished from the export credit component of the Japan Export–Import Bank's loans to export suppliers.

[6] *Asahi Evening News*, Jan. 18, 1965, p. 7.

[7] *Ibid.*, Oct. 26, 1964, p. 7.

[8] *Japan Times*, Jan. 23, 1965, p. 10.

port sales or exports through a trading company. Trading companies were allowed to deduct from their taxable income one percent of the proceeds from export sales. In no case, however, was the amount deductible allowed to exceed 80 percent of the income arising from exports. By this means, the income tax of large trading companies was reduced by 20 to 30 percent.

An alternative method of computation was introduced in 1961 (firms could avail themselves of either, but not both). According to the second method, if exports in a given year exceeded a firm's "normal exports"—defined as the average during a specified base period—80 percent of income in excess of the normal income from exports was not subject to tax. For small firms with no previous export experience, this provided a considerable export incentive.[9]

The above methods made it possible in some instances for firms to earn a higher net income by selling goods at a low price abroad than they could earn by selling at a higher price at home. This fact explains why in the past, from the point of view of the individual exporter, the issue of "dumping" has been far from straightforward, and it was an important argument in confrontations concerning the dumping issue.

In accordance with a commitment by Japan at the conclusion of the Anglo-Japanese Treaty of Commerce and Navigation (ratified April 4, 1963), Japan agreed to accept the provisions of GATT Article XVI (4), as of March 31, 1964. The commitment was reaffirmed during the negotiations for Japan's admission as a full member of OECD, and became effective on the agreed date. The article states that

[9] In this context, it is interesting to read the recommendations for British policy offered in a study prepared by a group of Conservative Members of Parliament: "We do not subscribe to the view that every manufacturer should become an exporter, and we think it a pity that the Government has in the past devoted so much of its effort to encouraging the small exporter." Conservative Political Centre, *The Expansion of Exports* (Plymouth: Clarke, Doble & Brendon Ltd., Oakfield Press), March 1963, p. 4.

contracting parties shall cease to grant either directly or indirectly any form of subsidy on the export of any product other than a primary product which subsidy results in the sale of such product for export at a price lower than the comparable price charged for the like product to buyers in the domestic market.

Japan's acceptance of the article required it to terminate the export income deduction system, which according to GATT was interpreted as a subsidy.

In place of tax remission on export income, a series of new measures was introduced effective April 1, 1964. The first measure revised the prevailing method of allowance for depreciation on fixed assets for corporations engaged in export business. Prior to April 1, 1964, additional depreciation (over and above regular depreciation) because of exports was permitted only if the amount of export sales during the current period exceeded that of the preceding period. In that event, the additional rate of depreciation had been calculated as follows:

$$\frac{\text{amount of export sales in the current period}}{\text{total sales in the current period}} - \frac{\text{amount of export sales in the prior period}}{\text{total sales in the prior period}}$$

Under the former system, if domestic and export sales increased at the same rate, the permitted additional depreciation would be zero. Thus, regardless of the amount by which it had increased the absolute volume of its exports, a firm might receive no benefit whatever. This was especially adverse to traditional industries such as textiles and sundry goods which find it difficult to increase their export ratio. On the other hand, it was favorable to firms newly entering the export field. In any event, effective April 1, 1964, the amount of additional depreciation (again over and above regular depreciation) was to be computed by multiplying the ordinary depreciation allowance for a specified period by the following:

191

$$80\% \times \frac{\text{export sales for preceding accounting period}}{\text{total revenue in preceding accounting period}}$$

The new formula was favorable for firms employing a high proportion of fixed assets. The procedure of accelerated depreciation merely permits a greater offset against taxes in earlier years to be balanced against a smaller offset in later years. In effect, it constitutes tax deferment or an interest-free loan to producers for the period during which depreciation was accelerated. The total allowable depreciation does not, of course, exceed the cost of acquisition of the assets. Thus the procedure does not constitute a tax exemption and it cannot be classified as a subsidy within the meaning of GATT Article XVI.[10]

A second measure begun April 1, 1964 permitted the exemption from tax of an amount placed to the account of Reserves for Cultivation of Overseas Markets.[11] The rationale of this measure was to encourage firms to open and maintain new overseas markets regardless of the state of their earnings. It permitted manufacturers to place in a reserve account a maximum of 1.5 percent (0.5 percent in the case of trading companies[12]) of the proceeds received from overseas transactions in the preceding accounting period. No maximum limit on the reserve accumulation was specified in the law; however, due to a compulsory procedure for disposition of the reserve, there was a virtual limit on the amount of the reserve.[13]

[10] During FY1963, the last year of the export income deduction system, the amount of tax subsidy amounted to ¥23,521,000,000. Had the new system of tax deferral been in effect during that year, the amount of tax deferral would have been ¥25,407,000,000. Ministry of Finance, Tax Bureau, *Shōwa 39, Sozei Oyobi Inshi Shūnyū, Yosan no Setsumei* [Incomes of Tax and Revenue Stamps, Explanatory Budget, Fiscal Year 1964], Jan. 30, 1965, p. 5.

[11] This did not apply to exports of technology, which were the subject of a special procedure described below.

[12] The profit ratio on sales of trading companies is approximately one-third or one-fourth that of manufacturers for export.

[13] Disposition of the overseas market development reserve was prescribed as follows: "The balance of the reserve must be restored to income for tax purposes at a minimum rate of 20 percent of the reserve

A third measure permitted the exemption from income of an Overseas Market Development Reserve for Small or Medium-Sized Enterprises. "The amount assessed by an 'authorized commercial and industrial association' on its member corporations and credited to its Overseas Market Development Reserve account may be deducted from income of the member corporation, but the amount deductible shall not exceed 2.5 percent of the proceeds obtained by the corporation from 'overseas transactions.' " An "authorized commercial and industrial association" is one "designated by the appropriate minister for which at least 20 percent of the products of its members are related to 'overseas transactions.' "[14] Thus the tax advantage to small enterprises is relatively greater than that to larger enterprises in the corresponding measure for a market development reserve referred to above. However, in order to avail itself of the privilege of this law, the small firm must be a member of an export association. In effect, therefore, the law encourages small firms to form such associations, which are much more readily subject to the control of the government than a host of individual small firms, as such. In particular, because of inadequate accounting practices, it is often difficult for the tax authorities to identify income derived by small firms from exports as distinguished from income derived from domestic sales. Administration of the market development reserve provisions by export associations relieves the government of this problem.

Requirements for the release of funds from the market development reserve for small firms are identical with those prescribed for large firms as indicated above. Therefore

---

originally provided in each of the next succeeding five years. Additional amounts may also be required to be restored to income based upon the actual deductible expenses for overseas operations incurred in the years after the reserve was created." Price Waterhouse & Co., *Clients' Circular* No. 64/4, Tokyo, May 22, 1964.

[14] *Okura Zaimu Kyokai* [Monetary and Fiscal Association], *An Outline of Japanese Taxes, 1964* (Tokyo, Sept. 1964), p. 73.

in both cases the tax exemptions are only temporary and thus not classified as subsidies within the meaning of GATT Article XVI.

A fourth measure permits the establishment of an Overseas Investment Loss Reserve. This measure was inspired by a principal objective of Japanese foreign investment, namely the need to diversify and control sources of basic raw material supply. To a considerable extent, investment in foreign raw material sources takes place in developing countries, usually under conditions which are economically or politically risky. The present measure encourages such investments by permitting losses due to capital investments by specified firms in designated developing areas to be deducted as expenses. The amount of the reserve attributable to loss is limited to one-half the investment concerned. The amount credited to the reserve is immune from tax for five years,[15] but between the sixth and the tenth years, one-fifth of the reserve must be returned to the profits account annually. This arrangement also appears to be a device for tax deferment rather than tax exemption, but in any case it is immune from the provisions of GATT Article XVI inasmuch as that article refers to "products" rather than to "investment."

A fifth measure permitted a Special Deduction in Connection with Overseas Transactions in Technology. This measure attempted to strengthen the balance of payments through the invisibles account. For specified exports of technology, consulting services and shipping services, it granted an exemption from tax of up to 70 percent of the proceeds (although the maximum amount deductible could not exceed 50 percent of the income of the corporation during the period concerned, excluding income from immovable property and capital gains on fixed assets or securities). The allowance for deduction of income received from technological exports was introduced in 1959; prior to the present measure, however, the amount exempt from

[15] In this, as in other similar situations, it would be consistent with GATT rules for the government subsequently to further *postpone* the date as of which the reserve becomes subject to tax.

tax had been limited to 50 percent of the income of the corporation. In this case, which concerns invisibles, as in the case of measures referring to overseas investment, the requirements of GATT Article XVI, which refer to "products," do not apply.

Finally, a sixth tax measure designed for the promotion of exports introduced as of April 1, 1964 included a provision allowing for the deduction of hotel and traveling expenses of foreign buyers from the export income of Japanese sellers.

Tax revisions effective in the fiscal year beginning April 1, 1965 made no substantial changes in the new measures for export promotion established during the preceding year.

ECONOMIC CONCENTRATION IN EXPORTS

In historical perspective, the apparent backsliding that has occurred in Japan's antitrust and cartel policy since the days of the Occupation is neither extreme nor surprising. For beginning with the depression of the 1930s a high degree of cartelization had been sponsored and even compelled by the government. Starting from the premise that Japan cannot afford to waste scarce resources, the government encouraged the expansion of large producer units capable of achieving economies of scale and also the centralization and concentration of marketing channels. By this means Japan has endeavored at once to strengthen its competitive position abroad and its ability to defend the home market from powerful foreign companies. This attitude remains active at the present time. It is reflected in the insistence of MITI that competing firms sort out their activities and reduce the amount of overlapping; they are urged to arrive at a state of agreed specialization. From another point of view, centralized control of production and prices is consistent also with the government's desire to forestall market disruption abroad. Moreover, due to the importance of administrative guidance, as distinguished from statutory law, in the government of Japan, it is more

195

convenient—especially in the era of ostensible liberalization—to make "recommendations" or "suggestions" to a small group of large firms rather than to a large group of small firms.

The tradition favorable to economic concentration in industry is favorable to concentration in foreign trade as well. Among the various laws authorizing exemptions from the Anti-Monopoly Act (Law No. 54, 1947) is the Export–Import Transactions Law (Law No. 299, 1952), administered for this purpose by MITI. In accordance therewith, exporters and importers, domestic firms preparing goods for export, and dealers in such goods may under specified circumstances be authorized by MITI to agree on prices, quantity and quality restrictions, and similar matters. "At one time the FTC had to concur in such arrangements. Now only a filing with MITI is required. . . ." The formation of foreign trade cartels has accordingly become a commonplace.[16] In 1962, cartelized commodities constituted fully one quarter of total Japanese exports.[17] As of March 31, 1963 260 foreign trade cartels were known to be in existence.[18] Many of these were formed to administer the provisions of Japan's "voluntary" self-imposed export quotas. In some cases cartels are formed to transact business with Communist countries, which bargain with Japan through a "single channel" that would place a group of competing Japanese firms at a disadvantage. International cartels

[16] Michiko Ariga and Luvern V. Rieke, "The Antimonopoly Law of Japan and Its Enforcement," *Washington Law Review*, Volume 39, No. 3, Aug. 1964, p. 469, n. 121. See also, Japanese Fair Trade Commission, *Report on the Legislation on Restrictive Business Practices and Its Application in Japan*, submitted to OECD Commission of Experts on Restrictive Business Practices, Sept. 1964, which is the first issue of an annual report.

[17] *Mergers and Cartels in Japan*, Japan Industry Series, Trade Bulletin Corporation, 1964, p. A-37.

[18] Of these, 194 were formed under the Export–Import Transactions Law, 11 were formed under the Export Marine Products Industry Promotion Law (1954), and 55 were shipping conference agreements established under the Marine Transportation Law (1949). Hiroshi Ryori, "Cartels in Japan," *The Oriental Economist*, Jan. 1964, p. 27.

formed with partners abroad, however, may or may not be known to the Japanese government.[19]

In general, the effectiveness of export cartels in engrossing trade for the benefit of their members and in enforcing discipline among them with regard to the particular commodities within their jurisdiction is extraordinarily high. To the extent that cartels receive the blessing of MITI, they also receive MITI's assistance in enforcing discipline on outsiders as well.

The goal of agreed specialization is sought on the international as well as on the domestic plane. A statement by the *Keizai Doyukai*, Japan's Committee for Economic Development, for example, expresses it as follows: "We suggest that Japan and the U.S. work out detailed item-by-item arrangements regarding the division of labor for the production of heavy and chemical industry products."[20]

The tenor of official policy with regard to concentration in export marketing is revealed by the Supreme Export Council. This consultative body, created in 1954, includes economic cabinet ministers, the governor of The Bank of Japan, the president of the Export–Import Bank and various business leaders; it is presided over by the prime minister. It deliberates annually over the export target to be set for the year. In stating the target for 1963, the Council also recommended some instrumental steps to be taken in achieving it, including the following:[21]

To reduce the number of manufacturers in each market by means of a joint marketing or rotation system.

To push forward transactions through systematized or regimented channels.

[19] "While Japanese companies are required by the Anti-Monopoly Law to report all such restrictive agreements to the FTC for official clearance, there is evidence of deliberate failure to do so in many cases." *Asahi Evening News*, Jan. 11, 1965, p. 7.

[20] *Keizai Doyukai, Problems Confronting Japan in the Changing World Economy*, Tokyo, Oct. 1962, p. 6.

[21] *The Mainichi Daily News*, Monthly International Edition, June 1, 1963, p. 1.

To amend the Export and Import Transactions Law in such a way as to put freewheeling "outsiders" on the producers' level under control.

To conclude agreements on export price and quantity.

In the implementation of its foreign trade objectives, as in other matters, however, the effectiveness of government policy is impaired by competition and jealousy among its various agencies. The problem is described in a statement of the *Keidanren* (Federation of Economic Organizations), probably the most influential body of Japanese businessmen:[22]

> Notwithstanding the fact that promotion of foreign trade and economic cooperation is absolutely indispensable for the growth and development of the Japanese economy, positive efforts on the part of private enterprises for the promotion of export and overseas economic cooperation have been not a little impeded by needless competition and conflicts over authority among the government ministries, a situation caused by excessive overlapping of authority and other complexities inherent in our present machinery. . . .
>
> There exists at present a number of deliberative councils in connection with foreign trade, which call upon private citizens from time to time to express their views. These . . . should be either reduced, reorganized or abolished. . . .
>
> The respective areas of operation of the Overseas Economic Cooperation Fund and the Export–Import Bank should be clearly defined. . . . The ministries with jurisdiction over these government organizations should restrict themselves to appointment and discharge of the directors and to the necessary budget compilation for financing these institutions. Otherwise, these institutions should be given full authority to undertake their operations without interference.

[22] *Keidanren*, "Recommendations for Reform of the Foreign Trade Administration," *Keidanren Review*, Aug. 1964, pp. 42-45.

ECONOMIC COOPERATION

The chief complaints made by other donor nations against Japan's program of economic assistance are that it is insufficient in amount and that it has been designed principally to serve Japan's own industrial interests. On the first point there is room for argument in terms of Japan's ability to pay, but on the second, clearly, promotion of Japanese exports—especially those of the heavy and chemical industries—is one of its basic objectives.[23] A large (though declining) proportion of the flow of resources from Japan to developing countries has consisted of reparations; for this reason the transfer has been described as one of "economic cooperation" rather than "economic aid." The flow of resources is in effect a flow of goods, for all Japanese loans and credits are tied.

Japan's economic cooperation, moreover, is of a *project* rather than *program* type; that is, its purposes are narrowly specified. This also is conducive to the export of Japanese plant and equipment. The cooperation is almost entirely bilateral rather than multilateral, and apart from reparations and technical services there are no outright grants. Embarrassingly, after it reached the amount of $371 million in 1961, the total value of Japanese economic cooperation declined in successive years to $242 million in 1964. In proportion to national income, it also declined from 0.97 percent in 1961 to 0.44 percent in 1964 (Table 34).

The principal component of the economic cooperation program is suppliers' credit, which in 1964 accounted for 39 percent of the total. Suppliers' credit, provided chiefly through the Export–Import Bank, permits deferred payment for exports and is subject to strict commercial criteria. In several instances, for example, when the guarantee

[23] In 1962, for example, two-thirds of the exports of Japanese heavy machinery to the developing countries was supplied in connection with the economic cooperation program. MITI, *Keizai Kyōryoku no Genjō to Mondai-ten, 1963* [Present Condition of Economic Cooperation and Its Problems], Tokyo, 1964.

TABLE 34

Net Disbursements Under Japan's Economic Cooperation Program, by Year, 1960 to 1964

Category	Calendar Year (millions of dollars)				
	1960	1961	1962	1963	1964a
Total	250.8	371.1	281.9	264.9	242.3
Grants:	66.9	67.8	74.6	76.7	49.0
Reparations	64.7	65.4	71.0	72.2	44.4
Technical aid	2.2	2.4	3.6	4.5	4.6
Long-term credits:	76.5	198.1	131.1	99.4	140.2
Government loans	19.0	26.8	12.5	60.3	48.6
Suppliers' creditsb	64.0	170.4	126.1	47.9	94.0
Consolidationc	—6.5	0.9	—7.5	—8.8	—2.4
Private investment	77.1	93.8	69.1	76.7	45.0
Contributions to international organizations	30.3	11.4	7.1	12.1	8.1
Total disbursements in relation to national income (percent)	0.78	0.97	0.66	0.54	0.44

a Preliminary.

b Includes credits with a maturity of five years or more only.

c The "consolidation" account refers to refinancing by the Japanese government of commercial credits and the outstanding balances of Open Account transactions between Japan and other countries.

SOURCE: Ministry of Finance, December 1964.

of the central bank of the recipient country was not considered strong enough, the recipient country's reparations credits have been earmarked as collateral for the suppliers' credits. Incidentally, although the Export–Import Bank has a legal lending capacity considerably in excess of its actual loans and credits, the government requires that commercial banks participate in virtually every individual assistance transaction.[24] The Japanese supplier's contact with

[24] The aggregate amount borrowed and outstanding at any one time must not exceed three times the sum of the Export–Import Bank's capital and reserves, and the aggregate amount of loans and guarantees outstanding at any time must not exceed the sum of the capital reserves and the abovementioned limit of borrowing. (The Export–Im-

the Export–Import Bank is usually made through his own commercial bank. Allocation of the funds is generally made not to the overseas principal but rather to the Japanese supplier after approved arrangements have been made between him and representatives of the assisted country. As a result both of government restrictions on the range of commodities subject to approval and the manner in which transactions are processed, the supplying companies on the Japanese side are usually members of the *keiretsu* group. Thus economic cooperation also contributes to the growth and consolidation of big business in Japan.

Qualitatively, the loans extended by Japan are "hard": their maturities are comparatively short and the interest rates are high. Of course, this reflects the stringent conditions prevailing in Japan's domestic capital market. In the economic cooperation program, the minimum rate on government yen loans (principally to India and Pakistan) is 5.75 percent. The rates on private investment range from 4 to 7 percent on the portion financed by the Export–Import Bank and from 8 to 9 percent on the portion financed by the commercial banks. Suppliers' credit is extended at rates ranging from 5 to 7 percent.

Various reasons have been suggested for the insistence of the Japanese government that commercial banks participate, if only marginally, with the Export–Import Bank in the financing of economic assistance activities.[25] The most obvious effect of their participation is the effective increase in the interest rate on all transactions. Another effect is the involvement of the private banking system in the task of export promotion through the economic cooperation program. For example, by having committed their own

port Bank, *The Export–Import Bank of Japan: Its Object and Functions*, Tokyo, 1964, p. 5.) The bank is allowed to provide a maximum of 80 percent of funds required for individual export credit transactions, and up to 50 percent of funds required for foreign investments.

[25] See John White, *Japanese Aid*, Overseas Development Institute (London, 1964), p. 38.

funds, the banks are obliged to cooperate actively in screening and processing the loans.

Although it is often asserted that Japanese technical methods are peculiarly appropriate to conditions in Asia, in no year prior to 1965 did Japanese technical assistance amount to as much as $5 million in value. In one of its principal forms—technical training—linguistic difficulties have presented a barrier, for technicians are not usually multilingual. Technical assistance has also been provided in the form of pre-investment surveys, especially for projects which might result in subsequent orders for Japanese construction materials. In some cases, however, even when Japan has been invited to proceed with the actual construction of projects, the Ministry of Finance has failed to approve the loans which would make this possible.

Divided authority and rivalry among government ministries has impaired the effectiveness of the economic co-operation program. In the case of suppliers' credits, for example, actual disbursements are made by the Export–Import Bank, but they require the prior approval of the Ministry of Finance, the Foreign Ministry, and the Ministry of International Trade and Industry. In this instance, MITI's approval is the most important. Government loans and "consolidations" (see Table 34) also require the combined approval of three ministries, and in some cases the Economic Planning Agency must be consulted as well.

Evaluation of the nature, size, and effectiveness of Japan's economic cooperation activities is complicated by the fact that statistics as presented by the Japanese government are somewhat inconsistent with those published by the Development Assistance Committee of OECD. Lack of comparability results partly from differences in the classification of official as distinguished from private funds. In order to forestall invidious comparisons among recipients and competitive requests for increased amounts of aid, individual country data are not published by Japan. On a regional basis, however, Asia is by far the main recipient:

in 1963, 70 percent of total bilateral official and private transfers from Japan was extended to Asia.

A word remains to be said about Japan's general position in the role of donor nation. Since 1954, when Japan became associated with the Columbo Plan, its efforts have had a political *and* economic motivation. Politically, the objective has been to restore Japan's membership in the club of the "advanced industrial nations." As a member of this club, however, Japan's situation is ambiguous in several respects. For example, Japan is at once a contributor of capital to the World Bank and a borrower from the same institution. The conflict between the demand by developing countries for soft loans and the stringent conditions that prevail in Japan's domestic capital market emphasizes its immature status as a donor. Moreover, while borrowing heavily at short-term, Japan is under pressure to lend capital at long-term to developing countries. Although for purposes of economic assistance Japan is classified among the "advanced industrial countries," it has a long way to go before resolving the contradictions of its own dual economy. As distinguished from the developing countries on the one hand and the advanced countries on the other, Japan might be classified as a transitional or "middle-advanced" [*chūshin koku*] country, defined as one sharply dichotomized by its dual economy. In addition, there exists a practically desperate need for the improvement of social overhead facilities in Japan; thus potentially the aid program is highly explosive as a domestic political issue. Despite these difficulties, however, and the fact that among the twelve members of DAC Japan ranks in per capita national income at the bottom of the list along with Portugal, it ranks fifth in terms of the total value of economic assistance actually rendered.

Japan's position may also be contrasted with that of the "metropolitan" powers which retain special links with their former colonies or dependencies. The aid programs of such countries redound to their eventual commercial gain with much less explicit emphasis on export promotion than is necessary for an equivalent return in the case of Japan.

ECONOMIC DIPLOMACY

In the mid-1960s, as emphasis on a high rate of growth was succeeded by emphasis upon stable growth, commercial policy—known at the level of external affairs as economic diplomacy—likewise assumed a role of greater importance. For in view of the balance of payments constraint on the growth rate, stability in the expansion of exports had become a major factor in economic stability at large. In turn, the growth of exports was affected by barriers abroad, especially discriminatory barriers against Japanese goods. For example, one of Japan's principal aims in accepting the obligations of full membership in OECD—which is the principal source of the discrimination—was to acquire the privilege of confronting its other members on this issue on their own ground.[26] Another source of discrimination is the action of some members of GATT which by invoking Article XXXV of that agreement refuse to accept GATT obligations with regard to Japan.[27]

The degree of discrimination is difficult to determine statistically, since in other countries as well as in Japan

[26] OECD's aim in admitting Japan as a member of the club was somewhat different. When the event was impending in August 1963, a key OECD official remarked to me that its purpose was to induce Japan to accept a larger responsibility for aid, to "educate" Japan in terms of OECD concepts of liberalization, to obtain larger benefits from Japan as a market, and to have a place for discussion with Japan. With regard to OECD barriers against Japan, he argued that it was "in the interest of the Japanese themselves not to disrupt Western markets."

The members of OECD are: Austria, Belgium, Canada, Denmark, France, the Federal Republic of Germany, Greece, Iceland, Ireland, Italy, Japan, Luxembourg, the Netherlands, Norway, Portugal, Spain, Sweden, Switzerland, Turkey, the United Kingdom, and the United States.

[27] These are mostly developing countries. As of March 1965 they included: Austria, Cameroon, Central Africa, Chad, Cyprus, Congo-Brazzaville, Gabon, Haiti, Kuwait, Nigeria, Portugal, Sierra Leone, the Union of South Africa, Tanzania, Trinidad-Tobago, Uganda, Upper Volta, Spain, Dahomey, Senegal, Mauritania, Jamaica, the Ivory Coast, Niger, Kenya, Togo, Malta, Gambia, and Burundi.

the existence of formal restrictions is sometimes less important than the way in which they are administered. Also, the effect of total exclusion from a minor market may be of less importance than partial exclusion from a major market. The International Trade Bureau of MITI is of the opinion that at least up to 1965, discrimination has been a greater handicap to Japanese exports than all other trade barriers combined. Beyond this, little evaluation has been done.

It may be useful, however, to identify the items subject to discrimination in various major markets. It is convenient to designate the items at the four-digit level of the Brussels Tariff Nomenclature (BTN), which at that level contains a total of 1,097 entries. Within the strategic market area of the European Economic Community, as of May 1964 Italy was the chief offender against Japan, discriminating against 116 Japanese export items. France was second, discriminating against 68 items; Benelux and Western Germany discriminated against 33 items and 20 items, respectively. As compared with 1960, however, when France and Italy respectively discriminated against twice as many import commodities from Japan as in 1964, the situation was considerably improved (Table 35). Most of the items subject to discrimination fall in the categories of textiles, sundry goods, light machinery, and ceramics.

Besides the ECC group, some other countries of Western Europe are also a source of discrimination against Japan. As of May 1965, the number of Japanese commodities at the BTN four-digit level subject to discriminatory treatment by a selected list of countries was as follows (in parentheses is the number of items additionally subject to restriction in the imports of the specified country from OECD countries as a whole, Japan being subject to the latter restriction as well): Austria 389 (53); Denmark 30 (126); Greece 14 (97); Norway 75 (0); Portugal 1,037 (60); Spain 730 (367); and Sweden 47 (0).[28] Relations with the United Kingdom are discussed separately below.

[28] Ministry of International Trade and Industry.

In Japan's relations with the United States and Canada, discrimination is not enforced directly in the form of quota restrictions by those countries on imports from Japan, but rather indirectly in the form of limitations imposed "voluntarily" by Japan upon its own exports.[29] Controversy on this subject is vexed by the fact that there are three types of such voluntary control. The first type results from intergovernmental agreements, as in the bilateral cotton textile agreement between Japan and the United States. The second type of control is designed to forestall retaliatory action by protectionist interests abroad. The third type is a truly voluntary type of control motivated exclusively from the point of view of Japan's own interests.

In the case of Japan's cotton textile exports to the United States, the recent history of the pressure associated with the first of these three types of control is of considerable interest. United States policy on cotton textile imports has been complicated by the fact that the American government has been paying subsidies on raw cotton exports since 1956.[30] Therefore foreign users of United States cotton have received the benefit of the U.S. export price, and even those foreign mills not using United States cotton benefited because the world market price of raw cotton was forced down by the U.S. export price which was relatively low. United States mills have had to pay the supported domestic price for U.S. cotton and could not buy cheap foreign cotton because of U.S. import quotas. However, in order to remove the disadvantage of U.S. textile producers in the export market, they in turn have been paid an export subsidy, equivalent to the raw cotton subsidy.

[29] The history of voluntary export control in Japan goes back to the depression of the 1930s when quantitative restraints were imposed extensively in an effort to restrain the rise of import barriers abroad. In the postwar period they were reintroduced (1954) at which time they were applied to exports of knitted gloves and porcelainware.

[30] From 1956 to 1960, the export subsidies ranged from 18 to 24 percent of the price received by U.S. farmers for upland cotton. U.S. Department of Agriculture.

TABLE 35

Japanese Export Commodities Subject to Discriminatory Treatment by EEC Countries as of December 1960, December 1962, and May 1964

Discriminating country	December 1960: Total	December 1962: Total	Total	Number of commodities subject to discrimination at the four-digit level of the Brussels Tariff Nomenclature — May 1964			
				By specified country's customs area only	By two customs areas	By three customs areas	By all EEC.
Benelux	40	40	33	3[a]	5[e]	13[i]	12
France	357	179	68	19[b]	21[f]	16[j]	12
Italy	228	106	116	65[c]	23[g]	16[k]	12
West Germany	34	30	20	0[d]	5[h]	3[m]	12

[a] 7332, 5806, 5807.

[b] 2928, 2944, 3205, 3907, 4415, 5710, 6009, 6203, 7116, 7301, 8514, 8518, 8519, 9002, 9009, 9029, 9213, 9707, 9810. Excludes six agricultural commodities of no importance to Japan.

[c] 0206, 0301, 1001, 1101, 1102, 1604, 1902, 2923, 3702, 3901, 3903, 4010, 4011, 4012, 4013, 5001, 5002, 5004, 5007, 5102, 5103, 5305, 5505, 5506, 5507, 5601, 5602, 5603, 5604, 5666, 5808, 5917, 6107, 6108, 6109, 6110, 6111, 6201, 6603, 6910, 7019, 8203, 8315, 8406, 8415, 8435, 8440, 8462, 8501, 8515, 8520, 8521, 8523, 8706, 8707, 8709, 8712, 8901, 8902, 9017, 9023, 9102, 9104, 9705, 9802.

[d] Excludes commodities liberalized after January 1, 1965.

[e] Benelux and Italy: 5306, 5605, 5913, 6205, 9805;

[f] France and Italy: 3902, 5009, 6002, 6004, 6601, 7302, 7315, 8503, 8524, 9001, 9005, 9007, 9008, 9012, 9028, 9211, 9703.

France and West Germany: 5802, 5905, 6101, 6913.

[g] Italy and France: see "f" above.

Italy and Benelux: see "e" above.

Italy and West Germany: 5310.

[h] West Germany and France: see "f" above.

West Germany and Italy: see "g" above.

[i] Benelux, France, and Italy: 5101, 5508, 5805, 5809, 6106, 6401, 6402, 5907, 6908, 8209, 8214, 8441, 9801.

[j] France, Benelux, and Italy: see "i" above.

France, Italy, and West Germany: 5311, 6104, 8525.

[k] Italy, Benelux, and France: see "i" above.

Italy, France, and West Germany: see "j" above.

[m] West Germany, France, and Italy: see "j" above.

[n] 1912, 5104, 5307, 5509, 5607, 5804, 6005, 6102, 6103, 6105, 6202, 6911.

SOURCE: MITI, *EEC Shokoku no Tainichi Sabetsu Hinmoku Taiyō* [Situation of Japanese Commodities Subject to Discriminatory Treatment by EEC Countries], May 1, 1964.

In order to limit cotton textile imports to a level consistent with these arrangements, and at the same time to place any such limitations within a multilateral context,[31] the United States requested a conference under the auspices of GATT to prepare "Arrangements Regarding International Trade in Cotton Textiles." Nineteen countries, including Japan, participated in the conference for the "short-term arrangement" which was made at Geneva on July 21, 1961, and which was to take effect for one year beginning October 1, 1961. Thereafter the "Long-Term Arrangement Regarding International Trade in Cotton Textiles," with a term of five years, came into effect on October 1, 1962.[32] Standard principles of GATT to the contrary notwithstanding, the arrangement authorized importers to enforce quantitative restrictions on the import of cotton textiles and moreover conferred upon them the privilege of imposing unilateral sanctions in the event of their failure to arrive at mutually acceptable supplementary bilateral agreements with exporting countries. Under these auspices, the United States concluded a separate bilateral agreement with Japan for the year beginning January 1, 1962, which was succeeded by a three-year bilateral agreement, the latter being the object of much criticism in Japan.

Thus the immediate factors that led Japan to accept "voluntarily" the bilateral restrictions can be found in the provisions of the multilateral Long-Term Cotton Textile Arrangement, which is potentially highly punitive. For according to Article 3, if imports of cotton textiles "cause or threaten to cause disruption in the market of the importing country," restrictions may be applied against the exporting

31 Bilaterally, Japan had been prevailed upon as early as 1957 to "voluntarily" restrict its cotton textile exports to the United States. See Warren Hunsberger, *Japan and the United States in World Trade* (New York and Evanston, Ill.: Harper and Row, 1964).

32 As of Jan. 1, 1963, the 23 parties to the agreement were: Australia, Austria, Canada, Denmark, India, Israel, Japan, Mexico, Norway, Pakistan, Portugal, Spain, Sweden, the United Arab Republic, the United Kingdom (also representing Hong Kong), the United States, Belgium, France, West Germany, Italy, Luxembourg, and the Netherlands.

country. But the definition of "disruption" is left entirely to the discretion of the importing country (Annex C of the Arrangement) .[33] The extent of restrictions on imports, according to Annex B, may not exceed "the level of actual imports or exports of such products during the twelve-month period terminating three months preceding the month in which the request for consultation is made." Having imposed this restriction, the importing country may further limit imports from a particular supplier to an annual increase of five percent thereafter. However, an importing country might impose the 5 percent limitation on import expansion after a period of unusually low, rather than disruptively high, imports. This would effectively reduce the market share of the foreign supplier in succeeding periods when demand had recovered.

Another instance of voluntary export restriction of the first type occurs in Japan's relations with the United Kingdom. The commercial treaty[34] between the two countries provides for "safeguards" of two kinds; first, a general safeguard applicable to all products, and second, a safeguard for "sensitive items." Under the general safeguard, if imports into the United Kingdom "cause or threaten serious injury to producers of like or competitive products," and in the event consultation with Japan fails to provide a mutually acceptable solution, the United Kingdom is

> free to impose restrictions on the import of the Japanese goods in question notwithstanding the most-favoured-nation provisions of the Treaty. In an emergency these restrictions may be imposed at any time after consultation has begun. The Japanese Govern-

[33] Moreover, "disruption" would presumably have to be demonstrated in terms of statistical categories, but these also are not specified in the arrangement proper. Annex D merely suggests a list of categories which "is illustrative and should not be considered as being exhaustive."

[34] *Treaty of Commerce, Establishment and Navigation between the United Kingdom of Great Britain and Northern Ireland and Japan* (London, Her Majesty's Stationery Office, Nov. 1962), Cmnd. 1874. The treaty was ratified on April 4, 1963.

ment would have similar rights of action against British goods causing disruption of the Japanese market. Counteraction may be taken by the party whose goods are restricted in so far as the restricting Government has not been able to offer any compensation for its action.[35]

Regarding the sensitive items, which already were subject to export control by Japan prior to the treaty,

In general the criterion which has been applied for deciding that an item is sensitive is that there should be a strong presumption that, unless restrictions were continued after the coming into force of the Treaty, an increase in imports causing serious injury would ensue forthwith. Where this criterion is fulfilled the Japanese Government have agreed that supplies of Japanese goods to this market should continue to be restricted, since otherwise it would have been necessary to apply the safeguard procedure immediately. They have, however, been concerned to limit so far as possible the extent of the derogations from the Treaty obligations which would be involved. They therefore expressed the wish that for those kinds of sensitive goods for which it was possible for them to exercise effective control over export under their system of "voluntary export control," the control should be operated in this way instead of by way of restrictions on import into the United Kingdom. Under powers conferred by Japanese law the Japanese Government successfully operates voluntary export control on many kinds of goods going to other markets. Subject, therefore, to the necessary understandings about the way in which the controls would be operated, Her Majesty's Government were ready to meet the wishes of the Japanese Government in this matter.[36]

[35] Board of Trade, *Government Statement on the Anglo-Japanese Commercial Treaty* (London, Her Majesty's Stationery Office, Nov. 1962), Cmnd. 1875, p. 4.
[36] *Ibid.*, p. 5.

The second type of "voluntary" export limitation is likewise inspired by fear of retaliation. Instead of being established by intergovernmental formalities, however, it is introduced independently either by the Japanese government or by the group action of business firms in Japan in response to threats from abroad. In the past, business and labor in the United States have used various methods to induce "self-control" among Japanese exporters. One such method is simply arranging for the presentation of bills in Congress designed to control imports. Tariff Commission investigations may also be instigated by petitions from industry, which sometimes lead to Escape Clause action (Article 351 of the Trade Expansion Act).[37] United States restrictions against imports may also be invoked through the national security provision (Article 232) of the Trade Expansion Act.[38] Another source of harassment is the Anti-Dumping Act of 1921, which may be used in a discriminatory way due to the administrative methods (including suspension of customs appraisal during investigation of charges) by which it is enforced.[39]

[37] Cases in which the Escape Clause has been invoked with regard to United States imports are enumerated in the *Tariff Schedules of the United States Annotated* (1963), Appendix, Part 2 (Tariff Commission Publication 103), pp. 505-11. Eight principal commodities (watches, safety pins, clinical thermometers, lead and zinc, stainless steel tableware, cotton cloth for typewriter ribbons, sheet glass, and Wilton carpets) are specified, only two of which (lead and zinc and Wilton carpets) are of no importance to Japan. In a number of other cases where the Escape Clause was not invoked, Japan was nevertheless induced to impose voluntary export control. Examples of this kind include silk fabrics, paper hats, hooked rugs, umbrellas and umbrella ribs, baseball gloves, vinyl raincoats, ceramic ware, mosaic tile, wood screws, frozen tuna, canned tuna, plywood, and veneer sheet.

[38] Voluntary Japanese export control implemented to forestall invocation of this clause has included the following items: cotton cloth, secondary cotton products, woolen trousers, woolen hosiery, woolen gloves, woolen fabrics, and transistor radios.

[39] Other provisions of United States law which may cause difficulties for Japan include: the American Selling Price method of customs appraisal, Secs. 336 and 402 of the Tariff Act of 1930 and Sec. 2 (a) of the Tariff Simplification Act of 1956, as amended, 19 U.S.C. Secs. 1336, 1402, 1402 (a), (1958); Article 22 of the Agricultural Adjustment Act of 1933 (which figured prominently but was not invoked in the cotton

It has been observed that in some instances, Japan has failed to export to the United States even as much as permitted under Japan's own voluntary ceilings. In such cases, can it be said that exports are obstructed by the voluntary control system? There are several reasons for answering in the affirmative. In the first place, the quota is assigned not to a single exporter but rather to a number of firms, each of which may receive a small portion thereof. Since each exporter conducts his business *within* the limit of his subquota, it may easily happen that aggregate shipments fall short of the aggregate quota. In the case of the bilateral U.S.–Japan cotton textile arrangement, the export ceiling is specified not only for total cotton goods but also for a series of narrowly defined individual categories within the overall group. Transfer of unused quota allowances from one category to another is expressly forbidden. This strongly reinforces the tendency for aggregate quota allowances to remain unfulfilled. In addition, the arrangement specifies quarterly rather than annual limits on export shipments; transfer of unused quota allotments from one quarter to another is also prohibited. Altogether, these provisions strongly inhibit fulfillment of aggregate export ceilings, which explains some of the above men-

---

textile difficulties of 1962); penalties for fraudulent or willful under-valuation may be invoked under Sec. 592, Tariff Act of 1930, as amended, 19 U.S.C. Sec. 1952 (1958), which provides a way of harassing importers in cases where common errors are made in the filing of customs declarations; appeal of valuation by American producers, Sec. 516 (a), Tariff Act of 1930, 19 U.S.C. Sec. 1516 (a) (1958). There may also be delays in obtaining advisory administrative rulings and delays in obtaining judicial review of Customs Bureau decisions which do not result from statutes but which are legal restraints arising out of the complexity of the Tariff Act and its administration. These instances and citations were selected from *Beikoku Yunyū Kisei Kankei Hōkishu* [Collection of Regulations Regarding United States Import Restrictions], Ministry of Foreign Affairs, Economic Affairs Bureau, April 26, 1963. For further discussion of the same subject, see *Nichi-Bei Keizai Kankei no Shomondai* [Problems in the Economic Relations between the United States and Japan], edited by the Secretariat of *Keidanren* (Federation of Economic Organizations), *Keidanren* Pamphlet No. 82, Dec. 1964.

tioned dissatisfaction with the arrangement on the part of the Japanese.

In Japan's exports to the United States, "nearly seventy items" are subject to the self-imposed restrictions of the first and second types mentioned above. The commodities upon which they were imposed, moreover, comprised one-third of Japan's exports to the United States during 1961-63.[40]

A third type of voluntary export control may be construed as one inspired purely by Japanese self-interest. In this category, controls introduced by the government are to be distinguished from those originating at the business level. From the government's point of view, it is in the national interest to achieve stability in exports, which is conducive to their long-term growth. The government is also anxious to eliminate "excessive competition" among Japanese traders, which runs prices into the ground and thus reduces incentives to export. Another government objective is the diversification and upgrading of Japanese exports: by restricting the physical quantity of exports it induces the sale of items with a higher unit cost. In general, the government does not like to acknowledge the existence of some of these quotas for fear of arousing fresh demands abroad for further restraints. During the Occupation following World War II, the Japanese government also enforced minimum export prices (known as "check" or "floor" prices). Formally, these have gradually been abandoned in favor of quantity controls.[41] Quality control is another dimension of government export re-

[40] Masatoshi Tanibayashi, "Voluntary Control Applied to Japanese Exports to the United States," an address presented to the Third United States–Japan Businessmen's Conference, Tokyo, May 23, 1964. The "items" enumerated above, however, refer to commodities as defined in individual export limitation agreements. They are not expressed at any specified level of refinement of the commodity classification code; therefore some may be widely, and others narrowly, defined.

[41] Informally, however, they are still enforced through "administrative guidance" in some cases, for example, in electronic goods. In practice, this means that if the price is too low, while the export license will not be *refused*, it will simply not be *granted*.

strictions, as provided for in the Export Inspection Law (Law No. 97, 1957). As of 1965 commodities representing approximately half the value of all exports are subject to inspection before export. Private inspection firms or associations designated by MITI are in charge of about three quarters of the commodities, the remainder being inspected by government agencies. The design of commodities and the timing of shipments may also be subject to government export control.

Private firms, on the other hand, have their own reasons for desiring export restriction, some of which overlap those mentioned above. Elimination of "excessive competition" is desired in the interest of supporting prices and profits, as well as of stabilizing output and income. Export quotas are also instigated in order to preserve the market shares of established producers or trading firms—especially in declining industries such as textiles. The quotas are transferable and are sometimes sold. There may be some difficulty in distinguishing one type of "voluntary export control" from another. In some instances, for example, where it is claimed that the controls have been "involuntarily" imposed at the insistence of the United States, it appears that the quantity of exports is restricted to *all destinations.* Such comprehensive restraint suggests a purpose other than that of concern for orderly marketing in the particular area which produces vulnerable import-competing goods.[42] The difficulty of distinguishing public from private interests is also compounded by the ambiguous role of the export associations. On the one hand, they enforce the self-imposed export restrictions of private firms; on the other, the export restrictions imposed by the government (either independently or in collaboration with foreign governments) have also been largely delegated to the export associations for enforcement. In any given instance, it may be difficult to determine whose interests are principally at stake.

---

[42] However, it could be argued that global restrictions on exports are a precaution against evasion of individual country quotas by trans-shipment of goods.

The legal basis for Japanese export controls is found in the Foreign Exchange and Foreign Trade Control Law (Law No. 228 of December 1949, as amended). Requirements for the registration and licensing of exports are given in the Export Trade Control Order (Cabinet Order No. 378 of December 1949, as amended), issued under the foregoing law. As mentioned above, export restrictions as implemented by private parties are authorized under the Export and Import Transactions Law (Law No. 299 of August 5, 1952). In accordance with this law, exporters as such, or in some circumstances exporters in combination with producers, may conclude agreements to prevent sales abroad at unduly low prices or to prevent harmful or unnecessary competition in particular markets. "The exporters entering into such agreements need only report to MITI on the establishment of a voluntary export control agreement and get its approval. Requests for MITI validation of individual shipments are not required on these commodities. MITI has indicated that its information on this latter category is far from complete since it suspects that considerably more private control agreements are made than are reported officially."[43]

The present trend is increasingly for industries to implement their own self-restriction through the export associations. Each of these is dominated by either one or a few large firms, usually trading companies. The dominant firms express their wishes to the government and in many cases the government responds with rules and regulations which it requests the export associations to enforce upon their members. In the event that "outsider" firms decline to join an association sponsored by their industry, or to submit to its discipline, they may be ordered by the government to do so. As one exporter expressed it, "MITI wants the associations to be powerful so that it can transmit

[43] United States Embassy, Tokyo, Memorandum on "The Current Status of Japanese Voluntary Export Controls to the Western Hemisphere," Dec. 26, 1961. For a breakdown of reported export control agreements by type, see MITI, *Tsūshō Hakusho* [White Paper on International Trade], 1963, p. 595.

its orders to them and have them enforced, especially in cases where there is no apparent legal basis for the order MITI wants to have enforced."

In some cases, as in trade with the United Kingdom, export restriction is enforced by licenses issued by the Japanese government or its agents. In other cases, the restriction is imposed through import licensing by the country of destination. Sometimes, however, as in Japan's export of restricted commodities to West Germany, a "double-check" system—both export and import licenses being granted by the selling and buying countries respectively—has been used. Another device is the use of a designated "trade channel." To insure orderly marketing in the United Kingdom, for example, in some instances the Japanese government has designated the Japanese firm authorized to handle specified exports from Japan and the British government has designated the authorized importer in England. The designated exporter on the Japanese side— usually a large firm—then collects orders from a number of other Japanese companies, as well as from its own customers abroad.

Evasion of the quotas and other export controls is of course a fine art in Japan. For example, quotas have been evaded by sending components (for radios, for example) to Hong Kong or Taiwan where they were assembled and shipped to the destination for which the "Japanese quota" had already been fulfilled. In some cases, such as baseball gloves, cheap grades of the commodity under quota have been shipped not under their commodity name but rather as "toys." On the whole, however, it cannot be denied that the export control system has been relatively effective.

Incidentally, by exerting upward pressure on prices, "orderly marketing" has had a tendency to improve Japan's terms of trade. This pressure has been exerted particularly on the commodities in which traditionally Japan has competed on a price basis. At the same time, in the category of heavy and chemical goods, Japan lacks the competitive power to be able to offer conspicuously low prices. These factors, together with the fairly steady postwar depression in the prices of primary products—which constitute Japan's principal imports—help account for the favorable terms of trade which in recent years has been a distinctive feature of its foreign trade. Being the product of the above indicated mixture of causes, however, favorable terms of trade have not necessarily been always an unqualified advantage to Japan.

Relevant to the topic of the terms of trade, as well as to the problem of "dumping," is the matter of dual pricing. There are various reasons why the export price *should* be lower than the domestic price of some commodities, and various ways in which the charge of dumping can be avoided when the export price actually is lower. In the first place, unit export prices should be lower than domestic prices of particular commodities because larger quantities are sold in export than in domestic transactions. Second, the method of financing is more advantageous to the producer in the export market than in the domestic market. A considerable interval may elapse before goods manufactured for the home market are sold and the producer's costs reimbursed, while in export transactions his costs are usually reimbursed with little delay. In many instances, moreover, the process of production for export is itself financed by a letter of credit opened for this specific purpose. Third, besides the avoidance of delay in payment, export shipments are subject to much less risk of nonpayment than domestic shipments. Fourth, production for export ordinarily takes place in accordance with given specifications of size, quantity, color, and other dimensions. Often production for domestic sale is done on speculation, with consequent remainders of unsold merchandise. Fifth, in export sales the foreign buyer pays all delivery and advertising charges, whereas in domestic sales the producer pays for advertising and distribution. Sixth, in the event that a raw material has been imported in bond for the purpose of manufacturing an export product, the export price may be legitimately lower than the domestic price by as much as the import duty saved. In actual practice these factors are often reflected in unit export prices which are lower than domestic prices for certain commodities.[44] This may be accomplished by the device of segregating a particular model or design of a standard article for export sales only; in the case of television sets, the distinction may consist in a minor modification of the wiring. Thus it can be claimed that there is "no domestic price" for the product in question and accordingly no possibility of dual pricing.

Another concern of Japan's economic diplomacy is the subject of tariffs, especially those of the United States. It may be argued that since United States tariff rates make no distinction concerning the country of origin of merchandise, and since a given tariff applies equally against all suppliers, no discrimination is possible in the U.S. tariff system. Nevertheless, there is evidence that its pattern of rates has a relatively adverse impact on Japan. That this effect is not entirely unintentional is suggested by evidence such as the following: "In 1934 the United States Government increased the duty on tuna canned in oil from 30 percent ad valorem to 45 percent ad valorem to equalize the difference in the costs of production in the United States and in Japan."[45]

Discrimination is implied if it can be shown that the

[44] Japan is not the only country which practices dual pricing. For example, in a letter to *The Financial Times*, the President of the British Board of Trade was quoted from *Hansard* as saying, "Dual pricing is a dangerous subject for us to raise, as we ourselves go in for a great deal of dual pricing. There was an article in *The Financial Times* only a few days ago quite openly listing some of the products in which Britain goes in for dual pricing." *The Financial Times* (London), July 16, 1963.

[45] United States Tariff Commission, *Bonito Canned in Oil, and Tuna and Bonito, Canned, Not in Oil; Report on the Escape-Clause Investigation* [GPO C1. No. TC 1.9: 187] Report No. 187, Second Series, p. 14. The statement is quoted here as an exceptionally rare example of official frankness. The considerations to which it alludes remain relevant to government policy-making, but current official statements about such factors are much more guarded.

tariff rates on the commodities imported from one principal supplier are consistently higher than the rates imposed on commodities from other principal suppliers, particularly where the comparison is restricted to suppliers which are the source of a well-diversified list of United States imports. On this basis, it can be shown that the United States places a disproportionately heavy burden on imports from Japan. For in the first place, commodities such as textiles and sundry goods, which figure prominently in the list of United States imports from Japan, have been subject to tariffs which are high in relation to the average height of United States tariffs.[46] This can be verified by inspection of a valuable tariff analysis prepared by the Committee for Economic Development.[47] Disregarding primary products, the commodities subject to rates of 30 percent or more constitute practically a representative list of Japan's principal exports.[48] Second, and more important, the ratio of duties collected on imports from Japan in relation to the value of those imports has been consistently higher —in almost every one of the 15 tariff schedule categories— than the corresponding ratio on imports from other principal United States suppliers.[49]

Trade with the Communist countries ("centrally planned economies," in United Nations nomenclature) is another subject of sharply rising importance in the field of Japan's economic diplomacy. Exports to the Soviet Union

[46] See testimony by Peter Kenen in *Hearings* before the Subcommittee on Foreign Economic Policy of the Joint Economic Committee, U.S. Congress, Dec. 4-14, 1961, p. 222.

[47] Committee for Economic Development, *Comparative Tariffs and Trade* (Washington, March 1963). This study presents the United States tariff in terms of the Brussels Tariff Nomenclature. It is particularly useful because it provides the ad valorem equivalent of specific rates for a large proportion of Schedule A categories.

[48] According to an internal secretariat note of the GATT, dated Aug. 13, 1963, 18 percent of the 5,064 United States tariff rates were at an ad valorem level of 30 percent or more, as contrasted with only one percent in the case of the European Economic Community.

[49] Effective Aug. 31, 1963, the *Tariff Schedules of the United States Annotated (1963)* (Tariff Commission Publication 103), containing eight major schedules, superseded the former 15-schedule classification.

have increased steadily and impressively (from $60 million in 1960 to $182 million in 1964) while exports to Mainland China after the rupture of relations following the Nagasaki flag incident of 1958 have increased in a striking but markedly unsteady fashion (from $3 million in 1960 to $153 million in 1964). Trade with the USSR and Mainland China constitutes about three quarters of all Japanese trade with Communist countries. In promoting exports to the Communist countries, the Japanese government professes to observe the principle of "separation of economics from politics."

There is no treaty basis for trade with Communist China since Japan does not recognize the Peking government. Trade is conducted, however, through two quasi-officially sponsored channels. The first, inaugurated in accordance with the "Three Principles of Trade with Japan" enunciated by Chou En-lai in 1960, consists of trade between China and Japanese firms designated by Peking as "friendly." There are approximately 300 such firms which are either independent entities or dummy firms operating in behalf of other—conceivably "unfriendly"—principals. In 1964 transactions through the friendly firms, which are conducted on a cash basis, constituted 56 percent of the total bilateral trade with Communist China.

The second channel for trade between Communist China and Japan is by way of the Liao–Takasaki agreement (known as "L-T trade"). This five-year agreement, formally the "Japan-China Overall Trade Agreement," was signed in 1962 by Liao Cheng-chih, chairman of the Sino-Japanese Friendship Association, and his Japanese counterpart, Tatsunosuke Takasaki, who was formerly minister of MITI. In charge of the agreement on the Japanese side is the Japan–China General Trade Liaison Office, a quasi-governmental agency. The "friendly firms" mentioned above handle chiefly small-scale items, whereas the L-T arrangement was concluded for the purpose of financing exports of plants, equipment, and vessels from Japan to Communist China.

The difficulty of maintaining the "separation of economics from politics," however, is illustrated by events of the "Yoshida letter" controversy. The letter was delivered in May 1964 by former Prime Minister Shigeru Yoshida to the Nationalist government in Taiwan in response to its protest over the financing provided by Japan's Export–Import Bank to Communist China when the latter purchased a vinylon plant from the Kurashiki Rayon Company. Apparently the Yoshida letter, which was never published, conveyed the assurance that Export–Import Bank financing—which was construed by Taiwan as constituting "economic aid" to Communist China—would thereafter be withheld in any subsequent trade between the mainland and Japan. Subsequently, an L-T contract for the sale of a freighter was signed between Communist China and the Hitachi Shipbuilding and Engineering Company. The terms of the contract specified merely the amount and timing of the payments and made no reference to whether or not Export–Import Bank financing would be used. Later, the Japanese government, reversing the precedent of the Kurashiki Rayon case, refused to authorize use of the bank's facilities on the ground that participation by a government institution would not be compatible with the "separation of economics from politics." Peking, however, took the view that Japan's policy was the result of intervention by Taiwan: this constituted an "intolerable interference" by Taiwan in Sino-Japanese affairs. Moreover, by "accepting" this interference, Japan was specifically accused of mixing economics with politics. Peking demanded that the Sato government repudiate Taiwan's intervention by authorizing the use of Export–Import Bank funds to finance the Hitachi contract. In typical fashion, the Japanese government never rejected Peking's demand; it simply never accepted it. Peking then annulled the contract as of March 31, 1965.

The cancellation of the Hitachi freighter contract caused a furor in Japan because due to the expected inception of the third Chinese Five-Year Plan in 1966 it was regarded as a test case for a major series of contracts for exports of plant and equipment from Japan to Communist China. If trade were to be interrupted at the outset of the plan, the adverse effect on Chinese demand for Japanese products would be of a long-term nature. The likelihood of such an adverse effect was increased by the growing competition among countries of Western Europe to seize the opportunity afforded by the collapse of Communist China's trade with the USSR, especially with regard to its need for capital goods.

In contrast with Communist China, the USSR has normal diplomatic relations with Japan, and a treaty of commerce and navigation signed between the two nations in 1957 provides a legal basis for their trade. For several reasons, prospects for expansion of Japan's exports to the USSR seem better than those for exports to Communist China. Among these are the thaw in relations between the USSR and the West,[50] the increased emphasis upon consumer welfare in the USSR, and Japan's proximity to Siberia, in which large-scale development activities are anticipated.

As in the case of trade with Communist China, however, an important bottleneck in exports to the USSR is the ability and willingness of Japan to provide long-term credit. In competing with Japan, countries of Western Europe have progressively softened the terms of their sales to the Communist countries. Another obstacle is the necessity of maintaining trade with each Communist country in a state of bilateral balance. These constraints, despite the principle of "separation of economics from politics," tend to enhance the role of government and thus of politics in the negotiations. In itself, no doubt, this role is not uncongenial to the Japanese government, whose propensity to

[50] To avoid incurring the possible retaliation of the United States, leading Japanese trading firms have in the past conducted their trade with the USSR through "dummy" firms. The dummies of Marubeni-Iida, Mitsui & Co., and Mitsubishi Shoji Kaisha have been Nihon Kai Boeki, Toho Bussan, and Meiwa Sangyo, respectively. *The Mainichi Daily News*, May 16, 1964, p. 4.

intervene even in commerce with non-Communist countries is well established.

---

13 · LIBERALIZATION AND ITS COUNTERMEASURES, A

In industrial circles the advent of liberalization was regarded with dread—descending on Japan from the West it was likened to a second coming of the "Black Ships." Trading companies were also apprehensive; the system of controls had provided them with the lion's share of the import quotas and they had been able to sell at a comfortable profit everything they were allowed to bring in. Of course, some benefit might have been seen by consumers, had they been consulted. Ultimately, however, the decisive lead came from the government. At that level, it was realized that liberalization would further expose Japan to external sources of business fluctuation and would complicate the problems of planning and economic control. However, it would quicken the progress of Japanese industry in its approach towards world standards. Liberalization was also the price of Japan's admission into the company of the "advanced industrial nations," which it dearly sought not only to enhance its position in the West but in Asia as well. Moreover, the prospective increase in Japan's dependence on exports, especially in the strategic modern sector where its task was to transform excess capacity into an eventual export surplus, required fresh efforts to breach import barriers abroad; in this respect, Japan's own liberalization would fortify its economic diplomacy. Principally for these reasons, in a typically realistic calculation, the Japanese government affirmed its economic leadership in the introduction of the liberalization program.

By April 1964, when the degree of so-called commodity import liberalization had formally attained a level of 93 percent, it seemed that the transition had been accomplished in a remarkably steady manner. Partly, this result was real, and partly it was only apparent. An important factor was the high rate of growth in the economy at large, which made it possible to assimilate a sharply rising level of imports. Imports were also sustained by the world market for Japanese exports, which had been relatively favorable during the flood tide of transition and which kept the merchandise balance from deteriorating as much as it might. The initial amount of dislocation was further reduced because the first import categories to be liberalized were those in which Japan's competitive power was greatest. At the same time, vulnerable industries undertook massive rationalization and technological investment programs, and were encouraged by the government to merge into large units capable of defending domestic markets by financial and institutional as well as technical means. This brings us to the fact that liberalization was not all that it purported to be, for countermeasures in the form of institutional and procedural restrictions were devised in depth. In particular, in the capital, as contrasted with the commodity, sector, measures introduced in the name of liberalization were construed by some observers as subjecting Japan's foreign commerce to more control than ever before.

However formally expressed, however apparently smooth, and by whatever means achieved—matters which are discussed below—it should also be noted that Japan's liberalization program in 1965 fell under a double shadow. In domestic affairs, the unsound basis of much industrial expansion began to drive large as well as small firms, and leading securities houses as well, towards the brink of bankruptcy. Externally, while Japan's door was opening, a wave of restrictionist policies issued forth from other countries. Among some of Japan's principal trade partners, such as the United States and the United Kingdom, these policies reflected structural balance of payments problems which were not likely to be solved soon. Simultaneously, in the world at large, there were queasy symptoms of a cyclical depression.[1] After a remarkable run of good luck in the timing of external and internal economic events since World War II, at this most critical juncture the coincidence was heavily adverse to Japan.

THE FOREIGN EXCHANGE CONTROL SYSTEM

The history of Japanese foreign exchange control begins with the passage in 1932 of the Law for the Prevention of Capital Flight. This was inadequate (for example, it failed to prevent capital flight through nonrepatriation of export proceeds) and it was superseded in the following year by the Foreign Exchange Control Law. A licensing system was added to the latter in 1937, and in 1941, at the outbreak of the Pacific War, the control system was expanded to include all foreign assets.

After the war, until November 1949, all external transactions were conducted under the supervision of the Occupation authorities. However, in March 1949, through the Foreign Exchange Control Board, authority over the foreign exchange control system was returned to the Japanese government. (The functions of this board were transferred to the Ministry of Finance in July 1952). In April 1949 the system of multiple exchange rates was abandoned and the external value of the yen was established at ¥360 equal to one United States dollar. In December 1949, with the advice of the International Monetary Fund, the Foreign Exchange and Foreign Trade Control Law (Law No. 228) became the basic law for exchange control; and in May 1950 the Law Concerning Foreign Investment (Law No. 163) became the basic law concerning long-term capital imports.[2] The purpose of these laws was to concen-

[1] As observed by the London *Economist*, "The international economic conjuncture is more worrying now than at any time since the end of the war. There is a definite danger of relapse into world illiberalism. It is conceivable that there could be a relapse into world recession. And too many of the government and central financial authorities of the world are looking fixedly in the opposite direction." March 13, 1965, p. 1,111.

[2] For further details see the publication of the Foreign Exchange Control Department, The Bank of Japan, *Outline of Japanese Exchange Control*, April 1962.

trate the nation's entire foreign exchange resources and the control of their movement in the hands of the government. Any individual acquiring a foreign claim could be forced to repatriate it and sell the foreign exchange proceeds to the government at an official price; no external liabilities could be created without the government's consent. Fundamentally, foreign exchange was allocated through the government's foreign exchange control budget; secondarily, it was allocated through the licensing system administered by the foreign exchange banks.

The foreign exchange budget was introduced in accordance with the provisions of the Foreign Exchange and Foreign Trade Control Law. It was formulated with reference to the long-term economic plan, first on a quarterly and then, after two years, on a semiannual basis. The budget was prepared in two sections—commodities (compiled by MITI) and invisibles including current and capital transactions (compiled by the Ministry of Finance). The commodity budget included three categories into which all imports requiring the use of foreign exchange were classified. The first category included Automatic Approval (AA) items for which, acting as agents for the government, foreign exchange banks would issue licenses automatically up to the uncommitted balance of foreign exchange made available by the government in this budget category. The import license provided permission for payment as well as for customs clearance of the goods. Second was the Fund Allocation (FA) category, including items for which importers were required first to obtain an allocation certificate from MITI, which then was presented to the foreign exchange bank in order to obtain the import license. The category included most foodstuffs, some raw materials, and other essential goods. As contrasted with the AA category, for which a fund of foreign exchange was budgeted for the category as a whole, individual commodities were budgeted within the FA category.[3] Importers could apply for allocation cer-

3 For an interesting discussion of the problem of the lag between the allocation and the actual use of foreign exchange funds in the budget-

tificates in this category only after MITI had issued notices specifying the particular items for which exchange would be made available. Originally, the government designated the countries of origin from which imports of FA items would be permitted. Also, a high degree of discrimination was practiced by MITI in the selection of applicants to whom allocation certificates were granted. Third was the Automatic Fund Allocation (AFA) category, which combined features of the first two. This category was designed to include items for which it was difficult to estimate import demand. Mainly it provided for imports of machinery and consumer goods. As in the AA category, there were no individual commodity quotas. However, it was necessary to obtain a MITI fund allocation certificate before receiving the import license from the foreign exchange bank; and MITI reserved the right to terminate issuance of these certificates at short notice. The process of commodity import liberalization consisted of transferring commodities from the FA to the AFA and AA categories.

Export commodity control was likewise established in accordance with the provisions of the Foreign Exchange and Foreign Trade Control Law. Although exports were subject to a minimum of restrictions, prior validation for exports was required, standard methods of collection for exports were prescribed, and the process of the repatriation of export proceeds was supervised.[4]

The invisibles section of the foreign exchange budget included both current and capital transactions. One of its chief objectives, apart from the effective allocation of foreign exchange, was the prevention of flight of capital. Auxiliary to the foreign exchange control budget, as mentioned above, imports of long-term foreign capital were subject to the Law Concerning Foreign Investment. Specifically, the scope of the latter included technological

---

ing process, see United Nations, *Problems and Techniques of Foreign Exchange Budgeting*, E/CN.11/DPWP.8/L.5, 20 Aug. 1963.

[4] Exports in fulfillment of contracts having a value of $100 or less were permitted without export validation, as of April 1, 1965.

contracts, loans with a maturity of one year or more, and purchases of corporate debentures or stocks by nonresident foreigners who desired the privilege of repatriating their investment or its earnings in foreign currency. Matters concerning the Foreign Investment Law are discussed further below.

Although gradual steps toward liberalization of current account transactions were taken by Japan during 1960-63, their aggregate sum was not sufficient to satisfy IMF authorities. In November 1963 Japan was advised by the IMF that it could no longer justify on grounds of defending the balance of payments the maintenance of foreign exchange controls on current transactions. There were, of course, social and economic reasons apart from the balance of payments which from Japan's point of view justified retention of controls. Among these were the protection of infant industries, protection of noncompetitive industries, and prevention of social distress in vulnerable geographical areas.[5] Psychologically, on the other hand, Japan was sensitive to the charge of being "economically backward" and to being classified among those conspicuously immature nations listed as exchange control countries. In any event, at the persistent urging of the IMF, as well as of the United States, effective April 1, 1964, Japan relinquished the protection of IMF Article 14 and accepted the obligations of IMF Article 8, which required that she remove all restrictions on payments for current transactions and on the convertibility of yen held by nonresidents. Earlier, on February 21, 1963, Japan had communicated to the GATT its accession to GATT Article XI and its relinquishment of the protection of GATT Article XII which permits quantitative restrictions on trade to be imposed to forestall any threat to its monetary reserves by a country in balance of payments difficulties.[6]

[5] If Japan wished to apply balance of payments controls for such reasons, it would be obliged by the terms of GATT Article XV to submit the facts to the IMF and to accept its determination as to whether the action would be acceptable.

[6] Under IMF Article 8, it is restrictions on *payments* for current trans-

Japan's credentials as a "member of the club" of advanced nations were improved further on April 28, 1964 when Japan was admitted as a full member of OECD. It thereby expressed its adherence to OECD requirements for the liberalization of capital movements and of current invisible operations.[7]

Prior to Japan's entry into OECD, two fundamental laws —the Foreign Exchange and Foreign Trade Control Law and the Law Concerning Foreign Investment—were the

---

actions which are prohibited. Theoretically, a country could avoid this prohibition by simply suppressing contracts or *transactions*, in which event there would be no occasion for payments. However, the provisions of this article must be read in conjunction with the provisions of GATT Article XI, which prohibits restrictions on *transactions*. Jointly, these articles leave no room for restriction of either transactions or payments on current account.

[7] See OECD, *Code of Liberalisation of Capital Movements*, May 1962, and the texts of amendments dated Oct. 1962 and May 1963. See also, OECD, *Code of Liberalisation of Current Invisible Operations*, Dec. 1964. Upon assuming the obligations of membership, however, Japan lodged reservations with regard to 17 items of the codes. Reservations in the category of current invisible operations concerned the following: technical assistance; authors' royalties, patents, etc.; reinsurance and retrocession; insurance business abroad; printed films; profits; dividends; tourism; and immigrants' remittances. In the category of capital movements, reservations concerned the following: liquidation of direct investment; personal capital of foreign nationals changing their country of residence; gifts between relatives; use of blocked funds; purchase by residents of foreign Member States of domestic securities on domestic markets; sale by residents of foreign Member States of domestic securities on domestic markets; commercial credits (less than one year); commercial credits (one to five years). These reservations are reported in the *Memorandum of Understanding Between the Organisation for Economic Co-Operation and Development and the Government of Japan Concerning the Assumption by the Government of Japan of the Obligations of Membership of the Organisation*, July 26, 1963. Incidentally, concerning some items with regard to which no reservations were expressed by Japan, the ambiguity of the Codes suggests that implicit reservations may be construed. For example, in Annex A, List 1 of the *Code of Liberalisation of Capital Movements* it is remarked that inward and outward movements of capital for long-term direct investment shall be authorized by members "unless, in view of exceptional circumstances, the Member concerned considers the transaction in question detrimental to its interest." These "exceptional circumstances," however, have never been defined.

basis of Japan's foreign exchange control system. Together
they defined the scope of foreign transactions by means of
"prohibiting all, but granting specified exceptions."
Liberalization, it might be thought, would approach the
matter from the opposite direction, "granting all, but re-
serving specified exceptions." However, in assuming its new
obligations, Japan rescinded neither the two basic laws nor
their auxiliary Cabinet Orders and Ministerial Ordi-
nances, such as the Foreign Exchange Control Order, the
Import Trade Control Order, or the Ministerial Ordinance
Concerning Control of Invisible Trade Transactions. Instead, the foreign exchange allocation procedure, which
had been implemented through the foreign exchange
budget, was abolished by appropriate amendments to the
basic laws, while the structure of the control system itself
remained latent and intact. For example, the following
here-italicized words in Article 52 of the Foreign Exchange
and Foreign Trade Control Law, which formerly said, "*In
order to effect the most economic and beneficial import of
goods within the scope of the foreign exchange budget* any
person desiring to effect import may be required to obtain
approval therefor as provided for by Cabinet Order,"
were changed to read, "*In order to effect a sound development of foreign trade and the nation's economy. . . .*"
Thus the legal framework was retained which would make
it possible either to enforce import control by means other
than exchange control or to restore exchange control as
such with a minimum of inconvenience.

Moreover, although the purpose of liberalization was to
terminate quantitative restrictions in commerce, by a singularly inopportune stroke the successor to the foreign exchange control budget, which became effective on April 1,
1964, was designated as the "Import Quota System." This
designation resulted from reasoning which began with the
premise that Japan's obligations under IMF Article 8 required that Japan remove all restrictions on "payments"
for current international transactions. The foreign exchange budget had been criticized as a system for the re-

striction of payments. Hence, it was argued, "the import quota system, which is based upon quantity, is a system of import restriction in the pure sense of the word and does not come under the category of payment restriction . . . as provided for in Article 8 of the IMF Agreement."[8]

In its external features, the import quota system was quite similar to the foreign exchange control budget system.[9] On the export side, restrictions were relatively few. However, "The Minister of International Trade and Industry may deny or attach conditions to the grant of license [for export] if he deems it necessary for the maintenance of balance of international payment and sound development of international trade or national economy." Exports sold in accordance with the "standard method of settlement"[10] could be certified by any foreign exchange bank, but exports with nonstandard methods of settlement, exports of plants, rolling stock or ships under deferred or installment payment terms, exports without exchange, exports of specified goods in short domestic supply, exports subject to import limitations abroad (such as cotton textiles), COCOM embargo items and other special types of exports required the approval of MITI in addition to bank certification. With

[8] Trade Bulletin Corporation, *The April 1964 Supplement to Foreign Investment, Foreign Exchange Control and Import Control System*, Book Two, Social and Economic Laws of Japan, Volume XXVI, April 1964, pp. 46-47.

[9] For a detailed account see "Explanation Paper to the International Monetary Fund," The Ministry of International Trade and Industry, April 1965; or *Manual of Foreign Exchange and Foreign Trade System in Japan*, Foreign Department, The Bank of Japan, May 1964.

[10] "Standard method of settlement" for exports means that the payment is received in terms of designated currencies: " (a) under irrevocable letters of credit issued or confirmed by prime banks with drafts to be drawn at sight or with usuance within 5 months after sight or 6 months after shipment, (b) in the form of advance payment within one year prior to certification, or (c) through bills with documents against payment or documents against acceptance (i.e., bills without letters of credit) to be settled within 5 months after sight or 6 months after shipment, if the export is destined to areas other than the United States and South East Asia." The Bank of Japan, Foreign Department, *Manual of Foreign Exchange and Foreign Trade System in Japan*, May 1964, p. 9.

the exception of authorized banks, designated trading companies, insurance companies and travel and transportation agencies, recipients of foreign exchange were obliged to promptly exchange it for yen.

Commodity imports under the import quota system were classified into the same four groups as under the former foreign exchange control budget system, namely imports requiring payment in foreign exchange,[11] imports without foreign exchange,[12] license-free imports,[13] and government imports.[14] Imports requiring payment in foreign exchange were likewise differentiated according to the previous system. The first category was designated, as before, the Automatic Approval (AA) category, and as before included items for which import licenses were granted automatically by the foreign exchange banks. Second was the Automatic Import Quota (AIQ) category, corresponding to the former AFA category, including items for which import licenses were granted automatically; for goods in this category, however, it was necessary to obtain an import quota certificate from MITI before applying to the foreign exchange bank for the import license. Imports within these first two categories were regarded as liberalized.[15] A question might

[11] See Article 4 of Cabinet Order Concerning Control of Import Trade (Cabinet Order No. 414, Dec. 29, 1949), as amended.

[12] These included gratuitous imports, imports paid for in domestic yen, and imports in kind, such as investment goods supplied by foreign companies as a contribution to their joint ventures in Japan. Imports in this category required a license from MITI. See Article 8 of Cabinet Order Concerning Control of Import Trade (Cabinet Order No. 414, Dec. 29, 1949), as amended.

[13] These included relief goods supplied without compensation, commercial samples supplied without compensation having less than a specified value, noncommercial quantities of personal supplies of specified commodities, and the like. See Article 14 of Cabinet Order Concerning Control of Import Trade (Cabinet Order No. 414, Dec. 29, 1949), as amended.

[14] See Article 20 of Cabinet Order Concerning Control of Import Trade (Cabinet Order No. 414, Dec. 29, 1949), as amended.

[15] An OECD trade mission to Tokyo in 1963 decided that the procedures by which AA and AFA imports were governed at that time corresponded to what within the Organization was usually described as "automatic licensing." According to OECD criteria, therefore, the

be raised concerning the need for two categories of liberalized imports rather than one. Indeed, in their licensing aspect, OECD authorities would like to see both categories abolished. As explained by MITI, licensing provisions were retained in the liberalized categories of the import quota system purely for statistical purposes rather than control. The licenses provide a much earlier signal of import activity than that afforded by customs declarations, and in a country so highly balance of payments conscious as Japan this is a matter of importance. Similarly, the distinction between the AA and AIQ categories was retained for the purpose of separately identifying relatively sensitive items which have been recently liberalized. Moreover, in order to make the liberalization program less unpalatable to the Japanese business community, it was expedient to distinguish AA from AIQ commodities so that the government could promise to watch AIQ items carefully and to take quick action in case of excessive imports.

Unliberalized commodities were included in the Import Quota (IQ) category, corresponding to the former FA category. For this class of imports, it is necessary first to obtain an import quota certificate from MITI, which is then presented with the application for import approval at an authorized foreign exchange bank. The quota commodities and the limit-amounts of individual commodity imports are determined on a semiannual basis by the Import Policy Section of MITI's Bureau of International Trade. In principle, the quotas are established on a quantitative basis except when this is "difficult or inappropriate" (as for sundry goods), in which case they are expressed in terms of value. When determining import quotas within the IQ and AIQ categories, the Import Policy Section is required to consult with the various production branches of MITI in order to take account of their overall estimates of supply and de-

former AA and AFA categories, and their successor AA and AIQ categories respectively, may be described as liberalized. See OECD Council Memorandum, "Japan-OECD Mission's Discussions on Trade Matters in Tokyo," CES/63.43, Paris, July 4, 1963.

mand for individual commodities. In coordinating the quotas with these estimates, consideration is given to the protection of infant industries, the degree of international competitiveness of established industries, levels of prices, investment and inventories, and potentially disruptive regional effects of imports.[16] The Import Policy Section also may—and ordinarily does—consult with private business firms whose interests are affected by the quotas it establishes. The actual size of import quotas, however, is not revealed; after a particular quota limit has been reached, MITI simply issues no more quota certificates. (Thus quota amounts can be estimated ex post by import statistics compiled with reference to elapsed quota periods.) The only publicly available information concerning import quotas is the list of commodities included in the IQ and AIQ categories, respectively.[17]

[16] An interesting example concerns the production of leather from hides, which traditionally has been included among the "unclean" occupations practiced only by the underprivileged *eta* or *buraku* class. Members of this class live in distinctly segregated areas of Japan and their occupational as well as geographical mobility is very low. Hence unrestricted imports of leather would cause acute hardship among these people, without the possibility of any early relief.

[17] See *Yunyū Kohyō Kainkei List* [Publicized List of Import Items], published semiannually by *Tsushō Sangyō Chōsakai* [Research Association of Trade and Industry], a quasi-official agency of MITI. In the April 1965 edition, 162 items at the four-digit level of the Brussels Tariff Nomenclature were specified within the IQ category. Thirty-nine of these were commodities exempted by GATT from the scope of Japan's liberalization program, such as (1) gold and silver, (2) commodities whose import is restricted in the interests of national defense, public morals or sanitation, (3) government imports, such as alcohol, salt, tobacco, rice, wheat, and certain machinery. About two-thirds of the IQ commodities are products of agriculture, forestry, fishing, or mining. Advanced types of large machinery are also importantly represented. The country of origin, as well as the quantity of IQ imports, is determined by the government. Incidentally, since import quotas are designed to satisfy only "basic needs," holders of quota certificates are assured of a satisfactory profit. However, quotas are often assigned on a rather arbitrary basis. Nevertheless, in order to forestall additional price increases, the government—officially—does not allow quota certificates to be transferred by one individual to another, inasmuch as the certificates would be exchanged at a premium which would then be incorporated in the price of the commodity.

An explicit countermeasure to liberalization of foreign exchange control exists in the form of the import prior deposit system. This was originally devised as an adjunct to the exchange control system at the advent of "private trading" under the auspices of the Occupation in 1949; it remained available for use as part of the control machinery which was not dismantled in 1964. The purpose of the prior deposit system is to restrain imports selectively; this is accomplished by the requirement that prior to granting an import license the foreign exchange bank must receive from the import applicant a deposit of an amount which varies inversely according to the "essentiality" of the goods. In Japan's chronically "tight money" circumstances, the device is particularly effective. During March 1964 to April 1965, for example, the schedule of required deposits in relation to the value of licensed imports was as follows:

35 percent: consumer and capital goods
5 percent: raw materials
1 percent: a very small number of items, including special raw materials for the manufacture of export goods and goods for the promotion of small enterprises

As an "antidepression" measure, on April 1, 1965 the government suspended the 35 percent requirement; the ratio for capital and consumer goods was reduced to five percent and that for specified "other" goods was set at 1 percent. In each case, the deposit is returned after 80 percent of the goods have been imported or if the import transaction has been canceled for a reason acceptable to the control authorities. In conversations with OECD officials who had criticized the prior deposit requirement as being inconsistent with the liberalization program, representatives of the Ministry of Finance argued that the system was merely a means of combatting inflationary tendencies in Japan. Representatives of MITI, on the other hand, argued that the system was a means of combatting "excessive competition." As compared with other forms of import re-

striction, such as tariff surcharges, the prior deposit system
has the merit of not immediately provoking increases in
the domestic prices of imported goods. It can also be used
as a countermeasure against what may be regarded by the
government as undesirable speculation in inventories of
imported goods. Similarly, the option of raising import
prior deposit rates provides the government with an additional tool for use in the event of balance of payments
difficulties. Apart from its merits in such situations, the
system has a constant adverse bias in its impact on small
and medium-sized firms as contrasted with large firms,
for the former characteristically operate with limited
financial means. To this extent it tends to implement MITI's
policy of inducing small firms to merge into larger units
and thus to combat "excessive competition." In offsetting
the effects of liberalization, moreover, the import deposit
system is of much potential significance since high prior
deposit rates can be assessed against AA as well as against
AIQ or IQ commodities.

---

14 · LIBERALIZATION AND ITS COUNTERMEASURES, B

COMMODITY IMPORT LIBERALIZATION

As indicated above, commodities in the AA and AIQ categories are considered to be liberalized. Following the OECD
definition, however, the *degree* of liberalization is calculated
in terms of a ratio whose numerator and denominator both
refer to commodities actually imported into Japan during a base period, namely calendar year 1959. The liberalization ratio is

$$\frac{B}{A - C} \times 100$$

in which, on a customs clearance basis, A is the value of
total imports during 1959, B is the value of imports in

1959 of commodities which at the current date under consideration are "liberalized," and C is the value of government imports during 1959. For example, if in the year 1959 raw materials constituted 49 percent of total private Japanese imports and if by 1964 raw materials had been entirely absorbed within the AA and AIQ categories, then 49 percent of Japanese imports would have been classified as liberalized in 1964 (despite the fact that in 1964 raw materials constituted only 39 percent of total Japanese imports).

Clearly, therefore, changes in the composition of imports between 1959 and the period currently under review have an important bearing on the size of the liberalization ratio. To take extreme examples, if a commodity had been entirely excluded from the import list in 1959 (or absent because of having been innovated after that time) the degree of liberalization could reach 100 even though the formerly excluded product remains excluded. On the other hand, if a commodity which had not been imported at all during 1959 were to be liberalized in a subsequent year, regardless of the size of imports of that commodity in the subsequent year it would contribute nothing to the degree of liberalization as calculated at that time.

In addition to its conceptual limitations, a further difficulty concerning the liberalization ratio is the fact that the Japanese government declines to release some information, without which it is impossible for an outsider to recalculate the ratio. In the numerator, B, the value of imports in 1959 of commodities which at the current date are included in the AA or AIQ categories, is classified as confidential information. In the denominator, the value of C, government imports during 1959, is likewise confidential.[1] These are only two of various matters concerning the liberalization program which are so classified. As already mentioned, the size of import quotas for unliberalized commodities is not revealed. The relation of imports to output of unliberalized commodities is likewise not

---

[1] I estimate this figure as $300 million.

published, although this could be estimated from available statistics. As officially calculated, however, on a customs clearance basis, the progress of commodity import liberalization has been as follows:[2]

Date	Liberalization Ratio (percent)
April 1956	22
April 1957	31
April 1958	33
April 1959	34
April 1960	41
April 1961	62
July 1961	65
October 1961	68
December 1961	70
April 1962	73
October 1962	88
April 1963	89
September 1963	92
April 1964	93
July 1965	93

No corresponding ratio is available concerning the degree to which ingredients of the balance of payments other than import commodities have been liberalized.

As indicated in the table, the degree of import liberalization reached a plateau in 1964 beyond which further progress will be difficult. The ratio of 93 percent attained at that time, moreover, is more favorable than the result which would be found by an alternative method of calculation. The latter would take account only of the value of imports of liberalized commodities in relation to total imports during any given year. Although this calculation has been performed by the Japanese government, the

[2] For an alternative calculation on a foreign exchange budget basis, see Nobuyuki Ikeda, ed., *Bōeki Jiyūka Ron* [A Treatise on Japanese Foreign Trade Liberalization], published by *Hōritsu Bunka-sha* [Law and Culture Publishing Company], 1961.

result has also been withheld as confidential. By my own estimate, the figure was 85 percent during 1964. It should be emphasized that as the composition of trade changes in time, the degree of liberalization in terms of this more realistic concept may actually deteriorate even though the "93 percent level" may remain constant.

Future progress in increasing the degree of liberalization will depend less, however, on formal increases in ratios as evaluated above than on the institutional and procedural means by which imports are administered. Prior to liberalization, the comparatively low ratio of imports to national income was of course partly attributable to the restrictive effect of the exchange control system. This was not fully appreciated by some who argued that from a balance of payments point of view there was not too much to worry about in introducing import liberalization, inasmuch as the ratio of imports to national income was lower in Japan than in many other countries.[3] The rather steady manner in which imports have increased following liberalization may be misundertood for a similar reason. Imports have certainly increased considerably since the advent of the liberalization program, partly because of increased production, partly because of increased consumption, and partly because of changes in the structure of industry. The actual amount of the increase, however, has been less than might have been anticipated. And the difference may be explained largely by the implementation of institutional and administrative countermeasures, concerning which further discussion follows.

TRADING COMPANIES

Among the factors that condition the impact of liberalization is Japan's "unique institution," the trading company [sōgō shōsha]. In contrast to the days of the foreign

[3] In addition to jeopardizing the commodity balance, liberalization also has a tendency to increase the level of invisible payments associated with commodity imports and the level of debt service on account of increases in capital inflow.

exchange budget when allocations for most of Japan's major imports were closely held by a few of these companies, it might be expected that liberalization would widen the distribution of import licenses. The ensuing increase in competition would constitute a separately identifiable source of expansion in the volume of imports. Instead, however, based on the leverage of their established position, the hegemony of the leading trading companies has increased rather than decreased during recent years. For the fiscal year ending in March 1965, 40 firms handled 81 percent of Japan's total imports, an increase of four percent over the preceding year.[4] Four giant firms alone account for more than one-third of Japan's total imports, and the rate of increase in their transactions exceeds the rate of increase in Japanese imports at large.[5] Each tends to serve primarily members of its own "group" and to avoid importing commodities that would compete "excessively" with the products of that group; however, group lines are not observed as rigidly as they were in the prewar period. Recently, in the name of "orderly importing," the major trading firms have also organized new means of cooperating with each other.[6]

As already mentioned, the giant trading firms are far more than specialists in particular commodities or even

[4] *Nihon Keizai Shimbun*, International Weekly Edition, April 13, 1965, p. 13.

[5] These include Mitsubishi Shoji Kaisha, Mitsui and Company, Marubeni-Iida Company, and C. Itoh and Company. During 1961-63, while the increase in total Japanese imports was 44 percent, imports transacted by the big four increased 55 percent. In terms of the value of their total annual transactions of all kinds, these are the largest firms in Japan, each being a member of the "trillion yen club."

[6] "Parallel with a trend among Japanese industrial corporations to refrain from engaging in excessive competition both in production, sales and equipment investments, moves are now afoot among major trading houses to establish a cooperative import system for some of the important international commodities." For example, "The soybean importers have . . . agreed to divide domestic customers among themselves and refrain from making sales to other customers than to those they are assigned." *Nihon Keizai Shimbun*, International Weekly Edition, March 2, 1965, p. 12.

foreign trade in general; their "integrated" activities include production, distribution, and finance on both the domestic and the international levels. They also possess powerful government contacts which prior to liberalization enabled them to engross the imports of strategic bulk commodities such as raw materials and fuels. As liberalization progressed, their preeminence was sustained by their key role in the economic complexes which buy and consume these commodities. To some extent, of course, Japan's growth provided import opportunities for new trading companies, but chiefly these were confined to shipments of finished and specialty goods in small lots, such as cosmetics or prepared food. It is a conspicuous feature of the institutional aspect of Japanese importing that even small shipments are usually arranged through trading companies rather than by consumers on their own account. Large shipments, on the other hand, are almost invariably transacted through trading companies, whose position is thoroughly entrenched for the following reasons.

One of the principal means by which major trading firms have maintained and increased their control of imports is the restriction of access to channels of domestic distribution. The distribution system for producer goods and for bulky commodities is tightly controlled; it is also difficult for new trading companies to obtain import commissions from large individual domestic buyers, regardless of commodity. One reason for the strength of the major trading firms in these situations is the fact that at the initial stage of processing the number of buyers of bulk commodities in most industries is small. For example, there are few steel mills and few large processors of raw cotton, and their allegiance to established trading firms is based on relations of long standing. Often, as in the import of iron and steel materials, imports are arranged jointly by a group of large mills; in this event, the channels of distribution are available only to established major trading companies.[7] Even

[7] About 80 percent of the raw materials used in the iron and steel industry is imported by the four leading trading firms.

when there are many buyers of imports of a particular commodity, the principal members of such a group will be found to have close connections with one or another of the major trading firms.

Second, it is common for trading companies to own shares in the industrial consumers of bulk commodities; on the other hand, the reverse may be true, or they may own shares in each other. In any case, it is usually difficult for an outsider to determine which of several firms is the parent company, for in Japan control is not necessarily associated with a majority stock ownership position. Third, the trading firm and the domestic buyer may be linked through their common relations with a particular bank. Marubeni-Iida, for example, has a special relation with the Fuji Bank, which acts as an intermediary in making contacts between Marubeni and the bank's other customers. Frequently, the special relation between a trading company and a particular bank is used by the former to obtain loans for its own customer; indeed, this is often an indispensable prerequisite for trading company sales. In such cases, the trading company usually guarantees the loans of its customer. It is very difficult for a newcomer either to make such arrangements or to offer such guarantees. Moreover, the giant trading firms—in which the funds of the leading banks are heavily committed— have access to credit on distinctly more favorable terms than would be available to any newcomer. The newcomer is an outsider, and leading banks are known to protect the trading firms with which they collaborate by refusing loans to them or to other rivals who need help in financing competitive imports.

Another link arises from the fact that the major trading firms act not only as suppliers of raw materials to their clients but also as suppliers of plant and equipment and as agents for both the domestic and foreign sale of the commodities they produce. Thus ties are formed at many levels and in many different contexts. The giant trading firms, furthermore, have both a tradition of responsibility and the resources with which to act responsibly. In the event defective goods are received, a buyer is much more likely to have satisfactory recourse to an established trading firm than to a newcomer.

For reasons such as these, newcomers may not avail themselves of their present legal opportunity to import bulk commodities. Formally, anyone is free to bring in soybeans, milo, corn, or barley. If he were to do so, however, it would be difficult for him to find a buyer. Sometimes small or insecure buyers will deal with a small trading company, but the sale is likely to depend on the ability of the trading company to provide credit as well as goods. Transactions with small buyers are usually highly speculative, and where bulk cargoes are concerned the amounts of money involved are so large that loss in only a few such transactions may permanently cripple a new trading company.

Besides the restriction of domestic channels of distribution and finance, the newcomer would find that in bulk commodities (which constitute three quarters of Japan's total imports) the number of major foreign sources of supply may likewise be small or that desirable foreign suppliers already have long-term sole agency contracts with the leading Japanese trading firms.[8] Established giant trading firms sometimes obtain such exclusive contracts after providing investment or development funds to their foreign suppliers, particularly in the case of mining. This is known as "tying the supplier with money." On the other hand, from the foreign supplier's point of view, even if he wished to take advantage of the fact that quantitative restrictions had been removed from the import of his commodity into Japan, he might find that he is still restricted by the bottleneck of the exclusive agency contract he has signed with the distributor in Japan. Imports of manufactured goods are especially subject to this form of restriction, for if the distributor in Japan is not an aggressive salesman, the foreign supplier cannot bypass him by

[8] In the case of iron ore, for example, in 1965 there were only fifteen major individual suppliers to Japan, located in ten different countries.

appointing other agents. Furthermore, the Japanese government itself is in some instances a bottleneck between foreign suppliers and domestic consumers. All imports of rice and wheat, for example, are subject to allocation by the Food Agency of the Ministry of Agriculture and Forestry. Only about 10 to 13 principal trading companies are given licenses to import these commodities. A similar situation prevails with regard to other "government imports."

Liberalization, moreover, does not automatically create expertise. Many agricultural import commodities require complicated specialist knowledge. (For example, it takes about twenty years to train a good wool buyer.) Other reasons for the entrenched position of the giant trading firms include their control over storage and shipping facilities in Japan, experience in arbitrage and futures speculation, well-established contacts and sources of economic intelligence abroad, knowledge of foreign languages and foreign business practices—none of which can be readily duplicated by newcomers.

Although the above discussion specifically concerns newcomers, many of the same or similar considerations limit the role of small firms outside the mainstream of the big business network. Typically, small independents operate in areas of marginal profitability or small turnover, or in situations requiring a lot of bothersome attention to detail which large firms consider to be not worth their trouble. Should any of these limitations be overcome, the small firms are subject to being wiped out at short notice.

TARIFFS

While liberalizing imports through the gradual termination of exchange and other controls, the Japanese government received persistent appeals from the producers of import-competing goods in Japan for an equivalent amount of added tariff protection. Imposition of tariff duties for the protection of infant industries is consistent with GATT rules and with Japan's new IMF and OECD obligations; however, the demand for protection came from declining or backward, as well as infant, industries, and from interests which simply wished to maintain their customary preeminence in the domestic market. In this conflict between private and national interests the government's attitude was ambivalent. For it was well aware that true liberalization would promote its economic program of both liquidating the backward sector and impelling the modernization of leading firms. If Japan could achieve sustained rapid growth the difficulty of reallocating resources would be minimal and the home market would not necessarily be jeopardized. The economic program, however, was not immune from political realities.

Postwar tariff reform was inaugurated in 1951 under the auspices of the Occupation. Until that time, Japan's tariff structure had been substantially unchanged since 1910, the 43rd year of Meiji, when the Customs Tariff Law based on the German system was adopted. At the prompting of the Occupation, and as a means of smoothing the way for Japan's accession to GATT, the rates of the 1951 revision were established at a low level. Since comprehensive exchange control was in effect, the revised rates were of little consequence to Japanese industry at the time. The tariff reform, however, was incomplete, for the commodity structure of the prewar system, consisting of 943 items, remained out of date. Many postwar products, such as petrochemicals, were subsumed with commodities "not elsewhere specified," thus giving indiscriminate application to the tariff rate of that category.

A second postwar tariff reform was introduced in 1961. On this occasion changes in the structure of industry were recognized. The chief purpose of the second reform, however, was to take account of the government's decision to adopt principles and a schedule of foreign trade and foreign exchange liberalization.[9] The 1961 reform included three elements. First, a new tariff classification, the Brussels Tariff Nomenclature, including 1,097 items at the four-

[9] Taken in the meeting of the Ministerial Council on June 24, 1960.

digit level, was adopted.[10] Second, a new set of tariff rates was adopted, incorporating many changes both upwards and downwards. Increases were imposed principally upon those items whose liberalization was being most persistently demanded by the West, upon competitively weak agricultural products and commodities newly emerging from Japan's heavy and chemical industries. Decreases were allowed for items that had become essential for the expansion of the new industries and for items Japan was already producing on an export basis.

The third element of the 1961 tariff reform was the introduction of methods to increase the "flexibility" of the system. The basic rates are statutory levies which can be changed only by action of the Diet. Temporary tariff reductions are subject to ministerial option, but temporary increases likewise have to be approved by the Diet. To provide means of quick administrative protection in case of need, new tariff instruments were created. One of these was the "emergency tariff system," which could be invoked when "increased imports of foreign goods injure or are liable seriously to injure" domestic industries. In this event, statutory rates may be raised by administrative action within the limits of the difference between overseas prices and wholesale prices in Japan. Similarly, GATT concession rates may be retracted or increased, although in this case negotiations must be conducted with GATT partners concerning compensation to be provided by Japan. Another innovation was the tariff quota system, which for the benefit of consumers permitted imports within a specified quota at a low or zero rate of duty, but beyond which, for the benefit of producers, higher rates become effective.[11] The tariff quota system bears some of

[10] For statistical reporting of commodities actually cleared by Japanese Customs, however, a system based on the United Nations Standard International Trade Classification (SITC) is used.

[11] As of April 1, 1965, the following 12 items were subject to tariff quotas: maize (other than for feed), molybdenum ore, lumps of nickel (unalloyed), high-speed steel, silica sand, gypsum, manganese ore, antimony ore, mercury, antimony trisulphide, camphor, and superphosphates.

the same family characteristics as the foreign currency quota system, which makes it inconsistent with the liberalization program.

TABLE 36

Changes in Japanese Import Tariffs, by Year, 1960 to 1964[a]
(number of commodities)

Date effective (Japanese fiscal year, beginning April 1 of the year specified)	Increases	Decreases
1960	2	3
1961	251	386
1962	86	31
1963	14	10
1964	20	44

[a] The commodities for which tariff changes are summarized here were identified chiefly at the four-digit level of the Brussels Tariff Nomenclature, although in some cases they reflect changes at a more refined level. Changes in 1960 are expressed in terms of the Customs Tariff Code of 1910, which was still in effect at that time. The data include both statutory and administrative tariff changes.

SOURCES: *Sangi-in Okura Iinkai Teishutsu Shiryō* [Data Submitted to the Standing Committee for Finance of the House of Councillors], March 6, 1961; *Kaisei Zeiritsu Ayobi Genkō Zeiritsu* [Table of Comparison, Revised Tariff and Current Tariff], Bureau of Customs, February 1962; *Kanzeiritsu Shingi-kai Tōshin* [Report of Customs Tariff Council], Bureau of Customs, December 1962; *Bōeki Nenkan* [Foreign Trade Year Book], Japan Tariff Association, 1964.

In 1961 and 1962 the actual implementation of liberalization proceeded at a faster pace than originally scheduled. As countermeasures, additional tariff reforms were made in those years for the assistance of industry, agriculture, and mining. A device introduced at that time was the assessment of rates by volume as distinguished from the usual method of determining duties by value. By this means, home goods may be protected by subjecting to a higher rate of duty those commodities which are imported more cheaply than usual by virtue of being shipped in bulk. Another device was the method of selective levies, by which tariffs may be imposed either in terms of value or in terms of volume, depending upon which is higher. A seasonal tariff was also introduced, which with regard to oranges, for example, permitted a high tariff for the benefit of producers during the domestic delivery season from December to May and a lower tariff for the benefit of consumers during the rest of the year. A weapon against "cheap foreign goods" was also created in the form of "antidumping duties," which authorizes the imposition of extraordinary duties equivalent to the dumping margin. An evident source of the protectionism in Japan's tariff system may be found in the method by which changes in tariff rates and procedures are inaugurated, namely through the Tariff Deliberative Council, an advisory organ to the Ministry of Finance whose recommendations are usually accepted without change. The council is composed principally of business leaders representing production, finance and trade; it also includes vice ministers of interested ministries and a few scholars.[12]

In addition to those already mentioned, another protective device is that of "voluntary contributions" which are sometimes elicited as a countermeasure to the liberalization process. Imports of copper ingots, for example, were liberalized as of April 1963; at the same time, importers of copper were prevailed upon to make "voluntary contributions" amounting to ¥27,000 per ton. The amounts received were then distributed as a subsidy to domestic Japanese copper mines.[13]

[12] In a study of selected regions, Balassa has found that ". . . the elimination of duties on manufactured goods would lead to the largest relative increases in imports in Japan (39.9 percent), followed by the United States (38.2 percent), the United Kingdom (30.9 percent), the European Common Market (28.2 percent), and Sweden (14.0 percent)." Bela Balassa, "Tariff Protection in Industrial Countries: An Evaluation," *The Journal of Political Economy*, Dec. 1965, p. 593.

[13] From April 1963 to March 1964, small and medium scale mines which lacked their own smelting facilities received ¥16,000 per ton of copper content produced by them. From April 1963 to Feb. 1964, large mines which possessed smelting facilities received ¥10,000 per ton. Thereafter, the copper subsidies were successively revised; they were terminated as of March 1965.

A similar, but not "voluntary," procedure for the assistance of the coal industry was introduced in 1962. At that time, a duty of 12 percent was levied on imports of crude and fuel oil, 10 of the 12 percent being earmarked for the benefit of users of domestic coal.[14] Similar arrangements were made for the benefit of domestic crude oil production and the petrochemical industry in Japan.

MITI also made an effort to compensate for the abolition of the export income tax deduction system, which was terminated at the end of March 1964. This took the form of rebates for tariffs paid on imported raw materials used in the production of exports. By October 1965 the rebates were to be effective for all export products.[15]

Despite the tariff reforms, as the liberalization program took root an increasing number of discrepancies in the amount of protection enjoyed by various industries was steadily revealed. Because of outside demands by both developed and developing countries for tariff cuts by Japan, however, it has become more difficult for the government to resolve these discrepancies by selective increases in the basic rates.[16] Instead, special devices such as those described above will be increasingly relied upon in the future for purposes of adjustment, as well as for retaliatory or countervailing actions.

Nevertheless, through the tariff reforms a high degree of protection has been accumulated by a number of sensitive commodities. These special cases provide a bargaining reserve for Japan's economic diplomacy, especially in the struggle to overcome discrimination against Japanese prod-

14 "The power industry gets four percent as a general coal price subsidy to cover the cost difference between coal and oil, and an additional six percent as an incentive to use more coal in excess of minimum annual industry consumption quotas." *Asahi*, Jan. 21, 1965.

15 *Nihon Keizai Shimbun*, International Weekly Edition, May 4, 1965, p. 1.

16 In 1964, one-fourth of the total amount of Japanese customs revenue was obtained from duties on sugar. One-fifth of the total was received from duties on petroleum. Ministry of Finance, *Shuyō Hinmoku betsu Kansei Shūnyū Gaku Hyō* [Table of Customs Revenue by Major Commodities], June 1965.

ucts abroad. For the government would like to make further tariff concessions contingent on the withdrawal of such discrimination. On the other hand, a form of discrimination practiced by Japan against many other countries, including some of its own principal trade partners, results from the fact that contrary to their method Japan imposes tariff duties on the CIF rather than upon the f.o.b. value of imports.[17]

"STRENGTHENING OF INDUSTRIES"

At the level of the individual producer, policies designed to strengthen the hand of Japanese firms against new foreign adversaries in both foreign and domestic markets are chiefly of three kinds: modernization, mergers, and the formation of combinats (a standard term in the Japanese heavy and chemical industries, indicating "complexes"). Their objectives lie on both the engineering and the economic levels, and as countermeasures to import liberalization they are clearly consistent with both the export promotion program and the plan to liquidate the dual economy.[18]

As sponsored by the government moreover, policies conducive to the strengthening of enterprises (*keizai kyōka*) are usually designed to enhance the government's own power of intervention as well. The propensity of government policy in this respect was clearly shown in 1963 during the death throes of the foreign exchange control budget. At that time a highly controversial bill, originally entitled "Bill for Strengthening the International Competitive Power of Designated Industries" (later renamed "The Temporary Measures Bill for the Promotion of

[17] This has the incidental effect of discouraging imports by air freight, for the higher cost of such freight increases the base upon which tariff duties are calculated.

[18] When the Japanese government declares that backward small firms must be rationalized or liquidated, it is speaking in economic terms. When it declares that they must be protected and supported, it is speaking in political terms. Similarly, the defense of small firms is invoked as a reason for resisting the incursion of "giant foreign firms," but the aggression of giant domestic firms against the small is simply accepted as a fact of life.

Designated Industries") was sponsored by MITI. Although the language of the bill referred to the promotion of rationalization through mergers and the need for achieving optimal scales of production and management, in effect its objectives were to revoke the provisions of the Anti-Monopoly Law concerning economic concentration and to create a wide, nebulous area within which MITI could intervene in the affairs of business. The degree and vagueness of the proposed government intervention led to the bill's defeat. Had the issue been contested during a less buoyant period, however, as during the recession of 1965, the outcome might well have been different. Indeed, during the latter year, when structural defects in the Japanese economy were becoming painfully evident, it seemed that inevitable further moves for the extension of government control—which in the first instance would take place as rescue activities—would prove to be irresistible.

"Strengthening of industries," while a legitimate objective as such, is at the same time a euphemism for one of the processes by which industry's leading strings are tied together and shortened, thus facilitating intervention by a government which accomplishes its purposes as much by invisible as by visible controls. MITI's policy of strengthening industries in the form of encouraging mergers and economic concentration at large has been highly successful. The number of mergers increased steadily during the 1950s, when their average annual number was 372, to a peak of 997 in 1963.[19] In 1964 there were 864 mergers. During the period 1947-64, the total number of mergers was 8,226.[20] By far the majority of these have taken place

[19] Japanese Fair Trade Commission, *Report on the Legislation on Restrictive Business Practices and Its Application in Japan*, Sept. 1964. Mergers between foreign and domestic firms are not legally possible since they are not provided for in the Commercial Code.

[20] Contrary to practice in the United States, Japanese merger statistics include only figures for situations in which one firm absorbs another by means of the latter's legal dissolution. Cases in which mergers have effectively occurred by means of stock acquisition, interlocking directorates or transfer of assets are not included in the merger statistics. Because of the nature of legal reporting requirements, these

among small and medium-sized firms; and many have occurred in the field of wholesale and retail trade.[21]

Recently, however, the statistics include an increasing number of mergers among large firms. Mergers resulting in an after-merger capital of more than one billion yen increased from nine cases during 1957 to 45 cases in 1963; in 1964 there were 44 such cases. It is ironic that whereas Zaibatsu dissolution was undertaken by the Occupation authorities in the name of economic democracy, their reconstitution is now being pursued in Japan in the name of import liberalization. In its current program the government is also involved in the apparent contradiction of advocating import liberalization as a means of sharpening the competitive power of Japanese industry while at the same time it deplores what it refers to as "excessive competition," the implication being that the government wants Japanese firms to be able to compete with foreign firms but is reluctant for them to compete with each other.

The mechanism by which Japan's enormous postwar expansion has been financed in the face of a capital shortage is in itself conducive to mergers, especially during times of recession or even during a pause in the rate of expansion. At such critical times, the prerogatives and policies of the banks become paramount. Typically, to shore up their own investments, they then salvage those of their clients on the brink of bankruptcy by forcing mergers between them and more solvent clients—the latter being in no position

---

residual categories are incompletely compiled by the Fair Trade Commission. The number of mergers accomplished by interlocking directorates alone probably exceeds the number of mergers as narrowly defined by the Commission. Nevertheless, in the opinion of the Commission, the latter serves as a satisfactory indicator.

[21] Mergers among small firms have been assisted by Article 3 of the Small and Medium Business Modernization Financial Assistance Law (Law No. 115, 1956), which provides for loans by the national government to prefectures which assist mergers of specified kinds, and also by Article 8 of the Small and Medium Business Modernization Acceleration Law (Law No. 64, 1963), which provides for tax reductions for new corporations formed as a result of such mergers.

to resist since they too operate with a high proportion of borrowed funds. In boom times, leading banks follow the complementary policy of sponsoring affiliation among their clients in order to create viable industrial empires; each of these, with a bank symbiotically at its head, may then hope to survive the aggressive expansionary drive of rival empires.[22]

Technically competent as well as incompetent firms often find themselves financially vulnerable because of the standard practice in Japan of relying heavily on borrowed funds rather than upon self-supplied capital. One of the techniques of empire-building is to lend an attractive small firm funds for expansion at an immoderately generous rate and then to foreclose its property at the first moment it stumbles in meeting its obligations. It is interesting that discipline even within the ranks of the Mitsui group —which since the Occupation has contained more "individualism" than the Mitsubishi group—has been tightened recently following financial troubles among its members.

Although duplication and overlapping of facilities is regarded by the government as a waste of national resources, this in itself does not provide a motive for mergers from the point of view of individual firms. In enterprises where capital requirements are huge, however, as in shipbuilding, petrochemicals, or the automobile industry, the risk may be too great to be sustained by a single bank or financial complex. Under these circumstances, rival forces and their backers may find it convenient to join forces.[23] This gives rise to a distinction between the prewar Zaibatsu and their present-day successors. For in

[22] In the foreign trade sector, the degree of concentration of bank control is reflected in the fact that two-thirds of total Japanese foreign trade is transacted through five banks (percent of total shown in parentheses): Bank of Tokyo (25), Fuji Bank (12), Mitsubishi Bank (11), Sanwa Bank (9), Sumitomo Bank (9). Fuji Bank, Foreign Division, Dec. 1964. These shares remain rather stable from year to year.

[23] For example, both the Industrial Bank of Japan and the Fuji Bank finance Nissan Motors.

the prewar system, consolidations occurred almost exclusively among brother enterprises, whereas now they occasionally cut across group lines.[24]

One of the chief bottlenecks to mergers, however, is the personnel problem of reassigning executives. To avoid losing their jobs, top managers often seek to form cartels as an alternative to mergers. Sometimes a large firm which seeks to "broaden its base" may wish to acquire the specialist services of a particular small firm, but not its financial or other difficulties. In this case, the small firm may become informally affiliated with the large firm as its "satellite."

According to the original principles of the Antimonopoly Law,[25] many of the recent mergers among major enterprises would have been unacceptable to the Fair Trade Commission. The law has been progressively diluted, however, and has good prospects of being further diluted in the future. Also, the criteria devised by the Fair Trade Commission in interpreting it have been conspicuously loose. Indeed, "There has been no merger on which the Commission acted to prevent the merger."[26] A summary of the rules regarding mergers hitherto applied by the Fair Trade Commission is as follows:[27]

1. In cases where mergers were permitted unconditionally, the market share was always less than 25 to 30 percent.

[24] An excellent example occurred in the affiliation in April 1964 of Mitsui Steamship Co., Ltd. and Osaka Shosen Kaisha, Ltd., which were members of the former Mitsui Zaibatsu and Sumitomo Zaibatsu, respectively. (The new company is known as Mitsui O.S.K. Lines, Ltd.)

[25] Law Relating to Prohibition of Private Monopoly and Methods of Preserving Fair Trade (Law No. 54, 1947).

[26] Statement of Kikuzo Watanabe, Chairman, Fair Trade Commission, on "Japanese Legislation and Its Application," at 7th Session, Committee of Experts on Restrictive Business Practices, Organization for Economic Cooperation and Development, Oct. 21, 1964.

[27] Trade Bulletin Corporation, *Mergers and Cartels in Japan in Legislative and Fact-Finding Aspects* (Japan Industry Series), Tokyo, 1964, pp. 15-16.

2. Even in cases where the market share was 25 to 30 percent or more, mergers were permitted unconditionally in any of the following cases:

   a. Where there are strong competitors (including foreign competitors)

   b. Where it is very easy for new entrepreneurs to advance into the field of trade concerned because of existing technological, capital, and market conditions. (Therefore a merger of smaller enterprises usually does not come into question. If such merger causes monopoly profits, big enterprises will readily obtain entry.)

   c. Where a merger cannot create market controlling power (price controlling power) for the reason that the capacity of customers is much larger than the combined capacity of the companies concerned.

   d. Where the peculiar field of trade to which the merging companies belong is declining in prosperity due to such reasons as the emergence of substitute merchandise and where such decline is considered likely to continue in the future.

   e. Where it is evident that strongly competitive merchandise will be introduced from abroad in the near future as a result of the liberalization of foreign trade. (Certain nonferrous metals may be cited as examples.)

A case of special importance illustrating the application of these rules was the reconstitution of Mitsubishi Heavy Industries, Ltd. in June 1964 by the merger of three former Mitsubishi Zaibatsu companies.[28] Although the new firm's market share considerably exceeded 30 percent in some of

[28] Mitsubishi Nippon Heavy Industries, Shin Mitsubishi Heavy Industries, and Mitsubishi Shipbuilding and Engineering (Mitsubishi Zosen). The reconstituted company became the second largest firm in Japan (excluding trading companies) in terms of total assets as of Sept. 1964.

its product lines, the Fair Trade Commission ruled that substantial restraint of competition was obviated by the fact that most of its products were produced on order rather than for inventory; therefore the merger was accepted.[29]

Overlooked by most Western observers is another important instrument—the combinat system—which has been used in the postwar period for the strengthening of Japanese industries. The combinat refers to the technical combination of a set of physically contiguous plants which look like a unit and operate like a unit but which are owned by various firms which retain their separate identities. Thus the complex is economic rather than legal. It draws on diverse or even rival sources of capital and illustrates a prime form of rationalization or economizing in the use of capital. The prewar zaibatsu combine differs from the combinat in that the combine's component companies were not necessarily assembled either technically or even geographically, and it was financed by a single parent source of capital.

As a method of organization, the combinat achieves economies of scale without commensurate investment risk on the part of its individual component firms. For example, it permits the utilization of what in technically separate plants would be waste products and it permits the common use of utilities such as electricity, water, and steam. Theoretically, it may be organized by either large or small enterprises, but its chief examples in Japan are in the petrochemical industry where capital requirements are huge and where the component firms are themselves very large. In petrochemicals, the core of each combinat is a naphtha cracking company, which is physically inte-

[29] An excellent statistical evaluation of the degree of change in economic concentration over time is given in *Nippon no Sangyō Shūchū* [Concentration of Industry in Japan], compiled by the Economic Department of the Fair Trade Commission, published by *Tōyō Keizai Shimpo-sha* [Oriental Economist Company], 1964. See also, *Kōsei Torihiki Iinkai Nenji Hōkoku* [The Fair Trade Commission Annual Report], 1964.

grated with an oil refinery, an electricity generating plant, and others. Some of the component firms may be, but need not necessarily be, related by means of stockholding or interlocking directorates. On the other hand, there are examples of "vertical combinats" in which the entire constellation of plants forming the complex is under a single ownership or has been financed by a single source of capital.[30]

The formation of combinats is subject to government control, which has been exercised in such a way as to increase the degree of economic concentration in Japan. In the petrochemical industry, applications for permission to make combinat investments are screened by the Petrochemical Cooperative Consultative Council, composed of present members of the industry and representatives of MITI. Approval by MITI depends upon the recommendations of the council and—with special reference to liberalization—MITI's interpretation of the Foreign Investment Law. Recently, however, MITI's decisions have been adverse to "late starters," that is, firms which failed to obtain a foothold prior to 1962.[31]

In general, the government means to encourage the combinat method of organization, as recommended by a recent basic study of Japanese industrial structure.[32] For the purpose of "increasing the degree of cooperation in production," as recommended by the study, the government has extended loans through the Japan Development Bank for combinat activities in the petrochemical and foodstuffs industries, while elsewhere, as in the automobile and shipbuilding industries, outright mergers have been instigated as the price of Development Bank loans.

[30] These are *keiretsu* combinats, formed by zaibatsu successor companies, such as the Mitsui petrochemical combinat at Iwakuni or the Sumitomo petrochemical combinat at Niihama. Another example is the Yawata chemical-steel combinat at Tobata.

[31] *Nihon Keizai Shimbun*, International Weekly Edition, June 22, 1965, p. 3.

[32] *Sangyō-Kōzō-Chōsa-Kai Tōshin* [Industrial Structure Investigational Association Report], Industrial Structure Investigational Association, Nov. 1963, p. 44.

OTHER COUNTERMEASURES

A few further examples of countermeasures to liberalization might be briefly noted.

Foreign movies were liberalized in July 1964, prior to which the import quota had been 275 movies each year. It was feared that the advent of liberalization would loose a flood of foreign films upon Japan, and a new quota system was contemplated that would require Japanese movie houses to exhibit domestic films during a certain portion of the year. As it turned out, however, no great increase in movie imports occurred and no legal countermeasure was taken. However, by "administrative advice" of the government, major movie houses which previously had shown only foreign films voluntarily decided to set aside forty days each year in which only domestic films would be shown.[33]

Limitations on the import of crude oil were removed in July 1962. Simultaneously, however, the volume of production was put under control by means of a *throughput* limitation enforced on each refiner. The limitation was administered by the Petroleum Association rather than by direct government regulations as such. Thus, in effect, the restriction on imports of petroleum remained substantially the same as when subject to quota.

In the amendments to the national tax legislation presented by the Japanese government to the Diet in 1965, a countermeasure to liberalization was presented in the form of a provision for the benefit of mining. In order to facilitate the establishment of reserves for mine exploration, the smaller of either (a) 15 percent of the gross amount of sales from specified kinds of mining products, or (b) 50 percent of the net income from such sales was permitted to be set aside in the form of a reserve which would be exempt from taxation, provided that the funds were actually used for mine exploration within a period of three years.

[33] *Mainichi Daily News*, Feb. 12 and Feb. 16, 1965.

A plan for the restriction of nonferrous metal imports was announced by MITI in July 1964. The restriction was to be accomplished by the formation of a nonferrous metals import cartel which was to be given a virtual monopoly of imports of copper, lead, and zinc in ore and metal form.[34] A similar arrangement was planned by importers of bananas, who found that after their liberalization in the spring of 1963 the domestic price of bananas had declined "excessively." The problem was to be solved by the establishment of a Banana Importers' Association which would be charged with the task of "streamlining banana import channels."[35] These developments are consistent with the recommendations contained in the study of Japan's industrial structure cited above. According to the study, "It is extremely important to prevent too much competition in imports"; instead, "the arrangement of order in import transactions is desired, such as the strengthening of cooperation among importers, or between importers and consumers, if necessary."[36]

A piquant episode occurred in connection with the liberalization of automobile imports, which was repeatedly delayed because Japanese makers felt threatened by the financial as well as technical resources of foreign rivals. Financially, it was feared that when cars could be imported freely foreign firms would extend installment credit to Japanese buyers on terms that could not be matched by domestic companies. In preparing for the liberalization of automobile imports, therefore, MITI and the Ministry of Finance decided to forestall "excessive sales competition" by limiting the amount of funds that could be brought into Japan for the financing of installment automobile sales.[37]

In the meanwhile, however, foreign automobile makers

34 *Asahi Evening News*, July 17, 1964, p. 7.

35 *Mainichi Daily News*, June 5, 1965, p. 4.

36 *Sangyō-Kōzō-Chōsa-Kai Tōshin* [Industrial Structure Investigational Association Report], Industrial Structure Investigational Association, Nov. 1963, p. 107.

37 *Nihon Keizai Shimbun*, International Weekly Edition, July 21, 1964, p. 4; and *Mainichi Daily News*, Jan. 17, 1965, p. 4.

were forming their own plans for the anticipated installment credit competition. The Ford Motor Company requested permission to remit $1 million to the Kintetsu
Motors Company for the promotion of Ford sales in Japan.
Under the Foreign Investment Law, permission was denied by the government. Thereupon the Ford Motor
Company deposited the sum of $1 million with the
National City Bank of New York; based on this deposit,
the bank's Tokyo office extended a loan of an equivalent
amount in yen to Kintetsu Motors.[38] This tactic proved
to be very unpopular with the Japanese authorities.[39]

A final countermeasure which might be mentioned in
this group is the "Buy Japanese" program, which prevails
at two levels: at one level it is promotional, at the other it
is enforced by ordinance. The former, directed at the
general public, was introduced by MITI in 1961 with a "Buy
Japanese" campaign headquarters; in 1964 the observance
of "Domestic Product Recognition Week" was inaugurated. One of the chief tasks of this effort was to persuade
Japanese that their own merchandise is of as high quality
as foreign goods.

The mandatory aspect of the "Buy Japanese" program
appears in the field of government procurement. On the
surface, the Japanese Cabinet ordinance concerning this
subject is distinctly liberal.[40] In contrast with the United
States "Buy American" policy, it specifies no restrictions
concerning the prerogatives of Japanese government
agencies in procuring supplies from whatever source they

[38] *Japan Times*, July 10, 1964, p. 14.

[39] During times of credit stringency in Japan, a similar circumven-
tion, the "swap loan," has been employed. In this variation, an exchange nonresident opens a "free yen" (convertible) time deposit in
an authorized bank by remitting foreign currency to Japan. The free
yen deposit then forms the basis for a yen loan extended by the bank
to a Japanese borrower designated by the foreign depositor. Officially,
this procedure also is proscribed by the Ministry of Finance.

[40] Emergency Account Ordinance Concerning Budgets and Settlements of Accounts, September 25, 1963 (effective Dec. 13, 1963).

desire.[41] This contrast is the basis for claims such as the following:

> There exists essential and substantial difference between the measures taken by . . . America and Japan. Your Buy American campaign has been legally reinforced by the Buy American Act, as well as the Buy American legislation in 41 states in the United States. On the contrary, in Japan there is no legislation nor restriction of buying foreign goods as in your country.[42]

The restriction in Japan, however, is at a less obvious level. Instead of limiting the choice of procurement agencies in buying government supplies, the Cabinet ordinance simply confines the submission of bids to "eligible" suppliers. For 14 categories of goods which in the past included substantially all the commodities procured from foreign suppliers, only designated companies were permitted to submit bids following the effective date of the ordinance. This virtually excludes foreign firms from making sales to the Japanese government since it is unlikely that any foreign firm would be so designated.

[41] The United States policy requires American government agencies to purchase goods offered by United States suppliers if the price differential between United States and foreign goods is less than 6 percent. In areas suffering a business depression, a price differential of 50 percent is allowed.

[42] "Buy American and Ship American," Supplementary Paper by Katsumi Yamagata, Chairman of the Board, Yamashita Shin-Nihon Shipping Co., Ltd., presented at the Third Japan–U.S. Businessmen's Conference, Tokyo, May 23, 1964.

15 · LIBERALIZATION AND ITS COUNTERMEASURES, C

CAPITAL IMPORT LIBERALIZATION

As in the case of policies for the strengthening of enterprises, policies for the import of capital likewise have a double aspect: they are designed to increase Japan's competitive power while acting as a brake to the liberalization process. It is in the implementation of such double-edged policies that Japan's system of *gyōsei shidō* [administrative guidance] rises to a fine art.

Although there is no legal difference between "direct" and "indirect" foreign investment in Japan, it is useful to observe the administrative distinction in attempting to analyze government policy, inasmuch as the former is discouraged while the latter is encouraged.[1] As mentioned above, the legal basis for the import of capital is given in the Law Concerning Foreign Investment (Law No. 163, 1950, as amended), briefly FIL, which in general provides for the induction of long-term capital (more than one year), while the import of short-term capital (one year or less) is governed by the Foreign Exchange and Foreign Trade Control Law (Law No. 228, 1949, as amended), briefly FECL. Transactions under the former law are subject to *validation*, whereas transactions under the latter are subject to *licenses* or *approval*. Validation conveys the guarantee that repatriation of the principal and "fruit" (interest, dividends or royalties) of an investment will be permitted. Licenses convey a similar, but in some cases more restricted, guarantee.

Direct investments by foreigners include (1) stock investments made with the purpose of participation in management (otherwise known as "joint ventures"), subject to the FIL, and (2) establishment of branches or factories, concern-

[1] In practice, this emphasis in Japanese policy is the opposite of that in other OECD countries. In the case of France, however, there are likewise restrictions against United States direct investment.

ing which "notification" must be supplied to the competent minister (the one within whose province the proposal principally lies) through The Bank of Japan. If a branch or factory so established is to receive funds from abroad, permission must first be granted under the FECL.

Indirect investments include: (1) stock investments made through the securities market in Japan;[2] (2) acquisition of corporate debentures or beneficiary certificates of loan or securities investment trusts;[3] (3) acquisition of bonds or American or European Depositary receipts;[4] and (4) ac-

[2] Stocks listed on the securities exchange are classified as either restricted or nonrestricted and are subject to validation under the FIL. According to Article 4 of the Cabinet Order Concerning Exceptions to Standards of Validation, etc., Based on the Law Concerning Foreign Investment (Cabinet Order No. 221, July 1, 1952), the following are specified as restricted: water supply business, transportation by bus, truck, rail, air or water; public communication services (including broadcasting stations); gas or electricity business; shipbuilding; banking; mining; and fisheries. For investment without the purpose of participation in management, acquisition by foreigners of the stock of a restricted enterprise up to an aggregate of 10 percent will be automatically validated by The Bank of Japan; a foreign individual may acquire up to 5 percent of the stock of such an enterprise. (Incidentally, although foreigners are discouraged from making investments in basic industries or utilities in Japan, this is precisely the kind of investment which Japan pursues abroad in order to control and diversify its own foreign sources of raw material supply.) The stock of an unrestricted enterprise may be acquired by foreigners up to an aggregate of 15 percent, again with the exception that no individual may acquire more than 5 percent of the stock of the enterprise. In practice, foreigners have not been particularly discouraged from making portfolio investments (stock purchases) in basic industries.

[3] When the period from date of acquisition to the date of redemption is more than one year, validation is required under the FIL; when the period is between six months and one year, license under the FECL is required. In principle, acquisition for a period of less than six months is not permitted.

[4] At the *acquisition* stage these are subject to license under the FECL. ADRS and EDRS were devised for the convenience of foreign investors who wish to acquire Japanese stocks abroad. Outside the Japanese securities market, there are three ways in which a foreigner may acquire Japanese stocks: (a) purchasing shares in a foreign investment company (investment trust) which invests in Japanese stocks; (b) purchasing convertible debentures offered for public subscription abroad by Japanese enterprises; or (c) purchasing the depositary receipts of a foreign depositary organization. Depositary receipts carry the same

quisition of claimable assets in the form of loans.[5] Overlapping the distinction between direct and indirect foreign investment in Japan, technological assistance contracts are usually discussed as a separate category.[6]

The effectiveness of government policy in encouraging indirect foreign investment in Japan while discouraging direct investment is suggested by statistics for these two categories respectively. Between March 1949 and September 1964, total foreign capital introduced into Japan under the FIL amounted to $3.6 billion; of this, only 5.9 percent took the form of equity capital with management participation.[7] In value, the management participation stock amounted to $213 million. In addition, direct investment in the form of the establishment of branches or

---

rights as the original Japanese stocks held by the depositary (or in practice by its Japanese custodian), but they avoid some of the practical inconveniences of transactions in the original share certificates. At the stage of *issuance*, these securities require the "prior understanding" of the Ministry of Finance.

[5] Foreign currency loans (or loans from the proceeds of foreign currencies converted to yen) to Japanese firms, wholly owned foreign subsidiaries, joint ventures or branch offices in Japan or foreign firms are subject to validation under the FIL for loans with a maturity of more than one year or license under the FECL for those of one year or less. (Yen loans within Japan by authorized branches of foreign banks do not require validation or license.) For loans which are of an amount less than $300,000, whose period of maturity is more than three years, whose purpose is to finance the manufacture of other than amusement or luxury goods, and whose interest rate is "reasonable" (that is, no higher than the prevailing interest rate in the country of the lender rather than the rate prevailing in Japan), validation will be automatically furnished by The Bank of Japan. Applications for loans under other circumstances are reviewed by the respective competent ministries. Loans which might be construed as "direct" rather than "indirect" investment are subject to substantially identical rules.

[6] Class "A" contracts are those whose duration is longer than one year. These are subject to validation under the FIL. All other technological assistance contracts are Class "B" and are subject to license under the FECL. Since April 1964, even technological contracts without compensation concluded between foreign parent companies and their branches in Japan must be licensed under the FECL.

[7] Bank of Tokyo, *Semiannual Report, April-September 1964*, Dec. 1964, p. 39. During the same period, loans accounted for 65 percent of foreign capital, bonds 16 percent, and all other securities 19 percent.

factories of parent companies abroad—subject to license under the FECL—accounted for the induction of only $10 million during the same interval.

Of particular interest is the composition of the capital contributed by foreigners to joint ventures in Japan. In terms of its geographical origin, approximately three-fourths of the capital inflow for the purpose of managerial participation during the postwar period has been acquired from the United States. By type, more than one-half of the foreign contribution has been in the form of technological assistance, for which an equivalent value of stock equity was created.[8] The role of this foreign technology has been far more critical than its absolute amount would suggest, for it has been recruited chiefly at the very frontiers of Japan's petroleum, machinery, and chemical industries.[9] The strategic nature of foreign investment is indicated, moreover, by the fact that although the ratio of validated foreign management equity to the total paid-in capital of Japanese corporations was only 1.29 percent in 1963, the Japanese government has felt impelled to adopt a highly defensive attitude towards it, as further described below.[10]

[8] *Ibid.*, p. 44. In practice, the transfer of some technology is almost a prerequisite for the validation of a joint venture arrangement, especially if the joint venture is of considerable size. Technology in the form of patent licenses, know-how or machinery and equipment may be capitalized, in addition to which the foreign partner may also contribute cash.

[9] Owing to the progressive development of laborsaving devices in the United States, some technology and machinery which is already obsolete in the U.S. may be appropriate for use in Japan. A considerable amount of secondhand machinery has been acquired by Japan in the form of foreign contributions to joint venture arrangements. There are no published statistics, however, on the amount of such imports. In the *Yushutsunyū Tōkei Hinmoku Hyō* [Statistical Classification of Commodities for Japanese Foreign Trade], the only categories which identify secondhand commodities are #735-361,2, referring to used ships and boats.

[10] The ratio of validated United States management equity to the total paid-in capital of all Japanese corporations was 0.92 percent in 1963. Ministry of Finance, Securities Bureau, Enterprise Finance Section, *Hōjin Kigyo Tōkei Nenpo* [Annual Report of Statistics of Business Corporations], 1963.

Behind the policy that has determined this critical—and conspicuously narrow—role of direct investment by foreigners in Japan lies an ambivalent attitude on the part of the government. From a national point of view, the case in favor of the introduction of foreign capital has rested chiefly upon the need to overcome the technological lag which resulted from Japan's isolation during World War II, and second on the shortage of domestic capital. The government acknowledges that foreign capital has contributed greatly to the satisfaction of these needs; however, it argues that the favorable result is purely a consequence of its care in selective screening. As seen by the government, its problem is how to acquire foreign capital sufficient in quantity and quality for the acceleration of Japan's economic development without thereby incurring balance of payments difficulties or surrendering control of home industry to foreigners. Dread of being "colonized by foreign capital" is perhaps the deepest of these motives for restriction.[11] It is reflected in the particularly severe screening process applied to capital which seeks admission for the purpose of management participation. Japanese firms are highly vulnerable to loss of indigenous control because of

[11] This is enhanced by the government's fear of losing its own power to dominate business through the system of informal ministerial controls. For in some respects, joint ventures may be less responsive to suggestion than firms wholly managed by Japanese nationals. Partly, this is because foreigners are not much involved in the "web of relations" compounded of school loyalties, family and social connections, and the like, which transcends the visible boundaries of government and business organization. Partly, because of their cultural differences, foreigners may fail even to perceive the signals to which "members of the club" respond. At the same time, of course, as outsiders, foreigners are likewise excluded from the benefits of the system. This gives rise to a nice question concerning the proper attitude to be taken by United States firms which often complain that the provisions of the Treaty of Friendship, Commerce and Navigation between Japan and the United States notwithstanding, U.S. firms do not receive unqualified "national treatment" in Japan. From a legal point of view, it is not altogether clear that they would be better off receiving such treatment than they are now as objects of "discrimination," for if they were "members of the club" in the full Japanese sense, they would be implicated in arrangements that would render them immediately liable to prosecution under U.S. antitrust laws.

266

the characteristically high proportion of borrowed assets with which they are financed. If equity capital were to be introduced by foreigners into any particular enterprise to a degree reflecting the average ratio of equity to total assets prevailing in the United States, the Japanese share of the proprietorship would be quickly swamped. Foreign equity in joint ventures, however, is very rarely permitted to attain a level of 50 percent, and validation of applications for foreign participation even to the extent of 40 percent hitherto has been very difficult to obtain. An application for the acquisition of management equity for cash unaccompanied by technology would not be validated. Moreover, the Japanese government favors the introduction of technology on a licensing or purchase basis rather than in exchange for equity participation by foreigners in Japanese corporations.[12] By the same token, acquisition by foreigners of wholly owned subsidiaries in Japan is extremely rare, and there are virtually no examples of wholly owned subsidiaries which are allowed to engage in manufacturing activities. The fact that at a given time no Japanese company even exists in the field of a proposed wholly owned subsidiary is by no means considered a sufficient reason for its validation. On the contrary, exclusion is then explained by the argument that entry in these circumstances would constitute foreign domination of a Japanese industry in the highest degree. It is argued further that if a commodity is sufficiently needed by Japan, domestic firms will sooner or later enter the field, which foreigners should not be allowered to preempt.[13]

[12] In addition to serving the purpose of withholding control from foreigners, it has been cheaper for Japan to finance imports through portfolio borrowing of foreign capital than to obtain them by allowing direct foreign investment. Similarly, home control has been maintained and effective cost has been minimized by obtaining foreign technology through licenses and patent arrangements (equity payments being made only where there is no alternative).

[13] The countries of Southeast Asia regard their imports of Japanese capital with the same ambivalence as Japan regards the inflow of equity capital from the West. Although Japanese capital and technical assistance are urgently needed, it is feared that they will be accompanied

However, "foreign domination," together with control of capital imports for balance of payments reasons, are among the more muted themes of the government's case against unrestricted entry of foreign capital. Concerning the latter, even if not negatively expressed, the balance of payments criterion for MITI's restrictive policy is implicit in the fact that the strongest affirmative argument an applicant can offer in support of his application for validation is that the proposed capital import will either increase exports or reduce imports. During periods of instability, capital imports render the economy even more unstable; in periods of comparative stability, they add to the structural problem of finding offsets for the long-term increase in payments of interest, dividends and royalties. Psychologically, the repatriation of profits may also suggest to the Japanese that he is being "exploited" by the foreigner, who can merely reply that the higher productivity of foreign capital is reflected in higher incomes which are a net benefit to the economy at large even if all profits are repatriated.

Although it is a professed objective of the long-term economic plan to "liquidate the dual economy," and although small, backward firms have been urged to become more efficient, merge or accept extinction, in the context of direct investment by foreigners the defense of these same enterprises becomes one of the official arguments in favor of a restrictive policy. Unrestricted entry of foreign capital, it is said, would force the liquidation of small domestic firms in an abrupt and socially inequitable manner. It is also claimed that the "excessive competition" of Japanese firms for foreign technology would if unrestricted result in unnecessary duplication of facilities and excess capacity. Moreover, an agreement to refrain from export competition in third markets with the foreign supplier of

by economic domination by Japan. Shinobu Ichikawa, "The Actual Conditions of Five Southeast Asian Countries," *Diamond*, Dec. 7, 1964 (as translated by the Translation Services Branch, United States Embassy, Tokyo).

technology or the foreign parent of the Japanese subsidiary is more often than not a part of the price paid for technological imports. To this extent, therefore, the benefits of collaboration with foreign capital are considerably circumscribed both for individual firms and for the Japanese economy at large.

Motives and arguments aside, how is the government's ambivalent attitude towards direct investment in Japan reflected in the formal criteria by which it controls capital entry? The criteria are formulated at various levels. First, in the Memorandum of Understanding by which Japan became a full member of OECD, a vague and potentially restrictive statement of intentions concerning Article 1/1 (Undertakings With Regard to Capital Movements) of the OECD Code of Liberalization of Capital Movements is expressed as follows:

The Government of Japan will in future deal with all applications for inward and outward direct investments in the spirit of the item in question and will disapprove applications only in exceptional cases where serious detrimental effects to the economy are to be feared.

Concerning inward investments consideration will be given in particular to the following factors:

    a. co-ordination of industrial development with special regard to small and medium enterprises;
    b. maintenance of full employment;
    c. internal and external financial equilibrium.

Regarding outward direct investments the chief consideration of the Government of Japan will be the balance of payments position, without prejudice to exceptional cases in which detrimental effects for the Japanese economy are to be feared.[14]

14 *Memorandum of Understanding Between the Organisation for Economic Co-Operation and Development and The Government of Japan Concerning the Assumption by The Government of Japan of*

269

Second, on the domestic level, the criteria embodied in the Foreign Investment Law are both comprehensive and forbidding; as administered, they could be used to support practically any action which the authorities deem expedient. In Article 8, the FIL specifies two classes of criteria, positive and negative, which are prefaced by an injunction concerning the balance of payments:

> The competent Minister shall apply the following standards in validating contracts prescribed in this Law, and priority shall be given to those which will most speedily and effectively contribute to an improvement in the international balance of payments.

According to the positive criteria, those transactions may be approved which

1. Directly or indirectly contribute to the improvement of the international balance of payments, or
2. Directly or indirectly contribute to the development of essential industries or public enterprises, or
3. Are necessary for the revival or continuation of existing technological assistance contracts concerning essential industries or public enterprises.

Negative criteria to be observed by the competent Minister require that the following shall *not* be validated:

1. Contracts whose provisions are unfair or which contravene laws or regulations;
2. Contracts whose provisions are deemed to have been concluded in a manner not free from fraud, duress or undue influence;
3. Contracts deemed to have an adverse effect on the rehabilitation of the Japanese economy.

The law also forbids the validation of any contract for which authorized means of payment is not provided.[15]

---

the Obligations of Membership of the Organisation, July 26, 1963, Part III.

[15] According to Japanese government regulations prevailing in 1965, four separate categories of yen were established, these being distin-

The practical meaning of typically vague and discursive Japanese legal phrases such as the above can be known only by the way in which they are administered. At this third level, in terms of internal ministerial rules and regulations *(naiki)*, criteria become more precise. The *naiki* of the various ministries concerned with the validation process (principally the Ministry of Finance, the Science and Technology Agency, and the Ministry of International Trade and Industry), however, are unpublished; their contents must be inferred from the pattern of decisions—to the extent that these become known—as handed down by ministerial secretariats in due time. The policy that prevents foreigners from obtaining a majority stockholding position in joint venture companies under any but the most exceptional circumstances, for example, is a policy embodied in the *naiki*.

There is evidence that in recent years there has been a shift in emphasis from the "positive" to the "negative" criteria regarding direct investment.[16] Such a shift can be readily accomplished because of the informal and confidential nature of the *naiki* method of control. The *naiki* are subject to sudden change; they are also subject to negotiation. Usually, however, it is the foreign party's proposal for direct investment which is renegotiated under ministerial auspices when it is submitted for validation or licensing.

---

guished from one another in terms of convertibility, transferability, and ownership by a resident or nonresident. The categories were as follows: (1) free yen (or "nonresident convertible yen"); (2) nonresident yen (or "nonresident transferable yen"); (3) nonresident other yen (or "nonresident blocked yen"); (4) resident yen (or "regular yen"). A separate treatise could be written on the consequences of these distinctions, which in themselves constitute a barrier to liberalization, as for example with regard to the acquisition of shares and the remittance rights of shareholders.

16 This seems, for example, to be the sense of the Cabinet "Understanding" of June 28, 1963: "As regards direct investment such as the establishment of joint corporations, introduction shall be recognized unless the national economy is adversely affected, assuming a more elastic attitude than ever in the examination of contract conditions." *Official Trade Bulletin*, June 11, 1964, p. 6.

By the account of applicants who have been exposed to the process, contract changes imposed by MITI at the validation stage conform to a clearly discernible model. As a counterpart to each actual proposal, MITI constructs an "ideal contract" comprising—with reference to each of the proposal's dimensions considered separately—the most favorable terms which have ever before been validated in comparable contracts. As described by one foreign party to a joint venture contract, the process of renegotiation then proceeds as follows:[17]

First the MITI official points out that some other Japanese company already possesses part of the technology you propose to bring in; he tells you to take that part out of the deal: Japan is not interested. Second, he points out that whereas you are asking for 7 percent royalty, some other Japanese company made an agreement to acquire a similar kind of technology at 5 percent (he doesn't mention that there was a very high down payment in that case). Next he observes that you are asking for a large down payment; some other Japanese company made a similar arrangement with a much smaller down payment (he doesn't mention that the royalty rate was rather high in that instance). Other terms, such as the length of the contract, market territory, percentage of foreign-owned equity, training fee, or the number and rank of foreigners participating in direct management, are likewise renegotiated. No detail is too small for MITI's attention, and the fact that the Japanese and foreign parties to the proposal were already in agreement on all details before it was submitted for approval is of no consequence. Furthermore, you cannot ask MITI in advance what they will

[17] The proposed contract must be accompanied by a statement giving full details of the proposed plan of operations, a description of the benefits which will be obtained by the Japanese participant, an explanation of the technology provided by the foreign partner, a statement of the importance of the technology to Japan, an estimate of future results to be obtained, and detailed information about the home country affairs of the foreign partner's company.

settle for as a guide to the conduct of your relations with the Japanese partner. They require that your proposal be completely worked out before they will discuss it.

Often, therefore, terms which are acceptable to the prospective Japanese partner are determined to be "unfair" by the Japanese government agency which reviews the contract for validation. There is a distinct "tendency to insist that terms in new agreements be less favorable to the foreign firm than those in previous agreements." Also, "There appears to be a definite policy of requiring that the terms in a renewed licensing agreement be less favorable to the foreign interest than were those of the original agreement."[18] The authorities also require that the scope of proposed joint ventures be defined as narrowly as possible, which limits the potential area of expansion of their activities.

Selective control over the admission of foreign equity capital into Japan is exercised not only by means of the government screening process but also in effect through the veto power held by the trading company or by the industry cartel with which the Japanese partner may be associated. The opposition of either of the latter may be enough to defeat any plans not already defeated by MITI. The foreign entrant may thus have to deal not only with his ostensible partner but also with as many as three additional shadow partners. If he is unaware of the rules of the game by which these parties collaborate, the foreigner may fail to understand why his Japanese colleague "changes his mind" or makes promises which he ultimately cannot fulfill.

18 United States Embassy, Tokyo, Memorandum, "Introduction to Foreign Participation in Technological Assistance Agreements and Equity Investments in Japan," by Andrew B. Wardlaw, December 1, 1962, pp. 19 and 21. These and many other restrictive aspects of the criteria for validation were still strongly entrenched in 1965, with little prospect of being relaxed. For some evidence, see Trade Bulletin Corporation, *Guidelines to Foreign Investment in Japan, Establishment of Joint Ventures and Conclusion of Technological Assistance Contracts, 1964-65* (Tokyo, 1964), pp. 96-108.

Concerning the outflow as contrasted with the inflow of capital, the process of liberalization has been clearly asymmetrical, for whereas the procedural aspects of validation provide an effective countermeasure to the inflow of direct investment, the repatriation of foreign capital and its earnings has been substantially freed. Partly, the unequal rate of progress results from the fact that it is more difficult to distract outside attention from the realities of capital repatriation than from those of capital inflow. Also, the reservations lodged by Japan with regard to its obligations under the OECD Code of Liberalisation of Capital Movements are more restrictive on capital inflow than on repatriation of capital.[19] A measure for the liberalization of remittances with regard to a miscellaneous group of current and capital invisibles was introduced by a ministerial ordinance at the end of 1963.[20]

Nevertheless, in a very important instance, an increase in the liberalization of capital outflow has been offset, or more than offset, by new procedural requirements imposed on capital inflow. This occurred as part of the preparations made in July 1963 for Japan's then impending assumption of the obligations of IMF Article 8, which requires that members relinquish their "restrictions on the making of payments and transfers for current international transactions." Prior to July 1963 there had been two classes of

[19] The chronology of the liberalization of equity capital repatriation was as follows: In 1950, when the Foreign Investment Law was passed, the foreign investor was guaranteed only remittance rights on the dividends earned by his investment. In July 1952 stock principal remittance was permitted two years after the date of investment in five annual installments, allowing full repatriation within seven years. In June 1960 stock principal remittance was permitted two years after the date of investment in three yearly installments, allowing full repatriation within five years. In May 1961 stock principal remittance was permitted in full two years after the date of investment. In Aug. 1962 the two year waiting period was reduced to six months. In April 1963 practically all deferment requirements on capital repatriation were abolished; actual remittances, however, were still subject to license.

[20] Ministry of Finance Ordinance No. 58, *Ministerial Ordinance Concerning Control of Invisible Trade Transactions*, Nov. 2, 1963. Remittances were liberalized for an additional list of invisibles effective Dec. 18, 1964.

274

foreign investment in Japan, those possessing and those not possessing remittance privileges for invested capital and its earnings. Those lacking remittance privileges were "yen-based" investments, made without validation under the FIL.[21] It was hoped by nonresidents acquiring shares on this basis that sooner or later liberalization would proceed to the point where repatriation of even such investments would become possible.[22] Yen-based investment, moreover, afforded the only practicable route by which a nonresident could acquire a wholly owned subsidiary in Japan.

The hoped for stage of liberalization arrived in July 1963, at which time in fulfillment of its IMF obligations Japan permitted the capital and accumulated earnings of previous yen-based investments and technical assistance contracts to become remittable in installments.[23] Simultaneously, however, an emphatic countermeasure was adopted: all further unvalidated yen-based investment was prohibited. At the moment of its ostensible liberalization, therefore, the system of yen-based investment was actually abolished. After July 1963 all nonresident acquisitions of company shares became subject to either validation or ap-

[21] As an exception to Article 11 of the FIL, which requires that "A foreign investor desirous of acquiring stock or proprietary interest in a judicial person established under the Japanese laws and orders shall obtain validation of the acquisition concerned from the competent Minister in accordance with the Ordinance of the competent Ministry," the Cabinet Order Concerning Exceptions to Standards of Validation, Based on the Law Concerning Foreign Investment (Cabinet Order No. 221, July 1, 1952, as amended in Oct. 1957) provided that validation was not necessary where stock was acquired "without intention to receive foreign payment of fruit or principal withdrawn."

[22] Since the foreign exchange laws require that all exports from Japan must be paid for in foreign exchange (which must then be surrendered to The Bank of Japan for yen), it was not legally possible to repatriate yen-based foreign investments in the form of unrequited merchandise exports. Nor could repatriation be legally accomplished by the underpricing of merchandise exported by the Japanese subsidiary.

[23] As of March 30, 1964, the total of yen-based foreign investments amounted to $140 million in book value, with accumulated profits of $40 million. Trade Bulletin Corporation, *Guidelines to Foreign Investment in Japan, Establishment of Joint Ventures and Conclusion of Technological Assistance Contracts, 1964-65* (Tokyo, 1964), p. 7.

proval in accordance with the provisions of the FIL or the FECL.[24] The net change in conditions of remittability was appraised by a Ministry of Finance official, who remarked, "Although Japan may be forced to open the front door, she cannot be prevented from closing the back door." In the same stroke, the freedom of a nonresident foreigner to acquire a wholly owned subsidiary in Japan was also substantially foreclosed.

The countermeasure of forestalling the accumulation of earnings while liberalizing the remittability of those earnings was thus effectively invoked against nonresidents insofar as their acquisition of Japanese company shares was concerned. However, an alternative path to yen earnings remained available to foreign firms since they were free to open branches of their own companies in Japan without validation or approval and with a minimum of formalities. Prior to July 1963 a foreign company was obliged merely to send a simple notice to the Japanese government stating that the branch had been established. With the liberalization of remittance privileges for nonvalidated investment and its earnings, nonresidents would be given a fresh incentive to introduce new branches of nonresident firms which would result in a further accumulation of remittable yen beyond that of the earnings of branches already established. As an accompanying measure, therefore, the liberalization of July 1963 was reinforced by restrictions on the establishment of new branches in Japan. These were of particular interest insofar as they reveal the administrative as distinguished from the statutory aspect of countermeasures to liberalization. From a legal point of view, the Japanese government was enjoined from creating a license system for branches of United States corporations

[24] Abolition of the yen-based system was accomplished by amendment of Article 4 of the Cabinet Order Concerning Exceptions to the Standards of Validation Under the Foreign Investment Law, amendment of Articles 7 and 14 of the Foreign Exchange Control Order, amendment of Articles 1 and 2 of the Ministerial Ordinance Concerning Control of Foreign Securities, Immovables Abroad, Etc., and the Ministry of Finance Notification No. 181 of 1965.

because of the "national treatment" provisions of the Japan–United States Treaty of Friendship, Commerce and Navigation. Therefore, a "report system" was introduced instead, which as administered turned out to be very much like a validation system. According to its provisions, any foreign firm which wished to establish a branch in Japan after July 1, 1963 was required to submit a report to The Bank of Japan explaining in detail its proposed business operations. However, transmittal of the report, in itself, does not constitute compliance with the reporting requirements: before the branch may open for business, it is necessary for the report to be "accepted" by The Bank of Japan. Acceptance, in turn, has several prerequisites; for example, the bank requires an explanation of the "purpose" of the foreign company in establishing its branch in Japan. A complete explanation of "purpose" includes information which enables the bank to appraise the potential impact of the proposed branch on the activities of existing Japanese companies in the same field. If the consequences seem undesirable, the report will simply not be accepted by the bank. Of course, an impetuous nonresident is at liberty to proceed without acceptance. Should he do so, however, he can confidently be expected to meet with difficulties in his future encounters with the Japanese government, banks, and even with business associates of the branch. For example, the critical role of "acceptance" may be seen in the context of a still additional requirement effective beginning July 1963 which states that remittances of "necessary business funds" from overseas to branch offices in Japan are subject to approval in advance by the Japanese government. A license from the Ministry of Finance is also necessary for any guarantee by a head office abroad with regard to a loan by a branch, for any payment by a head office abroad in behalf of a branch, and for similar transactions.[25] Finally, after acceptance has been granted,

[25] These restrictions were introduced by amendments to Ministry of Finance Notification No. 192 of 1963 and to the Cabinet Order Concerning Control of Foreign Exchange (Cabinet Order No. 203,

the further requirement was added that following July 1, 1963 a report of operations must be furnished by each branch of a nonresident firm within three months after the end of each business period. Thus both the establishment and the operation of branches were brought under government scrutiny and control more directly than ever before.

In order to close the gap opened by the liberalization of remittance privileges, one major loophole remained to be covered. The loophole concerned the use of technology which when transferred gratuitously by the head office of a foreign firm to its branch or wholly owned subsidiary was free to enter Japan without government screening. Although the liberalization measures of July 1963 placed a heavy damper on the opening of new branches or the acquisition of wholly owned subsidiaries by nonresidents, those already established remained in a position to generate large profits by their own use of such transferred technology or by its sale or licensing to other firms in Japan for yen consideration. Prior to July 1963 the exchange-free transfers had been motivated by fear that if formal validation or approval had been applied for, the technology in question would fail to qualify under the standards of the FIL or the FECL, and foreign owners of such technology had preferred to acquire unremittable yen rather than receive no return at all on assets whose value might deteriorate over time. Following July 1963, when these yen became remittable, the loophole of course assumed extraordinary dimensions. Accordingly, by amendment of the FIL and the FECL, new rules became effective in April 1964 whereby all technological imports, including those received gratuitously from a foreign head office by its branch or subsidiary in Japan, and any act of yen licensing or sale of technology that a nonresident foreigner might perform through them with a Japanese firm, became subject to validation or approval

June 1950). Loans by nonresident firms to Japanese subsidiaries and guarantees of loans made in Japan by residents to such subsidiaries had already been subject to government approval before July 1963.

278

by the Japanese government. Periodically, moreover, announcements are published by the Minister of Finance and the Minister of International Trade and Industry specifying the kinds of foreign technology which Japan desires to import.

Ironically, after having registered many complaints against these restrictive policies, in 1965 the United States government emerged as a new ally of the interests attempting to stem the flow of equity capital into Japan. On the score of balance of payments difficulties, all capital outflow from the United States was officially discouraged. From Japan's point of view, this was a double-edged policy, for it tended to limit the flow of loans—upon which Japan has been predominantly dependent in the capital account—as well as equity. In the future, restrictions on the demand side may be even further offset by a relative contraction in the supply of foreign equity capital to Japan. For besides the discouraging official attitude of the United States government towards such investment by Americans, there is evidence that its rate of return has not satisfied expectations even during the period of Japan's most rampant economic expansion. The structural distortions which have been persistently revealed in the course of the growth process during recent years may have a further long-run dampening effect on the eagerness of foreigners to make either direct or portfolio investments in Japan.

---

16 · CONCLUSION

In this study I have attempted to analyze the interrelations of economic structure, performance, and public policy at the outset of Japan's liberalization program. The program was introduced at a delicate moment in Japan's transition to "advanced" status among the industrial nations of the world. The transformation of its industry was incomplete and its competitive power in the field of heavy and chemical industry—with some notable exceptions—was as yet weakly established. While liberalizing imports, Japan's traditional export position in third markets was being undercut by the output of cheap labor in the newly developing countries. Liberalization was introduced at a time, moreover, when structural defects evolved during the period of "miraculous" growth were reaping a harvest of their own. In particular, disparities were found in the relation between the structure of production and the structure of exports. Other structural problems included a deterioration in the capital structure of enterprises and a persistent deficit in the invisibles account of the balance of payments. These constitute a threat to the stability of the economy and thus to the liberalization program.

The increasing degree of economic instability in Japan is revealed, for example, by the acceleration in both the tempo and severity of cyclical fluctuations in the postwar period. This may partly be accounted for by the expansion of heavy and chemical goods output which are more subject to reversals in both internal and external demand than Japan's traditional staple and sundry goods. The increase in cyclical instability complicates the government's long-range plan to "liquidate" the dual economy, for in eliminating the backward sector—to which the "advanced" sector has habitually passed on the brunt of deflationary pressure during recessions—Japan ironically removes another of the traditional stabilizing forces of its economy.

A chief source of both structural distortion and cyclical instability is found in one of the key ingredients of the postwar growth rate, namely the competition for market shares among major enterprises and the speculative investment in plant and equipment which it evoked. While productive capacity steadily expanded ahead of home market demand, it was nevertheless essential for firms to maintain a comparatively high volume of output in relation to operating capacity. The reason for this was their high level of fixed cost, which included interest charges on inordinate amounts of borrowed funds and a labor force whose tenure of employment was largely on a life-contract basis. Consequently, in order to attain a break-even rate of production, firms engaged in cutthroat or "excessive" competition both at home and abroad. In the context of the latter, which occurred chiefly during periods of recession, we identified the phenomenon of "supply-oriented exports," which was an especially prominent feature of the long recession beginning in 1964.

Public policy was both a permissive and an enabling condition of these results. The role of government has been partly to sponsor industrial activities (by means of periodically revised national economic plans) and partly to coordinate and control them (by administrative guidance and by supervision of money and credit). In the expansion of supply capacity prior to liberalization, the home market, as distinguished from the foreign market, became the central arena of growth. Exploitation of the home market produced a further structural imbalance in the form of a disproportionate volume of investment in the private as contrasted with the public sector; social overhead facilities and housing were in chronic arrears. Typically, the periodic excesses of expansion were interrupted by constraints in the balance of payments; on these occasions the government would implement a tight money policy which would restrict imports and encourage exports. In this way the foreign market constituted a safety valve for excess capacity and had a stabilizing effect at the trough of the cycle. In the future, when it is complemented by more far-reaching fiscal policy, monetary policy will become a much less simple instrument to apply.

As the level of productive capacity rose through a series of such episodes, however, dependence on a sustained high volume of demand from abroad progressively deepened. Moreover, as both output and exports rise, and as the ratio of exports to output increases, a steadily increasing absolute amount of exports will be required to accomplish a given proportional improvement in the export ratio. If short-term gains are sought by the usual device of price-cutting, any appreciable increase in exports would be more likely than formerly to arouse resistance, if not retaliation and discrimination against Japan. Therefore, by virtue of becoming steadily more dependent on foreign markets for the maintenance of its growth rate, Japan's reliance as heretofore on the supply-oriented export mechanism to correct the balance of payments or compensate for deficiencies in home demand will in the future prove to have destabilizing rather than stabilizing consequences.

These facts have an immediate bearing on the strength of the Japanese government's commitment to the import liberalization program. The program itself includes two chief categories—imports of commodities and imports of capital. The government's attitude towards both categories is restrictive, partly from motives of protectionism, partly for bargaining purposes, and partly because it appreciates better than foreigners the extent of existing structural disparities and the degree of economic vulnerability they imply for Japan. It is interesting that in the case of capital imports, however, by restricting direct investment in favor of loans, the government clearly places a higher priority on restriction of control by foreigners than on the attainment of stability in the balance of payments. For when times are slack, interest payments on loans remain an active liability, whereas direct investment (aside from the repatriation of capital which applies to loans as well as to investment) creates an obligation for payments in foreign exchange only when dividends are earned.

Clearly, Japan is one of the most balance of payments conscious countries in the world. If it were not, it could never have attained a high rate of internal growth with such a slender stock of external reserves. A high order of skill, and controls of a high order of effectiveness, have contributed to this result. The experience of economic management, and the confidence engendered by that experience, were prerequisite to the acceptance of the liberalization commitment despite the government's misgivings and ambivalence in doing so. As we have seen, moreover, what is important in the implementation of liberalization is not merely formal rules, but equally or more important, the interpretation of the rules and the procedural devices by which they are administered.

Inevitably, however, external events will now have a greater impact on Japan than prior to adoption of the liberalization program. In a setting of structural imbalance, this impact will be augmented by the steadily increasing role which foreign trade must play if the economy is to maintain a satisfactory rate of growth. The task of management will therefore become more complicated than ever before. The government is aware that policies which were "sound" during the period of "miraculous growth" are clearly unsound in less expansive circumstances. Whether or not it can correct the disparities or dispel the hazards which are a legacy of the former period, the government will surely attempt to suppress their symptoms as expressed in the leading economic indicators. In order to do so it may well invoke stronger administrative, if not statutory, countermeasures to the liberalization program.

INDEX

acceptance credit, 118
"accommodation bills," 181
"administrative guidance," 156,
158-70 *passim*, 215-16, 250-51;
and economic concentration,
195; and export prices, 213n;
and cinema imports, 258; and
imports of capital, 262-79 *passim*
"agreed specialization," 195, 197
Allen, G. C., 20
American Aid, 103, 135
Anglo–Japanese Treaty of Commerce and Navigation, 190
antidumping measures: by the
United States, 211; by Japan,
248
Antimonopoly Law, 196, 197n,
251, 254
antitrust policy, 195. *See also* Anti-
monopoly Law
Ariga Michiko, 196n
assets and liabilities: Japan's external, 110-12

Balassa, Bela, 248n
balance of payments, 123-54; prewar, 123-28; basic balance, 129-
43; recent trends in, 129-54; instability in, 143-46; statistics of,
versus foreign exchange statistics, 146-49; errors and omissions, 149-52; multilateral settlements, 151; crises in, 178-80;
invisibles account: prewar surplus in, 126; deterioration in,
134; autonomous versus induced, 134-37; "Special Procurement" category of, 135-36;
sources of deficit in, 136-38;
factors affecting, 139; role in
balance of payments difficulties,
184; and technological exports,
194; and liberalization, 239n
Bank of Japan, The, 179; "window guidance," 160, 176; strategic position of, 175; and interest rates, 187; and selective financing, 189; and imports of

capital, 263; screening of foreign investment, 277. *See also*
qualitative credit control
banks: city, 121; foreign, their
role in Japan, 56n, 120; "overloan" condition, 174. *See also*
The Bank of Japan; free reserves
Berrill, Kenneth, 25n, 65n
"black ink bankruptcy," 184
"blind trade," 152
Bronfenbrenner, Martin, 72n
Brussels Tariff Nomenclature,
219n, 245
bunker fuel, 138
business cycles: reference cycle
dates, 145n
"Buy American" policy, 261
"Buy Japanese" policy, 260

call market, 121n
capacity: excess, 47, 62, 79-82;
productive, 48
capital formation: share of GNP,
174
capital movements, 138; short-
term, 56; short-term versus long-
term, 132; outflow, 132n, 274;
dependence on, 139-43; composition of, 142; liberalization of,
262-79; foreign repatriation, 274.
See also credit; "clean loans";
flight of capital; foreign debt;
foreign investment in Japan;
"impact loans"; usance
cartels, 195-98; in foreign trade,
196-98; compared with mergers,
251, 254; in nonferrous metals
imports, 259
China, Mainland, 105-106, 125-26
chūshin koku, see "middle-advanced country"
"clean loans": defined, 116n
coefficient of export intensity, 107
Cohen, Jerome, 20
Columbo Plan, 203
combinats, 250, 256; and Japan
Development Bank, 257; and
MITI, 257

285

Date Due